A WORLD WAR II STORY TOLD THROUGH THE LETTERS OF
BOAT GROUP COMMANDER, JOSEPH B. MCDEVITT

ALL CAME HOME

★ PAUL K. McDEVITT ★

FOREWORD BY WILLIAM O. MILLER, REAR ADMIRAL, JAGC, U.S. NAVY (RET)

AllCameHome.com

Please visit our website to contact the author,
contribute to our blog, or share additional stories, pictures or
documentation about Joe McDevitt and The Amphibians.

ISBN: 0986341002
ISBN 13: 9780986341007

Cover and interior by Publish Pros (www.publishpros.com)

This book is dedicated to the memory of Joseph B. McDevitt
and to all other members of the naval amphibious forces during WWII

FOREWORD

How does one human being love another? How does a son love a father? As Elizabeth Barrett Browning tells us in her famous Sonnet 43, "Let me count the ways."

All Came Home is a touching tribute from a son to his father, and it asks and answers both of these questions; it is a meticulously researched effort by a son and a scholar who implicitly asks, "What was my father like before I came to know him?" How could life produce such a stern but loving father?" What crucible could have brought forth such a man, gentle and caring but still a man of steel?" This is not a story imagined by a clever author. It is the story of a life that really happened. It is the culmination of a son's life of admiration and respect and most of all of wonder. Much of it is told in the father's own words, which are skillfully interwoven into the events which molded the father's life, the ordeal of World War II and the part in it played by Joe McDevitt and by his ship, the USS *Leon* APA 48. But it is more than that. It actually is the story of a generation of young American men and women, millions of them, who fought and won WWII, and who did this in the face of formidable personal and financial hardships that it put them through.

I, too, knew, respected and admired Joe McDevitt. He was a valued mentor of mine. I first met him soon after this narrative ends, so I knew only the older one. I now know how the man I knew and served came to be. Paul McDevitt has described for me the foundation of a life which I saw blossom as Joe McDevitt became part of a coterie of

Navy lawyers who gave legal substance—and the name—to the Cuban Quarantine of October 1962, and who later became the chief uniformed lawyer in the Navy. He was one who earned not only Paul McDevitt's tribute but ours as well and who deserves the honor and respect accorded to an American hero.

As I read these pages, I could not help but remember the final words of a famous poem penned by Captain, later Vice Admiral, William G. Beecher, Jr., as he surveyed the great armada of American men-of-war assembled in Tokyo Bay on September 2, 1945, as the formal Japanese surrender took place. That poem, "By Nimitz - - and Halsey - - and Me," warns the Japanese never to attack us again and concludes:

"For we have a country with millions of men
Like Nimitz–and Halsey–and me"

Yes. And, one of those "millions of men" was Lieutenant Junior Grade, later Rear Admiral, Joseph B. McDevitt. And, yes, too, says Paul McDevitt, "Let me count the ways."

Respectfully submitted,
William O. Miller, Rear Admiral, JAGC, U.S. Navy (Ret)

PREFACE

In the summer of 2009 my wife Barb and I attended a McDevitt family reunion in South Carolina. We are a large, close family that spans four generations. We have great reunions. As we packed up the car to head home, my brother Dave approached me carrying a rather nondescript box and said, "Here, this is for you. It contains letters that Dad wrote home during the war."

This was our proverbial box in the basement. I have since learned that many families across this nation have discovered their own boxes and that many more stories about American heroes are being researched and written.

I returned home and put the box away in a closet. Sometime later, for reasons that I cannot recall, my thoughts returned to the box one weekend when Barb was visiting her Mother. I retrieved it and reverently unpacked its contents. My clearest recollection of that experience was learning the true meaning of the term "musty."

Every letter that I picked up and opened released a wisp of 65-year-old air. It was strong, dusty, and stale. The hair on the back of my neck stood up. My nerves tingled.

Then, I began to read. The contents were utterly disorganized as a whole, but they were fascinating item by item. When I finished, I tried rearranging the letters in approximately chronological order and read them through once again. After the second reading, I knew *unquestionably* that I had to tell Joe McDevitt's story. They *were* a great generation, those young men and women… all of them. We honor them best by telling and retelling their stories. So, a new story began.

This book is based on Joe McDevitt's letters to his Aunt Margaret. Three batches of letters chronicle key stages of his early life. The first stage began with his enrollment at the University of Illinois. That education fashioned a powerful learner and a consummate time manager. Also, as an accomplished musician, Joe learned the essentials of working harmoniously with others in both small and large group settings. He learned the importance of leadership.

A second batch of letters describes Joe's early training and professional development in the wartime naval reserve. This was an utterly transformative period of his life, as it was for many of his generation. The United States Naval Reserve Midshipmen's School V-7 Program was designed to make warriors from a new generation of college graduates. From day one, the Navy sought to identify and foster leaders, individuals who would be able to step forward in difficult circumstances and say, "Follow me." Joe McDevitt thrived in this environment from its earliest days.

The final batch of letters recounts Joe's experiences during and immediately following the Pacific war. Joe became an experienced and successful line officer, capable of planning, organizing, and executing arguably the most complex naval operation: Amphibious Assault. By war's end, he was an accomplished and highly regarded naval reservist. All of the lessons he had learned and the skills he had honed prepared him— and a whole generation of his cohorts—for successful postwar careers. Since his record thereafter has been well documented and fully recognized, that is where we will end this story.

My greatest challenge writing this book was "the fire." In 1976, my Dad's home in Clemson, South Carolina, burned to the ground. All of his possessions, including documents, pictures, letters, and memorabilia from the war were destroyed. The only remnants of his earlier life would be the letters that he had written "home" to Margaret Zimmer, the spinster aunt who raised him. Those letters, and the box in which Aunt Margaret stored them, remained with the Zimmer family for many years before finding their way back to Joe McDevitt after the fire.

My challenge was clear: to research and accurately reconstruct the substance of the experiences described in my Dad's letters during four years of college, eleven months of Navy training, and twenty-one months of Pacific warfare.

I started where we all start these days—the Internet. I followed the leads, and the piles of documents on the floor of my basement began growing.

The Internet led to the Holy Grail of World War II researchers—the National Archives in College Park, Maryland. After that trip, fully half of my basement floor disappeared under stacks of documents. Trips to the university archives on the campus of the University of Illinois at Urbana Champaign came next. My library at the University of Illinois Springfield loaned four volumes of Samuel Eliot Morison's incomparable history of the US Navy in the Pacific War. Then I began corresponding with staff at the National Personnel Records Center. Finally I visited Marilyn Seidel's house.

Marilyn's husband, Sam, served with my Dad aboard the USS *Leon* throughout their war years. Sam returned to Salisbury, Maryland, and built a career in insurance. He became a successful and esteemed member of the community, and, with Marilyn, raised their family. The Seidels also hosted the very first reunion of the crew of the USS *Leon* in June 1983. More reunions followed. By 2012, the Seidel's basement had become something of a depository for material regarding the *Leon* and her crew.

Marilyn graciously provided me access to this treasure trove for two days in March 2012. The mother lode was the lists of crew members who had attended ship's reunions. The lists were far out of date, but they were a start at finding the penultimate resource—surviving crew members of the USS *Leon*.

This discovery began the final and most emotionally challenging part of my research. With Barb working the Internet, we updated the lists and I began telephoning Dad's former shipmates. Unfortunately, I learned with each call that one after another of them had passed on to a higher post. That was the low point of this project. Had I waited too long?

Then one day, I made a call to Seymour, Connecticut, and Ethel Janega answered the phone. I introduced myself and explained briefly the purpose for my call. She replied, "Sure, you want to speak with my husband, Bill. Hold on a minute." The hair on my neck stood up; *all* of the nerves in my scalp tingled. Bill Janega was a member of L Division, the boat group division that my Dad commanded aboard the *Leon*. He was alive and well. We spoke for a while and Bill said, "Paul, did you know that Jimmie Hecht lives over in Southington? And I think Glenn Dickinson still lives up in Granville, Massachusetts." So off to Seymour I went, where I joined Ethel and Bill Janega and two other crew members for an afternoon of stories, pictures, and dinner.

There is no substitute for first-hand oral history. So before I left Seymour, I commissioned Bill Janega as my ex officio consultant ("Hi Bill, what's a Welin davit?"). We have had many conversations about the *Leon* and her crew's wartime experiences since that day.

When my basement floor finally disappeared under stacks of books, papers, documents, and pictures, I began writing. This is how *All Came Home* came to be.

INTRODUCTION

Joseph Bryan McDevitt was born to John and Mary (Zimmer) McDevitt in McGehee, Arkansas, on December 22, 1918. We do not know how Mary, who was raised in Harrisburg, Illinois, first met John McDevitt, who lived in McGehee. We do know, however, that they eventually married in 1915. In his early years John McDevitt, who was short and of medium weight, was reportedly a prize fighter.

In the early 1920s, John began working as a locomotive fireman and then as an engineer for the Missouri Pacific Railroad. The job was in Little Rock, Arkansas, so John, Mary, Joe, and his younger brother, Edward, moved to Little Rock in the early 1920s. John was often absent from home for prolonged periods of time riding the rails around the country.

John, Joe, Ed, and Mary McDevitt, circa 1922

In 1926, the McDevitt family traveled to Harrisburg for the marriage of Mary's sister, Esther Zimmer, a Harrisburg school teacher, to Mike Hanagan. Mary had not been feeling well, but as a member of her sister's bridal party, she insisted on making the trip. Sadly, her condition continued to deteriorate after arriving in Harrisburg, and she passed away from typhus shortly thereafter.

The story of the untimely death of Joe and Ed's Mother was reported in her obituary in *THE DAILY REGISTER*, the local newspaper, July 24, 1926:

WOMAN DIES HERE AT PARENTS' HOME
Typhoid causes Death of Mrs. Mary McDevitt of Arkansas

Mrs. Mary McDevitt, wife of John McDevitt of Little Rock, Ark., who came to Harrisburg on a visit a little more than a month ago, died at 9:15 o'clock last night of typhoid at the home of her parents, Mr. and Mrs. Peter Zimmer at 125 West Homer Street. She had been ill ever since the day she came to Harrisburg and was feeling very bad at the time she started to this city.

She came here to attend the wedding of her sister, Esther Zimmer, a Harrisburg school teacher to M. J. Hanagan, an attorney from St. Louis. She had a large church wedding and Mrs. McDevitt was one of the bridal attendants. She was very ill during the wedding ceremony, but did not complain, not wanting to mar the happiness of the wedding celebration.

During the wedding reception her illness was noticed and she was induced to go to bed, following which a Doctor was summoned. He diagnosed her illness as typhoid and one of her sisters, who is a trained nurse remained over after the wedding to help take care of her, but her ailment proved severe and she did not show any improvement. Several days ago it became known that she could not get well and all of the out of town relatives were summoned.

Her husband, who is a railroader in Little Rock, and their two children, Joseph, 8, and Edward, 6, were at her bedside when the end came last night. Death came very peacefully as a relief from intense suffering that physician-friends and loving relatives could not lighten.

Her parents, brothers and sisters are well known in Harrisburg, which was also her home for several years. Her brothers are: John and Stephen Zimmer of Evansville, Frank and William L. Zimmer of Detroit, and her sisters are: Mrs. N. B. Humm of Golconda, Mrs. M. J. Hanagan and Miss Margaret K. Zimmer of Harrisburg.

She was a member of St. Mary's Catholic Church and her funeral will be held at that church at 11 o'clock Sunday morning following which the body will be taken to St. Joseph's cemetery in Hardin County for burial. Burial is expected to take place at 1:00 p. m. Sunday.

John McDevitt never remarried and was unable, because of his work, to raise Joe and Ed following the loss of their Mother. They lived briefly with their Uncle John Zimmer, his wife, and four children in Evansville, Indiana. Times were tough in those days however, and two additional mouths to feed was a hardship. Eventually Joe and Ed were split up. Joe went to Harrisburg where he was raised by his Aunt Margaret Zimmer. She lived across the street from her parents (Joe's grandparents), Peter and Catherine. Ed went to Benton, Illinois, forty-three miles from Harrisburg, to be raised by Aunt Esther and Uncle Mike Hanagan.

From that point on, the brothers' contacts were intermittent: One day weekend visits, annual family reunions, summertime visits to their Dad in North Little Rock, and trips that Ed and his Dad would make to summer resorts where Joe was playing with a band. The brothers remained close, as have their families to this day.

Harrisburg, IL   *1926–1936*

The strong Midwestern roots that Joe reminisced about for the rest of his life grew during his ten years living with the Zimmers. That family included Grandma and Grandpa Zimmer, four uncles, three aunts, and twenty-one cousins. Perhaps because of this strong family support, Joe flourished in Harrisburg. While we don't know many specifics of his early years there, we do know that he began taking piano lessons early on. He quickly demonstrated both a strong interest and a remarkable musical aptitude. The occasional letters written by John McDevitt to Margaret Zimmer verify that John continually struggled to pay for Joe's music lessons while he lived with his Aunt Margaret. No one—save perhaps his music teacher—could have imagined the rich rewards that this investment would return throughout Joe's lifetime.

THE DAILY REGISTER
May 11, 1936

"Joe McDevitt, a pianist, and Clifford Bennett, a sousaphone player, leave Wednesday evening for Cleveland where they will participate in the national music contest."

We can find no report of the contest outcomes; we do know that Joe performed well. The inscription on a commemorative medal awarded by the National School Orchestra Association at Cleveland, Ohio, in 1936 reads:

National High School
Solo Contest
Piano
Championship

Carbondale, IL   *1936–1938*

After graduating from high school in June 1936, Joe attended Southern Illinois Normal University (SINU) in Carbondale, Illinois, for two years. Newspaper articles and archival copies of the 1937 SINU yearbook OBELISK offer a glimpse of his life as a freshman. He was a strong academic achiever; became a member of Kappa Delta Alpha fraternity; and was actively engaged in both drama and music. Joe became a member of the Zitetic Society, the oldest organization on campus, which focused on drama, art, and music. He also accepted membership in the highly regarded Little Theater. This organization provided serious dramatic training for twenty-five competitively selected students each year. All Little Theater members participated in its annual production which, in February 1937, was A. A. Milne's *The Dover Road.* Finally, OBELISK reported that over homecoming weekend Joe had appeared in a one-act comedy on Russian peasant life entitled, "*A Marriage Proposal.*"

Of course, Joe rarely wandered far from his music that year. He played in both the marching band and the university orchestra.

After his freshman year, Joe was honored as one of twenty "Leaders of the Hour" on the Carbondale campus. The inscription accompanying his picture read, "Versatile musician…"

During his sophomore year, Joe was again active in the Zitetic Society, the Little Theater, the marching band and the university orchestra, Kappa Delta Alpha, and also the Newman Club. The December 15, 1937, *ST. LOUIS POST- DISPATCH* identified Joe as one of six students appearing in the Zitetic Society's annual play, "*Sun Up,*" a production with a Kentucky hillbilly background.

At the end of his sophomore year, Joe was again recognized for his outstanding and versatile talents as one of twenty outstanding students. The picture and caption from the 1938 OBELISK appear below.

Outstanding Student:
Joe McDevitt … Musician, Thespian … Grieg and Goodman in either hand.

Although he was prospering at SINU, Joe made a crucial decision about his future during his second year. He decided to apply to the University of Illinois at Urbana Champaign to study law. Family lore has it that Joe's friends and family had always encouraged him to study medicine. For some reason however, perhaps the positive influence of his new Uncle Mike Hanagan, Joe chose to study "LAW IN THE GRAND MANNER" at Illinois. He enrolled in the fall semester of 1938. His letters home to Aunt Margaret began shortly thereafter, as does our story.

Washington DC   *1936*

Few Americans understood better than President Franklin D. Roosevelt in the 1930s the threat that Nazi Germany and Japan posed to the United States. Roosevelt was a true visionary. He understood better than his military advisors that, before America could fight a war, it had to *get ready* to fight. The president began urging, cajoling, legislating, and directing American industry to get on a war footing well before hostilities began.

One of FDR's earliest priorities was preparing the Navy for a two-ocean war. A first step was to work with Congress to enact the Merchant Marine Act of 1936. The act created a maritime commission to head an agency charged with encouraging the modernization of the US Merchant Fleet. Among the commission's initiatives would be a collaborative effort between the agency, Navy planners, and American shipyard owners to design, build, and commission a new generation of merchant vessels. When refitted to the Navy's specifications, these ships—manned by crews of reservists like Joe McDevitt—would help transform amphibious warfare as large attack transports. This new weapon was considered so important that its capabilities were not widely publicized until a Fortune magazine article in April 1945.

The battle before the battles had begun.

1

LAW SCHOOL

The University of Illinois was a large and sprawling campus when Joe McDevitt arrived in fall 1938. The campus was located in the adjoining cities of Champaign and Urbana. With over fourteen thousand students on campus, Illinois was arguably among the five largest university campuses in the country. Of the eleven thousand undergraduate students, approximately 130 were enrolled in the Preparatory to Law degree program offered in the College of Liberal Arts and Sciences. In turn, those graduates competed each year to join approximately 240 graduate students in the College of Law.

The effects of the depression were just beginning to lift on campus, and signs of a revived social life were appearing. Still, some claimed that the school spirit remained at an all-time low. A conservative campus culture clung to past traditions, though evidence of more socially liberal attitudes glimmered, e.g., growing acceptance of smoking, lipstick, and drinking among women students. The campus would also cling to its peacetime traditions as the shadow of war lengthened in the early 1940s.

The depression notwithstanding, the College of Law had prospered under the leadership of Dean Albert James Harno, its leader since 1922. A nucleus of highly regarded "permanent faculty" insured needed stability and continuity. A progressive curriculum based on changing conceptions of the law and of legal education earned growing respect among both academic and non-academic constituencies. The buildings and facilities were suitable, which was something of a victory after years of very tight budgets. The law library, the backbone of legal education, was one of the largest in the nation.

At Illinois, the law school leadership focused on the vision articulated by Oliver Wendell Homes in a centennial publication celebrating the University of Illinois:

> "The business of the law school is not sufficiently described when you merely say that it is to teach law or to make lawyers. It is to teach law in the grand manner, and to make great lawyers."[1]

Champaign, IL   *September 15, 1938*

Dear Aunt Margaret:

I know I really should have written sooner - but to tell you the truth I've been spending most of my time wearing out shoe leather. Boy I've never walked so much before in my life.

My roommate is a swell fellow and we will get along very well. I've met quite a few fellows and they are all friendly and likable. As yet I have worked only once ($1.50) which doesn't mean much since I have to eat. But I've made several contacts with one with the best bands on the campus. There is a possible chance that next week I can start on a "bean job" that will pay for my meals. If so that would be fine - but it is not at all definite. Anyway, the only thing I'm worried about now is getting started - after that I think things will come along OK.

---

1   LAW IN THE GRAND MANNER: A Popular History of the College of Law at the University of Illinois, Board of Trustees, University of Illinois, 1995.

I've been looking for that card from you for the past two days -
but no card. Remember what you said? Was your trip all right?

I forgot to tell you that you are not allowed to send written
matter in those laundry cases - one way to do it is to line it
with newspaper & stick a sheet underneath it.

I've had no mail as yet and don't think I don't miss it!!

Write soon.

Love,
Joe

Joe McDevitt's *first* letter home from the University of Illinois, and the very first sentence made this son laugh. Many readers who attended large state schools probably still recall (and shared) his dismay at the amount of walking we did. Wearing out shoe leather remains a rite of passage even today among college students.

This letter introduces three themes that recur in Joe's letters for the next seven years. The first was Joe's immediate focus on his finances. As future letters will confirm, he was careful and conscientious with his money from his first days at Champaign. It was *always* in short supply. With good reason... he was the first in his family to go to college and to graduate. He had underestimated the cost of a college education and would receive minimal financial support from his family.

Here's a secret. In his very *last* letter home from Champaign, Joe pledged to clear his financial slate, including paying his $10 graduation fee before leaving campus. To this day, however, his university transcripts contain the following note recorded in 1942: "Did not pay $10 diploma fee." A more accurate note would read, "Could not pay $10 diploma fee."

The second theme was the centrality of music to Joe's life. He relied largely upon his musical talent to support himself financially through four academic years at the university. On several occasions his commitment to music would seriously challenge his academic commitment to the law.

Finally, Joe concludes his first letter noting that he has received no mail from his Aunt Margaret. Future letters will confirm that his Aunt Margaret, unlike Joe, was not a faithful correspondent. In some letters the profound disappointment that Joe feels and expresses about her failure to write is so deep and personal as to be palpable.

Champaign, IL   *September 19, 1938*

Dear Aunt Margaret:

I may as well start now - I mean Sunday is going to be my letter-writing day and you can expect to hear from me every Monday. I got your special yesterday evening and was certainly glad to hear from you too. I'm ashamed to say so, but I must admit that I've been the least bit homesick. People here - outside of friends - are so cold and unfriendly.

But today I did meet one person who I like very much. It was Fr. O'Brien at St. John's Church. He is really an educated man and the students all like him so very much. In fact, half the people who pack the church are non-Catholics who like to hear him speak.

There's one nice thing about church here on Sunday and it is the eleven o'clock Mass. Now I won't have to worry about not waking up in time. I went to Benediction this evening and the church was packed. It only lasted 15 minutes. Father O'Brien really knows how to get them to come. If you remember, Dick Christaman liked him a lot.

Thanks a lot for the money you sent Aunt Marg - it will come in handy because I haven't found any work as yet. They have been having union troubles up here - and if it is ironed out I'll have a "bean job" that will take care of meals.

Gee, I'm so sorry you had so much trouble on the way back. When you come up again you must bring a man to drive - it's too far for you to drive all by yourself. I bet you and Alanda were very tired. You didn't tell me when - what time you got home - I'll bet it was late. Didn't Grandma raise the devil??? Ho! Ho!

Well, I register Tuesday - Political Science 1a, Political Science 4, Economics, French and Rhetoric. Sixteen hrs. That is a good load, especially if I have to work.

Well, I've got to get something to eat before I starve. It is now 9 P.M. and I ate at 10:00 A.M. I've stayed at the house all day except the two times I went to church.

I've heard from Ed once and Papa wrote. (He didn't send any money Ha! Ha! I feel so sorry for Dad - Gosh I wish he could live up here.)

Well, Auntie. I'll write again this week sometime & let you know how things turn out. You needn't write so often because I know you are busy.

Tell Grandma, Grandpa and Mrs. Harrelson hello for me. Also all others.

Love,
Joe

P.S. It's getting awfully cold here and everyone is wearing overcoats. If you get a chance please send mine up right away. I should have known enough to bring it. It's so cold my face and hands are chapped.

Joe had a clear plan in mind as he began his studies at Illinois. He needed two years of coursework to complete the prelaw program and to earn the A.B. LAS degree (Bachelor of Arts in the College of Arts and Sciences) in 1940. He would then apply to law school and earn the L.L. B. degree in 1942.

But there was a problem:

"That is a good load, especially if I have to work."

Champaign, IL   *September 26, 1938*

Dear Aunt Margaret:

Well, here it is the first day of school - I've been to two classes this morning and have two more this afternoon. And, frankly, I'll admit that things don't look so good. In fact, just now, I can't see how I'll be able to clear things up. When I came up I expected to get a job that would take care of my meals - but the union trouble between the Restaurants and the Musicians unions is still as bad as ever and it looks very much like the eight restaurants on the campus which formerly hired bands are not going to do so any ways soon. So that means I have to pay for meals.

Yesterday I registered and paid $35 tuition. I had to have the other $36 deferred - paying $3 for that privilege. That means if I pay it all within 10 days I get $2.00 back. But I have two months to pay it - by November 20.

I had to use all the $15 you sent me to buy books - and a little more besides - gosh but they are so expensive. I still owe Mrs. Wiggins $14 on room & by the end of this month the board will total $11. So before I could stand in the clear at all I would have to pay $36 + 11 + 4 or $51. Of course, as I said, $36 of that has two months to pay.

Mrs. Wiggins didn't begin serving until yesterday - so I had to eat until then. After I paid Warren $10 I had $35. It cost me $9 to live here for 10 days. That left $26. But during the time I've been here I made $14. So when I went to register I had $40. I spent $38 of that. So now Aunt Margaret you know just how I stand - I thought you'd like to know. It looks like the next time I'll get to work will be Oct 7 for $4. That's a long time off - but that's the way work is here.

I'm going to write my dad - of course I can't give him an explanation like the above - for I'm afraid he would not quite understand it. I don't know just what he will say though, because he just sent Ed $50 a week ago. I haven't as yet asked him for any extra money though. Because I really didn't think I'd need it.

I'm taking two Political Science courses, Economics, French, Rhetoric, and History. They promise to keep me very busy. I made the band which lets me out of military. But there again is another worry - I have to buy a band uniform which costs around $15 or $20 & I'm already supposed to have it. Gosh darn it, everything seems to go wrong. Some people have all the money. These kids up here have nothing to worry about - they let their Dads and folks do the worrying. I wish almost that I had just started out digging ditches - no worry. (I really don't but I've set a goal that will be hard to reach.)

Felts has it easy - he gets his board and room free at his brother-in-law's.

I've just been thinking that probably the thing I should do - but I'll wait to see what you think - and dad too - is to go and make a student loan. At least I'm going to inquire as to the particulars.

```
Well, I must close and go down to lunch. If you write dad, please
explain this to him will you Aunt Margaret, because I am afraid
he will think I am spending a lot of money foolishly, and that's
one thing I certainly am not doing.

Well, write soon Aunt Margaret when you find time - and tell
Grandma, Grandpa and Mrs. Harrelson hello for me.

Love,
Joe

P.S. It's awfully cold here. Please send my coat when you can -
and send my sweaters in the laundry bag.
```

The first day of school and he already sounded down and out. The cost of everything—including university tuition, books, and room and board—was apparently a shock compared to his earlier years at SINU in Carbondale. Perhaps he was just realizing that his challenge at the University of Illinois wasn't going to be the academics, but his finances. A law degree was indeed going to be "a hard goal to reach."

The labor problems between feuding unions were an especially unrelenting burden. These disputes were absolutely beyond his control. How was he going to support himself? The bills were already piling up faster than he could manage.

This letter also mentions that he had been accepted into the First Regimental Band, the famed Illini Marching Band. The First Regimental Band was a serious musical organization with a strong professional orientation. The band's repertoire that fall semester included fifty marching formations and thirty musical arrangements from which thirty-minute programs were presented at six football games, including the Notre Dame game in South Bend, Indiana, and the Northwestern game in Chicago.

Joe learned lessons in the marching band that would serve him well in his future. These were lessons about teamwork, about the relationship between practice and performance, and about detailed planning and flawless execution of formations for small groups and large. He learned about inspired leadership, about delivering flawless musical adaptations while executing complex drills in hot weather and bitter cold, and about performance under pressure. He learned all these lessons well. They became part of who he was, of how he perceived the world, and of how he managed his affairs.

Champaign, IL   *October 3, 1938*

Dear Aunt Margaret:

Sunday afternoon, - and letter writing time for me. I have about five or six to write - and first of all - you. It is about 3:30 and things are so very quiet, an ideal Sunday afternoon. I'm going to an organ recital at five and to the closing of Forty Hours Devotion at seven.

I received the laundry bag and box this week. The coat really fits into the picture here - it is getting colder rapidly and one feels good with plenty of clothes on.

It was really thrilling yesterday to know that I am a member of the University of Illinois Marching Band - which the announcer on the broadcast called "the best and most wonderful band in the world." I want you to hear it some time. I'll tell you when a good time will be. Papa sent me $30 this month so that now all I owe is $22 to the school which must be paid by November 1st - and my next month's board (I've paid for last month and room for this next). Union trouble is still going on and my job has not started yet. I hope that it will sometime soon. I'm sending Papa's letter so you can read it. I understand just how he feels - but this was the first time I had asked him for any extra money. He sent Ed $50 at the beginning of school. I wish I could get to work - but I've tried.

School is "no play" here. I never go anywhere except to the organ recital and to church - I haven't time. But I'm satisfied to do no more.

Please write when you have time. I certainly love to hear from you. It's kinda lonesome here.

Love,
Joe

Champaign, IL   October 17, 1938

Dear Aunt Margaret:

Can't write much because am busy right now studying for exams but I do want to get this document back to you in a hurry as you asked - and also I wanted to thank you for the socks. I must say you hit the nail right on the head in picking them out. They suit me just fine & the fellows all liked them.

I've been writing so much that my hand cramps & I can't write even a legible handwriting any more. I made a B+ on every one of the four exams I have taken so far & the older fellows say that that is about as good as you can get on the first exams. School is very interesting here & I like it fine.

Gosh, I wish you could come up Saturday. It is Dad's Day and the band is going to put on a good show. You couldn't possibly make it, could you? Gosh, I wish you could come up.

Man, it is cold here - & the band marches out in the cold two hours every evening. 32 degrees - freezing. I wonder if you could manage to pick me up a pair of gloves sometime please. Hands are

the coldest things about me. I'll take care of them. Make them
warm. I have been borrowing a pair of my roommate's. He has
a leather pair for class and another pair for knocking around
school.

Well, Auntie, tell everyone hello and thanks a lot for writing.

Love,
Joe

Champaign, IL   *November 2, 1938*

Dear Aunt Margaret, Grandma and Grandpa:

Just a few lines to let you know that I still live at 1104 W.
Illinois in Urbana. Gosh, but I miss hearing from you. It's
lonesome enough when I do get letters.

It's been so very warm here for the past week. I just about
burned up this afternoon. Turning weather though. It gets cold
enough for a top coat at night.

Next Saturday the band is going to Notre Dame to play at the
football game - special train - all expenses paid. It will be
broadcast so maybe you can listen in. I don't know what station
but it will be easy to find the Illinois - Notre Dame football
game. And Aunt Margaret, I wish you could send those black
shoes - please. I had to borrow a pair last Saturday. They were
too small & just about drove me nuts. I'll bet I looked like I
was walking on nails. Ha. Ha.

I've just come back from Benediction and Newman Club meeting.
We danced at the meeting and Father O'Brien was the chaperone.

The boys outnumber girls 4 to 1 at this school - so it's pretty hard to get with one. Father made each girl dance with about 4 boys. It was funny to see him hustling some embarrassed boy around & asking a girl to dance with him. They have meetings every Sunday night. Father is a "good egg." But he makes too long sermons. It takes an alarm clock to stop him. Church lasted almost two hours this morning. I saw lots of people nodding.

I haven't found a job yet and things look pretty bad - still maybe they will break.

How are you, Aunt Marge? And how are Grandma and Grandpa? And Mrs. Harrelson, or is she still there. Tell Mrs. Edwards and Doc Klein hello for me - and write soon.

Love,
Joe

P.S. I've gained 6 pounds - 151 lbs.

Aunt Margaret, Miss Margaret K. Zimmer, was a central figure in Joe's life. She was born January 16, 1894, in Hardin County, Illinois, the sixth child—third daughter—born to Peter and Catherine Zimmer. Margaret lived most of her adult life in Harrisburg, Illinois, at 120 West Homer, just across the street from her parents. She was 32 years old, unmarried, and without children, when her sister Mary died in 1926. She raised eight-year-old Joe McDevitt as if he were her own until Joe left for college at the age of eighteen.

Aunt Margaret was a professionally trained and certified nurse. She never had her own family and she outlived most of her siblings, so we know less about her than most of the Zimmers. We know for certain that family caregiving consumed much of her life, beginning with ten years spent rearing her especially active nephew. In fact, we know from several of Joe's earliest letters home that, even in his earliest college years at SINU, Joe especially enjoyed spending his summers with Aunt Margaret in Harrisburg because she owned a piano! He loved music and relished the prospect of spending an entire summer playing her piano. So we may assume that Margaret Zimmer's professional options and perhaps even social opportunities were limited during the "Joe McDevitt" period of her life.

Margaret Zimmer

Some years later, Margaret Zimmer also became the primary caregiver as her parents, Peter and Catherine, aged and required greater support. That burden seems to have fallen to her for several reasons. Many of her siblings had moved away from Harrisburg by that time and were unable to help. Also, medically trained siblings in those days often carried the heaviest burden of parental caregiving. So, for another period of her life, Margaret sacrificed professional and personal considerations to support her family.

When Margaret was not working at home, she held positions with several different employers in her career. We know she worked for a time at the Saline County Red Cross, because *THE DAILY REGISTER* in Harrisburg announced that, on May 22, 1945,

Margaret Zimmer would teach a streamlined, six-lesson course entitled Red Cross Home Nursing. At other times in her career, she performed volunteer work in Harrisburg and applied for, as well as held, nursing positions at hospitals in St. Louis, MO, and Benton, IL. Family letters suggest other appointments.

We can infer much about the relationship between Joe and his Aunt Margaret based on the tone and content of Joe's letters, although this would be entirely a one-sided perspective. Firstly, Joe was obviously a loving nephew, who cared deeply about his Aunt Margaret. He rarely closed a letter without expressing his strong feelings for her or promising to pray for her. In later letters, he refers to her as his Mother. Also, he was obviously comfortable using terms of endearment, e.g., Auntie or Aunt Marge. Altogether his letters seem to verify that he understood and appreciated the sacrifices she had made for him, that he felt very close to her, and that he tried conscientiously to express those feelings.

Also, Joe's frank and wide ranging discussions about virtually every aspect of his life suggest that he and Aunt Margaret had communicated often and well during his formative years. He wrote to her about virtually everything, from his dreariest lows to his cheeriest highs. Sometimes she was a sounding board when he was uncertain; at other times she was a financial consultant; occasionally, she was an intermediary between Joe and his Dad. He had obviously talked openly and freely with Aunt Margaret while growing up, so that writing to her in a similar manner came naturally to him. Perhaps *his* strong need to communicate explains the keen disappointment that he felt when Aunt Margaret failed to reciprocate so often.

Finally, from a strictly personal viewpoint, Joe's letters sometimes "feel" like letters between siblings, e.g., as between a younger brother and an older sister. Perhaps this tone reflects the nature of their relationship, perhaps not.

Champaign, IL   *November 21, 1938*

Dear Aunt Margaret:

Gosh, I'll bet you thought I wasn't going to write at all,
didn't you? I've been so busy this weekend - the band went to
Chicago and I didn't get back until early this morning. That's
why I haven't written.

I'll be down some time Wednesday or Thursday, I can't say when.
I had arranged to come with Felt's brother-in-law but he isn't
driving down so I have to find another way. There are several but
they charge too much - 4 or 5 dollars for round trip. I don't
want to pay that much at all. If anything happens & I can't
come I'll send a telegram so tell everyone not to worry if one
comes. But I'll get there - I want to come home so badly.

I'm making this letter short so I can get it in the morning
mail.

I received the money and can't thank you enough Aunt Margaret.
I'll pay you back fully for everything someday.

Love to everyone. I'll see you this weekend.

Joe

Champaign, IL   *December 14, 1938*

Dear Aunt Margaret:

I know I haven't written at all since I came back and I've been
intending to for the past week. But right now is really the

first time I've had to write at all. I've had exams coming so thick and fast that I didn't know which end is up. I've only written Dad once - I must write him too.

He wrote and told me he was getting me a pass to Carbondale - one for Ed and I from Carbondale to St. Louis - and a pass from St. Louis down. (He also asked me what size shirt and socks I wear. I don't want him to buy me anything - no telling what they would look like. What shall I tell him anyway?)

I can't leave here until noon the 23rd Dec. Now the question is that Dad expects us down there Christmas Day. If I go down the 23rd, we would leave Little Rock the evening of the 26th or 27th and be back in Carbondale the 27th or 28th accordingly. The vacation lasts until Wed. noon, 4th of January.

But the trouble is I won't be home during hardly any of your vacation. I don't know whether Dad will come up to Harrisburg or not. In his last letter he just said he "wished we could all go to Harrisburg."

I wrote Detroit and got a letter from Gertrude yesterday. She said that Uncle Frank doesn't have a car and that his business is very bad now - that she has just started working full time - that they just will not be able to make it down Christmas. So there's no planning on them coming.

I'm sending my laundry - and I will mark on a piece of paper the things to send back up. I want you to keep some of the shirts so I won't have to pack them in a suitcase over vacation.

Write and let me know what you want me to do Christmas.

Love,
Joe

P.S. I forgot that I will have to be back up here on Dec. 31 since the band I play with is playing in Kokomo, Indiana, New Year's Eve.

A job! With a band! Research at the University of Illinois Archives confirmed that Joe was now the pianist with the popular Johnny Bruce Orchestra, pictured below. Two other members who played with Johnny Bruce that fall are mentioned frequently in letters to come. The first is Warren Felts, AKA Felts, whose family kindly provided the picture below. Warren is in the back row, third person from the left. He was a talented musician from Harrisburg and the high school class president the year he and Joe graduated. He was probably Joe's first contact with Johnny Bruce. The second person is Dori King, seated with Joe at the piano. Dori was the orchestra's featured vocalist who soon became the first serious love of Joe McDevitt's life.

Johnny Bruce Orchestra, University of Illinois, Fall 1938

Champaign, IL   *January 12, 1939*

Dear Aunt Margaret:

I'm afraid I won't be able to write much because I've just
finished writing a 2000 word essay and my hand is plenty tired.

But I know that I really should write you - I should have written much sooner.

But final exams are only a week off and the work comes thick, fast and hard these days. I haven't gotten to bed before 2 o'clock any nite this week and get up at seven. I like to see Saturday morning roll around - I don't have to get up until 10 o'clock.

I've heard from Ed twice - he told me about going to Harrisburg and about how nice you were to him. He said that he was going to stay away from Benton as much as possible. I sure feel sorry for him. He is rather bashful and doesn't know how to act in many circumstances. It isn't his fault at all, we both know that. However, college should eventually work a change in him. He's hoping - and planning - to go down and be with dad on his birthday March 4. I should like to very much but can't.

My last exam comes Monday afternoon, Jan.30. I have off until the next Monday - a week. I don't know yet how I will get home - I can't afford railroad or bus this time. But I will let you know for sure.

Dad changed boarding houses. Mrs. Buckles wrote and told me that Mrs. Kaiser had raised h _ _ _ and blamed her. Ha. Ha. I was the one who changed his mind.

Well I'm worn out - I'll write soon about vacation.

Take care of yourself.

Love,
Joe

McDevitt Receives Honorable Mention In Essay Contest

SPRINGFIELD, Ill., March 8 — (UP).—Loretta Wright, Leland high school, LaSalle county, was the winner in a statewide essay contest on Citizenship and Naturalization, sponsored by Gov. Henry Horner, it was revealed today.

Second place in the contest was won by Esther Marland, Somonauk high school, and third place went to James Tobin, University High school, Urbana. Each of the winners will receive medals to be presented by the governor. Joseph McDevitt of Harrisburg was one of eleven to receive honorable mention.

Joe McDevitt earns honorable mention in essay contest
THE DAILY REGISTER, Harrisburg, Illinois

Champaign, IL   *February 9, 1939*

Dear Aunt Margaret:

I know I should have written sooner but I've been quite busy getting registered and getting started on the new semester.

I got back safe and sound early Monday morning. I came up on the train. It was all my fault that I missed my ride. I had forgotten that he told me to be in Carbondale at 12 o'clock. I told you 12:30 - so I was all wrong. Oh well, I was glad because I got to stick around with Ed and the fellows a little longer. I'll be here long enough.

Well, Aunt Margaret, I'm so very sorry that things have had to happen to you as they have. It's queer that it happened while I was home isn't it? What are you going to do? - I know that's a bothersome question, but you surely must have something in mind. I only wish that I were in some way to be of help to you. Maybe someday things will all be different. I owe you and Dad an awful lot & when I do begin to succeed, and I certainly hope I do, you two will be the first on my list. Time enough for marriage later. Write and let me know how things are.

I registered - 3 political science courses, a constitutional history course, and French. It's going to be quite a load to carry. I've got a lot of work to do tonight.

Well, Aunt Margaret, tell all hello for me and take good care of yourself. Write Dad if you get a chance and convince him that 60 yrs. isn't so old. I'm afraid he's beginning to worry about it. He's mentioned that he isn't a 'spring chicken' any more in his last three letters. I hate to see him get that way. It's bad enough now.

Love,
Joe

Champaign, IL   *March 27, 1939*

Dear Aunt Margaret and all:

I know it has been a very long time since I wrote you last - and I should have written much sooner. But I guess I have a pretty good excuse - now that it's safe to tell you.

I'm very sorry to hear that you had the flu, Aunt Margaret. I know that you've been having a lot of trouble lately and that things have been "in a whirl." That's why I haven't written to let you know how I was. Now don't worry when I tell you this because everything is OK now - and back to normal. I too had the flu, and pretty badly from what they tell me. I missed 2 1/2 weeks of school and just about worked to death trying to catch up. I was in the hospital most of that time - Father O'Brien brought me communion several times. He was very nice - and a lot of help. I've been to church and communion every morning at 6:30 since I got out. Got pretty weak - and hot - but I came out OK - I feel swell now.

This Spring weather we're having now sure makes it hard to study, especially when I have so much to do. I didn't let you know anything and gave specific instructions that you should not be notified - because I knew that you would probably come up and take me home - and you had your hands full already. I didn't know that you had the flu. I didn't let Dad know either - in fact I haven't told him yet. It wasn't that I was weakened - or in bad health - that I caught the flu. Everyone had it - there were thousands missing from school - all theaters, churches, public places were closed - and the hospitals were running over capacity. But as I said before - it has all cleared up and things are normal again. By Easter time you won't be able to tell that anything was wrong with me, although I've lost quite a bit of weight. I've been eating like a pig lately though, and gaining back my weight. Don't worry about it, because if anything were wrong I wouldn't be telling you about it yet.

Of course, there have been bad results. I had to use the money Dad sent for February and March to pay bills that it wasn't meant for. I'm rather behind with Daisy, I still owe $18.50 on my tuition which comes due April 1, but I'm going to have it deferred, and I haven't been able to get all my books - I still have five more to buy. I haven't been able to work at all - so things have been piling up. I don't know what a dollar bill looks like any more. So it looks like I will have to apply for a loan - as much as I hate to. There's an awful lot of red tape involved. I can get a short term loan - about a three month one. Or a long term loan which would be paid back after I get out of school - which is quite a gamble. I would rather get a short term one which I could pay back this Summer - if I can find a good job. Here's the way I figure what my expenses will be - and how much I'd have to meet them with.

Expenses:

Room & Board	
Behind because of sickness	$33.00
March	$34.70
April	$34.70
May	$34.70
	$137.10
Tuition (Due April 1, '39)	$18.50
Books	$15.00
Total Expenses	$170.60
Assets $35 from Dad for Apr., May, June	$105.00
Deficit	$65.60

So at the very least I need $65.60 - which divided over three months would be $21.86 a month. I don't know how much I'm going to get to work - there isn't very much to be had. But I figure I can make about $30 before school is out. But, I haven't listed incidental expenses such as meals on Sunday, church contributions, notebooks and paper supplies, haircut, cleaning and pressing, etc. which can't be figured very accurately - but which run about $5 a month. So if I allow only $15 for spending money or incidentals, that means that I can use only $15 of the $30 I make on expenses. So if I subtract $15 from the $65.60 deficit I listed before - it should be only $50.60 - or $16.86 a month.

So you see, Aunt Margaret, I would only have to borrow $50 or $55. They usually want you to make the loans larger than that. You and Dad would have to sign - a banker and some other official. I would have to pledge any insurance policy or other security, make out a budget & lots of other things. But it wouldn't take so very long - and there's nothing crooked about the loan. It's just that they want to be sure that they have good security. And I want you to understand this - and clearly too. I don't want you to do a thing about any of this. I've gone into detail about this because you're the only one I've got to explain things to - Dad wouldn't understand all the figures. There's one thing you can do - you mentioned that you were going to write Dad. Please let him know that I was ill a little while - but that I am OK now. I won't tell him just yet because he would probably worry. Find out what he thinks about the loan and let me know as soon as you hear from him. I don't want to be an obligation to anyone - and I know that I can pay it back myself.

Well, so much for sordid details. I hate to talk about them but I thought you might like to know how I stand.

Tell Grandma I'm very sorry I forgot about her birthday - I really didn't forget - it's because I was sick at the time and couldn't write. But I thought about her just the same - and I gave her one of my best birthday presents she could get. I had a Mass offered up for her on St. Joseph's Day - and went to communion for her - that she might be strong and happy, and have many, many more birthdays - and wished I could be with her.

And I've thought a lot about you, too, Aunt Margaret. I've been worried - but if prayers help - you'll come out on top.

Thank Mrs. Edwards for me for the nice job she did on my laundry - I didn't have much - but I am sending my bag in the morning (if I can borrow $.20 Ha! Ha! My, the life of a poor college student! Ho!) And listen, Auntie, if you have any extra underwear panties floating around - send them up because I'm almost naked all of the way round - except for shirts. I'll have to build myself a pair of shoes I guess. Ha! Ha! Oh well, warm weather is coming so I think I'll start a new style by going bare footed.

Tell Cecil hello for me - and the kids.

How is Grandpa. Is he starting a garden? Tell him hello too. I think I'll be able to get home Easter, but I'll have to spend all my time studying. I'll write later and let you know for sure. We get out Thursday, April 6, at noon and have to be back Monday, April 10, at noon.

Well, take care of yourself, Aunt Margaret - and the best of luck in everything. I'll remember you each day.

Write as soon as possible and let me know what you think - and what Dad says.

Love to all,
Your nephew, Joe

P.S. My address is 1104 - not 411.

Champaign, IL   *April 4, 1939*

Dear Aunt Margaret and All:

Sunday afternoon - and the best time to write a letter - at least for me. I'm rather tired though. Palm Sunday - reading the Passion - church lasted a long time. And the last 4 or 5 nights I haven't been able to sleep. I went to bed at 11 o'clock and didn't get to sleep until after 2 - and to top it all off I woke up at 5:30 and couldn't get back to sleep.

Well, anyway, I certainly enjoyed your letter and thanks an awful lot for the $2. It has certainly helped.

I suppose I'll be home sometime Thursday evening. I think I'm coming with Professor Nolen & his wife (Felts' sister.) So you can expect me - and don't worry about me getting there.

My tuition payment is due April 8, but I think I can have it put off until after Easter - so don't worry about that.

Well, it's getting about time to go to church. On Sunday evening we have a public questionnaire before Benediction which is broadcast for half an hour. I wish that you could hear Father O'Brien because he is certainly wonderful. But you couldn't get the station - it isn't that strong. But when you come up - when?? - I want you to hear him.

Tell Grandma and Grandpa that I will see them this weekend - and you. So until then -

Love,
Joe

Students on the Illinois campus largely learned about current events on and off campus by reading the *The Daily Illini*, the student-run newspaper and the only "daily" in Champaign. Foreign affairs' reporting was relatively limited during Joe's first semester, but what did appear was alarming to a generation of young Americans for whom the Great War was a repugnant memory. In Europe, the German military mobilized and Germany occupied Sudetenland, Czechoslovakia. Sudetenland was a region occupied by three million Germans, many of whom joined the Nazis after the occupation. In the Far East, Japan continued waging an undeclared war on China, while casting a threatening eye on the colonial possessions of England and France to the South. Virtually every nation with an interest or a possession in the Pacific was carefully watching Japan, a nation seemingly hell-bent on achieving regional hegemony.

Most American college students, however, continued to focus primarily on their studies, football games, rush week and dances... though not necessarily in that order.

Champaign, IL   *April 20, 1939*

Dear Aunt Margaret:

I've been writing a lot today and my hand is tired - so forgive my scribbling and short note.

How are you? And how are Grandma and Grandpa? Has it been raining as much there as here? It rains every day. I wish it would warm up. I got a cold Easter week-end and can't seem to get rid of it.

I'd have written sooner but I've been terribly busy studying for exams - I have two more tomorrow so I've got to get busy.

I paid Daisy the money you gave me - and it left me owing her $40 (including this month's room and rent, however.) When the meals are added it will be about $60, and if Dad sends me $35, I'll be behind about $25-$30, which is how much I told you I would be behind. Then I have to pay the union $15 to work up here. It looks like I will make about $30 this Spring playing, so I'll clear $15 or $20. But my union due is due the 28th of this month - and I won't be able to make that much by then.

Well, Aunt Margaret, I've just got to get to work. I'll write again soon. Write me - yes?

Love to All,
Joe

In short order, the news from Europe grew worse in Joe's first spring semester. Germany took over all of Czechoslovakia in March. The April 11 issue of *The Daily Illini* reported and pictured German troops whom Hitler was pressuring to improve fortification along the French front known as the Siegfried line. In May, Germany signed the "Pact of Steel" agreement with Italy and began negotiating a non-aggression pact with Russia which would be signed in August.

America maintained an official policy of neutrality in spite of continuing pleas for support and assistance from Europe. Behind the scenes, however, President Roosevelt used every means available to neutralize or outmaneuver America's isolationist sentiment and to assist Europe.

Champaign, IL   *June 11, 1939*

Dear Aunt Margaret:

Sorry I haven't answered sooner, but I have been very busy - and
out of town. I went to Chicago this week and got pretty good
results - I got a job out of it all. It starts July 15 - in the
north-eastern corner of Michigan - at a private resort, Harbor
Springs by name. It will pay $27.50 a week, but not expenses.
So living will have to come out of it - but I should be able to
save some. It will last from July 15 until Labor Day - and right
after that we will start working on the campus here.

So I figure I should get down to Little Rock as soon as possible
- and work until time to get back. Dad has sent the pass -
and I'm ready to go. I'll have to be back by July 1 to start
rehearsing so I won't be down there long at that.

Love,
Joe

After second semester classes concluded, Joe McDevitt was admitted to the College of Law at the University of Illinois for the 1940-1941 academic year.

The band that Joe and Dori played with that spring semester and during the summer at Harbor Springs, Michigan, was the Wayne Karr Orchestra. This was a new dance band on campus directed by Wayne Karr, another Harrisburg musician who first arrived on the Champaign music scene in 1936. An undated picture of the Wayne Karr Orchestra, taken probably in spring 1939, appears below.

Wayne Karr Orchestra, University of Illinois, 1939

The Harbor Springs engagement was at the Little Harbor Club, a well-known entertainment hot spot. That job would provide valuable exposure for the orchestra to a new, more upscale clientele. Harbor Springs was a posh resort area that attracted summer vacationers from Chicago in the south to Michigan's Upper Peninsula to the north. A 1940s Harbor Springs Chamber of Commerce brochure proclaimed that:

> "Summer residents here find the ultimate in... formal functions; there are excellent night clubs conducted on metropolitan standards with well-known orchestras and shows comprising professional talent. Among the outstanding clubs are: Little Harbor Club, Beach Club, and Harbor Point Club."[2]

The *Petoskey Evening News* announced in its Harbor Springs column on Friday, July 14, 1939:

> "Wayne Karr's Orchestra members arrived Wednesday night and will be at the Little Harbor Club. Included in the orchestra is Mr. Karr, Harry Lewis, Bix Jensen, Steve Sartorris, G. Karr, Dune Morrison, John Carson, Joe McDevitt and Delores King."

The Wayne Karr Orchestra—Joe and Dori—had hit the big time.

Harbor Springs, MI   *Aug 25, 1939*

Dear Aunt Margaret and All:

Just a few lines to let you know that I received your letter scolding me for not writing & I suppose that by this time you

---

2   Haynes, Virgil D. (2003) GREEN LIGHT A Collection of Photographs by Virgil D. Haynes. Edited by Cynthia Haynes. Harbor Springs, MI: Haynes Studio Productions, p. 141.

have mine scolding you for the same. You must not have gotten the others that I wrote you.

Well, I got a letter from Ed this morning telling me that he will arrive here in the morning on a little vacation. Glad he can come up. He is also going back to Carbondale I guess. He didn't write much - in fact he hasn't been answering my letters. I have been sending Dad money too - I have sent him $40 - so I guess I haven't done so bad, huh?

We have one more week here & although I hate to leave such a fine country I will be glad to get away. I thought for a while that we would get a job in Akron, Ohio - the Mayflower Hotel - but I guess not now. I would have stayed out of school since it would have paid at least $62.50 a week - most likely more. However, it may come through yet. If not we will go straight to the campus & start to work. We will leave here the 3rd or 4th and arrive in Champaign the 5th or 6th - then start to work the 7th for rush week. But I do wish I could see you some time before the hard work starts in because there are so many things to talk about which can't be put in a letter.

My address in Urbana will be the same - 1104 W. Illinois St. and you can send the rest of my clothes there. I'm sorry I didn't tell you that I did get the clothes you sent - I thought I'd told you.

How is Grandma? Does she remember me by my name when you mention it? Give my love to her and Grandpa.

Well, I have to write Dad and get to a rehearsal. Had to send union dues to Champaign so can't send as much this time.

Take care of yourself and I'll try to see you soon.

Love,
Joe

"I would have stayed out of school since it would have paid at least $62.50 a week…"

"… I do wish I could see you some time before the hard work starts in because there are so many things to talk about which can't be put in a letter."

This is an important letter written during an important juncture in Joe McDevitt's college years. The two statements above firmly suggest that Joe spent the summer of 1939 reevaluating his commitment to law school versus a future as a professional musician. The music seems clearly to have won.

As for the law, surely Joe must have been proud that he had completed his first year of classes and had been admitted to the College of Law. This program was an especially prestigious professional one at the University of Illinois. He was right on schedule for achieving his longstanding goal.

What price, however, would he have to pay? The academics had been brutal, especially in the spring semester when he spent 2 ½ weeks in the hospital and then several weeks afterwards catching up on his health and his studies. The young man who wrote that long letter of March 27 was feeling nearly overwhelmed by misfortune.

More importantly, his finances had been a shambles. He surely realized by then that, no matter how hard he studied and worked, he would suffer unrelenting financial hardship until the day he graduated. Three long, hard years to go…

And then… in the midst of a wonderful summer playing in a beautiful resort on Lake Michigan with the love of his life, along came a musical opportunity—presumably to include them both—in Akron, Ohio. The gig would pay $62.50 per week or more. That was *very* big money. No wonder he decided to drop out of law school. Returning to the meat grinder in Champaign was more than he could stomach given this new opportunity.

Still, we have to wonder—could Joe McDevitt's longstanding plan be decided by something as insignificant as a band gig in Akron, Ohio?

Yes, it could have... and was. The only reason that the Wayne Karr group didn't relocate immediately to Akron was that the gig fell through. Had it not, the nation would have lost a future lawyer of national prominence and perhaps gained a professional musician with immeasurable upside potential.

One might wonder also if this one single event perhaps sidetracked Joe's plans for a permanent relationship with Dori King. Perhaps *this* rather than the Akron job was the matter that he wrote "can't be put in a letter" to Aunt Margaret.

Joe, Dori, and the band returned to campus for rush week. That summer would not be the last time that he would have to choose between a future in music or a career in law.

Washington DC   *1939*

The US Maritime Commission continued to pay cash subsidies to American shippers to encourage domestic production of merchant ships. US ships operating on routes in direct competition with foreign shipping could apply for a direct subsidy to make up for the difference in operating costs, provided the route was of strategic value and the owners had credible plans for replacing older ships with new construction. Also, domestic shipyards were subsidized to the difference in construction costs with foreign shipyards, assuming that ship plans were approved by the maritime commission.

However, US ship construction remained painfully sluggish. Only twenty-nine new merchant ships were constructed in US yards in 1939.

FIRST YEAR OF LAW CLASSES

University archival documents, Joe's academic records, and an uncharacteristically limited volume of correspondence in his first year of law school suggest Joe's three priorities that year included law classes, music, and Dori King.

In August 1939, he registered for thirteen hours of coursework, mostly law. Now that he was largely finished with general education work, the serious work was about to begin.

First Semester 1939-1940		
Subject	**Course No.**	**Cr. Hrs.**
Contracts I	1a	3
Torts	2a	3
Possessory Estates	10	3
French	2b	4

Shortly after Joe began classes, the worst possible news arrived from Europe. Germany (and later the Soviet Union) invaded Poland. The Soviets then attacked Finland in November; they would have their hands full overcoming the Finns' heroic defense. War declarations by England, France, Australia, New Zealand and Canada ensued. America continued to proclaim its neutrality, reflecting the widely held view that the conflict was a European affair.

Wallace Dudley penned an editorial in *The Daily Illini* on September 8 that reflected the dominant student view on the Illinois campus in fall 1939:

So It Is, So It Is

"It starts. No one is exactly sure why; no one professes to want war. It continues and under its own momentum gains strength hourly until the clash of economic, military and moral force against force reaches the inevitable climax against which it cannot surge.

And then the war ends, as mysteriously as it began. The captains and the kings depart; another American may glance over the record of strife to compile new material for his "Evidence in the Case - Who's to Blame for the War." Another fuehrer may start on another "Mein Kampf."

War is twice waged - first on the battlefield, then in print. But never - not even on the same battle ground where the vanquished surrender, does war bring ultimate victory. Neither war nor its results are entered as assets on the national ledger.

So from here on the Illinois campus, where the nearest approach to an air raid siren is a fraternity dorm in the early morning hours when a battery of alarm clocks galvanize the brethren into action, we'll sit this European conflict out, if you please."

Joe was pleased to find his musical fortunes (and his cash flow) improve in his second fall semester on campus. The Wayne Karr Orchestra had become a campus favorite. Ads appearing in *The Daily Illini* announced performances by the Wayne Karr Orchestra two to three times monthly at the popular Park Ballroom. Some weeks the band played at the "Park" on Saturday evening, some weeks they played on Sunday, and some weeks they played on Monday or Wednesday evenings. In addition to Park Ballroom, the orchestra also performed at the new Bradley Ballroom in the Illinois Union and at private parties, including proms, rush parties, homecoming, Dad's Weekend, holidays, football weekends, even final exams. For all intents and purposes, the Wayne Karr musicians were full-time professional musicians that year.

Due in part to his heavy work schedule, Joe's academic standing suffered during the fall semester. The high expectations of the law school faculty played a role too. Even for a young, healthy college student, a steady regimen of early Tuesday morning law classes after late Monday engagements at the Park Ballroom was a challenge.

Joe's second semester class schedule included twelve solid hours of law coursework. The orchestra remained in high demand at the ballrooms and on the campus party and dance circuit. Joe was surely pleased that steady work was available, but one wonders if he sensed that he was academically over-committed.

Second Semester 1939-40		
Subject	**Course No.**	**Cr. Hrs.**
Contract I	1b	3
Torts	2b	3
Equity	12	3
Const. Law	22	3

While Joe was learning about contracts and torts during the day and solidifying his reputation as a superb musician at night, the world outside moved on… badly. The spring of 1940 saw the fall of Finland, while the Germans and Soviets prepared to attack Romania with its rich oil fields. In April and May, as the world watched in shock,

Germany employed its blitzkrieg (literally "lightning war") tactics to invade and conquer Norway and Denmark, then Belgium, Luxembourg, and the Netherlands.

Then there was Joe and Dori King. The first news we hear of Joe and Dori that entire academic year was the Mother's Day card that Aunt Margaret received in May 1940. Yes, indeed, Joe and Dori were still close.

Mother's Day card to Aunt Margaret, May 1940

Champaign, IL *May 1940*

Dear Aunt Margaret and All:

With exams going on - we are pretty busy right now - but I thought I ought to write you and let you know that everything is OK.

I don't know whether I will get home after exams or not. We are to play in Grand Lake, Colorado for the entire Summer (12 weeks) and will leave almost as soon as we get through here. Exams are over Monday; we play Tuesday and Wednesday nights, and Friday and Saturday nights, and leave for Colorado Sunday. And Dori graduates Thursday night, so I can't very well miss that.

I wish you could arrange to come up, Aunt Margaret, and bring Ed or someone with you. Thursday would be the best day to come, as we are not working that night (a week from tomorrow.) Dori's folks will be here from Little Rock, too. Say, she told me three months ago to thank you for that purse - she really likes it.

Well, I simply must close and get back down to work. I will certainly be glad when exams are over.

Love,
Joe

A record twenty-four hundred students graduated at Champaign on June 11, 1940. Unfortunately, the front page headline in *The Daily Illini* that morning was not about graduation, but about alarming news of the war in Europe.

FRENCH GOVERNMENT EVACUATES PARIS
GERMAN TANKS PENETRATE TO ENVIRONS OF CAPITAL;
TROOPS 35 MILES DISTANT

The Japanese were equally aggressive in the Far East. The China conflict continued and, as part of that war strategy, Japan seized French Indochina in June 1940. In an effort to control Japanese militarism, Australia, America, Britain, and the Dutch government in exile agreed to stop selling iron ore, steel, and oil to the Japanese. The western powers hoped that, since Japan imported fully eighty percent of the oil she consumed, her economy and her military would grind to a halt without imported oil. Japan viewed these embargoes as acts of oppression and secretly began making plans for war.

The war headlines weren't the only bad news. Joe would not receive his second semester grades until he returned from Colorado, but they would be his lowest since arriving on campus. He was granted no credit for both the contracts class and the torts class. Worse yet, his cumulative GPA for the first two semesters had fallen below the minimum acceptable level, and the law school faculty had dropped him from the college.

Pine Cone Inn, Grand Lake, CO   *June 22, 1940*

Dear Aunt Margaret, Grandma and Grandpa:

I'm really getting out of practice writing up here - all we do
is eat like horses and get 10 hours sleep every night. You won't
know me when I get back. I'm really feeling fine. I certainly
wish you could be out here with me. Dad and Ed are not coming
out until August since Ed is going to summer school.

I can't get over how beautiful it is - the only thing the matter
is the climate is so dry. Our lips and nostrils are dry all the
time - and it is hard to breathe - until we get used to it. We
use three blankets every night.

We make $15 a week plus room and board, which isn't very much. I won't have anything left when I get my debts paid. I owe about $80 so I may have $20, $30 left when the summer is over, I hope. Please, put in as many words for a job that you can. I'll do anything, anywhere that I can. But I would rather be in Harrisburg or Little Rock where living would not cost so much.

I've been broke for a week, we haven't had our first payday yet - tomorrow is the big day. I'll pay you for my laundry. If I can't find a better bargain on shirts than I have yet - I'll send them home. It would be cheaper I think. Dori is doing small things for me - she said to tell you hello and that she was awfully disappointed when she got that letter you sent to the Weavers and there was nothing in it for her. She's pretty homesick for her mother. But she'll get over that soon.

And, please send a couple of towels - I didn't bring any and I need them - also underwear and socks & shirts. No hurry though.

Please write often. I'll answer.

Love,
Joe

The Grand Lake resort area was located on the north shore of Grand Lake in what is now the Rocky Mountain National State Park. It was beautiful country.

The Pine Cone Inn was *not* an elegant, high profile nightclub. It was a honky-tonk kind of a dance club that packed in summer vacationers six nights a week for dancing to big time bands. The only way to close up at night and get folks out the door was to turn the lights out.

As Joe noted, the musicians performed for room and board and only a small bit of pocket change. But the music they played that summer was arguably the best and most enjoyable of their careers. No classes, a full house every night, crowds who never left the dance floor—what more could they ask for? They played their hearts out all night and then slept for ten hours in cool, crisp mountain air. They woke up and ate like horses in the morning and then headed out to explore the beautiful Rocky Mountain West until dinner time and another show.

There are no more letters from Grand Lake, but Joe McDevitt's photo album captured the sights of that summer. Some of the places they visited remain familiar landmarks today: Trail Ridge Road; Tunnel Highway Bridge; Picnic Rock above Grand Lake; Cascade Falls on Flat Top Mountain Trail; Adams Falls; Shadow Mountain Fire Lookout; Beaver Dam in Hidden Valley; Lone Pine on the High Drive. They saw it all together. Good times, good friends. It was a great summer.

Of course, Joe McDevitt especially enjoyed that summer, because Dori King, by now a superb vocalist, appeared with him every evening at the Pine Cone Inn. Who knows what futures they may have discussed as they walked the beautiful Flat Top Mountain Trail together? They were young and in love.

A careful reading of Joe's later letters suggests that they discussed a future together, including marriage. For whatever reasons, however, Dori sang with the Wayne Karr Orchestra through the early fall of 1940 and then returned home to Little Rock, Arkansas. They never saw each other again.

When Ed McDevitt's summer classes were over, he and his Dad took the train to Colorado and vacationed for a week with Joe and Dori at Grand Lake. The picture here is probably the only existing photo of the four of them together.

*John and Ed McDevitt, Dori King and Joe McDevitt
at Grand Lake, Colorado, Summer 1940*

Washington, DC   *June 26, 1940*

President Franklin D. Roosevelt announced the United States Navy Reserve Midshipman's School, to be widely known as the Navy College Training Program or V-7. The program was intended to quickly recruit thirty-six thousand naval reserve officers to command the expanding US fleet in preparation for an expected war effort. The original qualification for admission was a minimum of two years of college. However, low retention rates in the first classes led officials to raise the minimum requirement to a full college degree.

Graduates of the V-7 program were to be commissioned as ensigns in the US Navy Reserve (hereafter, USNR). Ultimately, most of the junior officers would enter active duty and become the backbone of the fleet in the Far East, known as the Pacific Theater. Those reserve officers would help to plan, organize, and lead invasion armadas against the Japanese all across the Central and Western Pacific Theaters. They would bomb and bombard Japanese defenders with a ferocity that was previously unknown in modern warfare. They would land many thousands of young, hard assault troops on enemy beaches and would supply them with tanks, napalm, and artillery until the beaches were secure. They would care for the wounded and help bury the dead as Allied troops searched caves, tunnels, and underground bunkers and killed every last defender whose military code of conduct, *bushido*, exalted dying for the emperor rather than surrendering.

When the band returned from Colorado, Joe McDevitt learned—probably while catching up on his summer mail—of his academic suspension. His first inclination was to sell any possessions of value and leave the university. However, his commitment to a law degree was steadfast. Upon further reflection, he returned home to consider his future and to consult with his Aunt, with Doc Klein, and probably with his Uncle Mike Hanagan, among others.

Postcard to Aunt Margaret, September 8, 1940

Joe seemed to have at least two choices. He had earned his A.B. (Bachelor of Arts) degree and could look for work, presumably as a musician. Or he could return to Champaign and petition the law school to resume his studies. For the second time, he found himself choosing between music and the law.

Joe chose to return to campus. According to family lore, the law faculty there advised him—clearly and unambiguously—to decide whether he wanted to be a full-time professional musician or a lawyer. The message was to advise Wayne Karr to find another pianist!

Joe petitioned for readmission, and his petition was approved on September 16, 1940. His reinstatement was not, however, entirely painless. It carried a financial penalty, which was the very last thing that he needed.

Finally, Joe resigned from the Wayne Karr Orchestra and registered for fourteen hours of law coursework.

This account of a difficult time in Joe's life leaves unanswered questions. How could he support himself without working? How would he pay room and board, tuition, books, and fees? He still had two more years of law school to complete. Joe loved his music, but from his very first letter we know that he played to pay for his schooling.

An educated guess based on comments in future letters is that Doc Klein, a close friend of the Harrisburg Zimmers, extended a loan to carry him through the coming year. Doctor John Klein was a general practitioner who, with his wife Magdalena, had moved to Harrisburg in 1934. He received his medical degree at the Chicago Medical School and treated patients from Harrisburg and surrounding areas until his retirement in 1969. Discussions with two surviving daughters suggest that the Zimmers were not only patients, but also close friends who probably first met the Kleins while attending St. Mary's Catholic Church. The daughters described their father as a caring man who "was always glad to help someone who was trying to make something of himself." Doc Klein may well have assured Joe's future by helping him out that year.

While Joe and the band were playing in Grand Junction that summer, a change in attitudes toward the war was revamping the political landscape across America. The cumulative effects of three factors may well have triggered the change. These included: pictures of German troops goose-stepping victoriously in eight capitols across Europe; the rapid collapse of France—a large and valued traditional ally; and the realization that only one democracy remained in all of Western Europe. Drew Pearson and Robert

Allen noted the change in their syndicated column "The Daily Washington Merry-Go-Round" carried by *The Daily Illini,* June 7, 1940.

> "Administration leaders are amazed at the speed with which pro-Allied sentiment is sweeping the country. Some of them say that they think the country is ahead of the President."

Not so. Just eleven days later, President Roosevelt took advantage of the new mood to request money for a true two-ocean Navy. By September 10 the request had been approved and an order placed for 201 new ships, the largest order ever placed by the Navy. A call for twenty-nine C3-S-A2 merchant vessel hulls was included in that order.

SECOND YEAR OF LAW CLASSES

As Joe began his second year of law classes, the passage of President Roosevelt's compulsory draft act changed the world for many young American males. The act required sixteen million five hundred thousand American males aged twenty-one to thirty-five to register for one year of compulsory military training. FDR asserted that this act signaled the United States was marshaling its strength to avert "the terrible fate of nations whose weakness invited attack."

To facilitate registration for college students, the act permitted on-campus registration, so that students would not have to travel to register with hometown draft boards. Further, the act provided for a voluntary enlistment program which allowed draft boards to first fill quotas drawing from voluntary enlistments and then, as necessary, from compulsory registrants. This provision would help many college students complete their studies prior to joining up.

By the deadline for registration, October 16, 1940, two thousand seven hundred forty students on campus who were not residents of Champaign County had registered.

Joe registered for five law courses that fall. Each was taught by a faculty member who believed that *his* particular course was the most important course in the curriculum. His would be a busy semester.

First Semester 1940-1941		
Subject	**Course No.**	**Cr. Hrs.**
Remedies	4a	3
Criminal Law	5	3
Sales	9	3
Agency	11	3
Trusts	16a	2

Champaign, IL   *Early October 1940*

Dear Aunt Margaret:

I'm sorry I haven't written sooner. Here I've had two letters and I haven't answered until now. I've been very busy this week since the six week exams have been given. I think I came out OK.

How is your hand coming along? It's just too bad that it had to happen when you were doing a work of charity - fate I guess. But I sure hope it isn't too badly burned Aunt Margaret, because I know you'd like to get back to work. Good luck.

Well, it looks like things turned out OK up here with me. They passed in my favor - you can read the letter. But I have to pay the school $22.50 Nov. 19 - so I'm not clear by any means. It will turn out OK though I know.

Heard from Ed. He seems to have had a good time Homecoming, but didn't say anything about how school is.

How are Grandma and Grandpa? I can't tell which of them is ill from Cecile's letter. Ask her to decipher the paragraph I send in this letter. I surmise that it must be Grandpa, although I know Grandma is not in the best of health either. Give them my love.

Tell Cecile that we have been debating whether or not to wear summer clothes - but our minds were made up last night when the temperature dropped about 20 degrees. Coats feel good now.

I heard from Dad yesterday. He is filled with thoughts about the strike - and has just gotten back from his examination at St. Louis. I'm writing him.

Well, Aunt Margaret, I must close so I can get your letter off in the mail. Tell Cecile thanks a lot for writing, but I hope you will be able to do so yourself soon. Take good care of your hand, and let me know how you are soon.

Hello to everyone - Mrs. Edwards.

Love to All,
Joe

P.S. I believe you could save money by not putting so much starch in my collars - I've changed my taste. Ha! Ha!

Joe was close to his grandparents, Peter and Catherine Zimmer. While living in Harrisburg, Grandpa Zimmer was probably the dominant male figure in his life. From what we know of both Peter and Catherine, they likely encouraged and fostered the personal strengths that would become Joe's hallmarks—a powerful work ethic and strong self-motivation.

Both Catherine (Seiner) Zimmer and Peter were German immigrants. The Seiners immigrated to the United States from Bavaria about 1857. Catherine was only 18 months old when the Seiners left Germany and traveled for three months on a sailing vessel before landing in New Orleans. They took a flatboat up the Mississippi River to Shetlerville, Illinois, and then traveled directly to Hardin County. The family settled on a farm adjacent to the one that a young Peter Zimmer would one day own.

Peter's Zimmer's father, Stephan Zimmer, was one of fifteen children of Karl Anton Zimmer and Regina Martin Zimmer who lived in Baden, Germany. Stephan came to the United States by himself around the year 1840. He was a pioneer farmer who settled in Pope County, Illinois. He met and married Louise Seidler and together they had nine children, the third of whom was Peter. Peter eventually struck out on his own, moving to Hardin County, Illinois. He settled on a farm and opened a blacksmith shop. A short time later, he met and married his neighbor, Catherine Seiner, in 1880.

Grandpa Zimmer spent his most active years at his blacksmith shop and later as a farmer. He and Grandma had twelve children, including four boys, four girls, and four children who died at birth or in infancy. The Hardin County Zimmers were a close-knit family who were very active in the Catholic Church. Three of their daughters would play especially important roles in the lives of Joe and Ed McDevitt. The first was the boys' mother, Mary, who was the oldest Zimmer daughter; the second was Margaret, who would raise Joe after Mary's death; and the third was Esther Zimmer Hanagan, who would raise Ed.

Thanks to the Zimmers, both Joe and Ed McDevitt grew deep Midwestern roots living with an extended family of tough, strong immigrants who helped settle Southern Illinois.

Champaign, IL   *Mid October 1940*

Dear Aunt Margaret:

Thanks for your letter, and thanks very much for sending up my underwear and things. I had forgotten all about leaving them there and couldn't understand what I had done with them.

I've been so very busy that I haven't had time to answer until now, and I don't have much time even now since I have to get over to the library in a short while. But I didn't want you to get the wrong idea by not writing soon.

I can well appreciate all the trouble you are having, and I wish there were something I could do to alleviate them. But you're wrong when you say that I don't appreciate all that you have done for me, and you must remember that as yet I have never been in a position to repay you for all that you have done. You can rest assured though that I won't forget it - and that I will more than make up for everything when I get on my feet.

I didn't go to the insurance office as you told me was possible. But at the same time I haven't had my teeth looked at as yet. I thought over what you said about the policy being more valuable as a policy than otherwise, in fact I had thought of that before. In a way you're right, but in a way one's teeth are just as important if you plan to live for quite a few years to come. And I haven't any other source of income with which to have the work done. I'm going to have an appraisal made by some reliable dentist to see just how much it will cost to have the work done. I'll let you know, and won't do anything about the policy until I hear what you say.

I don't know yet whether I will be able to get away over Thanksgiving or not. Dad will expect me to come down, in fact he has already told me he will be looking for me. I think I told you that last letter I wrote you that he was going to have an operation performed on his eye. He hasn't had it done yet, but is planning to soon, probably by Thanksgiving.

How is Grandma? Is she any better by now? I hope that she is, and I hope that you are not having to work too hard. I was really surprised to hear that you have some broken ribs. You didn't tell me just how it happened. Surely Grandma didn't cause it, did she? You really aren't strong enough to handle her in your condition, are you? I only wish that affairs could be cleared up in some way, so the worry on all sides would be eliminated.

I hate to quit writing so soon, especially since you wrote so much to me in your letter, but I simply have to be at the library by 7 p.m. and I just have time to get there. I'll write again soon and let you know how things are. Write when you have time and let me know how things are at home.

Love,
Joe

A careful review of *The Daily Illini* from September through December 1940 leaves several impressions. For the first time, war news regularly displaced other news in front page headlines. If one wanted to learn about football games, sorority pledges, or Dad's Weekend, one had to turn the page once or twice. Also, the word "crisis" appeared regularly in the war coverage of both the European war and the Pacific conflict.

Champaign, IL   *November 1940*

Dear Aunt Margaret:

You will probably be surprised at receiving this letter so soon
after my last one - I don't write this often usually, do I?

But Paul and Thelma got a letter from her mother today, in which
she said that you and she may come up this weekend, and I just
wanted to write and tell you that we really hope that you will
come up.

You can both stay right here with us in the apartment, for we
have lots of room. But her mother has probably already told you
that. She has already been up for one weekend. It won't cost you
anything for room or for meals - and you could probably help me
do the ironing, so you see I really do want you to come. HO! HO!
That isn't the real reason, you know that.

I got my glasses today - I couldn't do without them any longer.
I wrote Uncle Mike and asked him for the money, because I'd had
no answer from Dad. I haven't received the money as yet (I only
wrote Friday so I didn't expect it so soon), but Paul advanced it
to me. The glasses seem rather awkward just now, but I can really
tell the difference when looking at close print. I look like a
student now sure enough.

I got a letter from Dad this morning - he didn't send any money
- and he told me that he had been "all in, down and out" with
his back. He had to go to St. Louis today for an examination to
see if "he was crazy." He had dated the letter October 15, 1940,
but the postmark was November 1, 1940, so I guess he just had
his dates mixed. He said that he wanted to see me the "worst
in the world" and wanted me to come down during Thanksgiving
vacation. So I guess that I will go down. That's another reason I
wish that you would come up this weekend.

I asked Dori (she's back in Little Rock, you know) to find out
just how Dad is, in particular just how bad that trouble was

about his eyes. She asked Mrs. Buckles, who told her that it wasn't serious. But he has had that trouble with his back every winter and it gets pretty serious. It seems to be starting earlier this year. Dori told me to tell you hello, and that she hopes everything is running smoothly for you.

Well I must close and get to studying. I just wanted to let you know that I hope you will be able to come up, and ask you to write this week as to whether you can come up or not, so that we can make sure the rug is swept, the dusting done, and everything in place for your coming.

Write soon.

Love,
Joe

Five days after Joe wrote this letter, Grandpa Zimmer died at his home at 125 West Homer Street in Harrisburg after a short illness. He was 81 years old. Joe may have been at home for the Thanksgiving break when his Grandpa Zimmer passed. Peter Zimmer's obituary in *THE DAILY REGISTER* in Harrisburg reported that his health had been failing for some time and that death was due to a complication of diseases due to old age. Funeral arrangements were delayed because Joe's Aunt Margaret, who had been caring for her father, was sick with pneumonia. Peter was buried at St. Joseph's Cemetery in Hardin County, Illinois.

Joe's second semester course load was six courses, including the contracts I and torts classes that he was repeating from the previous spring term. His grades and class rank had improved and would steadily advance each semester until graduation. This was good news, of course, since he was surely on a watch list at the law school that year.

Second Semester 1940-1941		
Subject	**Course No.**	**Cr. Hrs.**
Contracts I	1b	3
Torts	2b	3
Bills and Notes	15	3
Trusts	16b	2
Titles	3b	3
Use of Books	45	1

World events continued on a threatening course in the spring of 1941. Headlines in *The Fighting Illini* reported regularly on the war in Europe and speculated about America's future role in it. The news seemed to worsen monthly.

- On January 6, contrary to still-dominant isolationist sentiment, President Roosevelt recommended a "Lend Lease" program that would provide aid to France and England.
- On April 16, Britain received its first "Lend Lease" shipment of food aid, and by December millions of tons of aid had been received.
- On August 9, President Roosevelt and Prime Minister Churchill met off the coast of Newfoundland and agreed upon the Atlantic Charter which contained eight points of agreement on the aims of the war.
- On September 29, President Roosevelt issued an order that German or Italian ships sighted in American waters would be attacked immediately.
- On October 17, the USS destroyer *Kearny* was torpedoed by a German U-boat off the coast of Newfoundland. On the 31st, the American destroyer USS *Reuben James* was sunk by a German U-boat, killing one hundred fifteen crewmen.

Summer Session 1941		
Subject	**Course No.**	**Cr. Hrs.**
Persons	s7	2
Wills	s18	3

This was a heavy load for summer school, especially since Joe had resumed working again with a new band. A front page article in *The Daily Illini,* June 4, 1941, announced:

Midnight Permission Granted Today

Miss Maria Leonard, dean of women, yesterday announced that the regular 10:30 p.m. deadline for women students has been extended until 12 midnight for the Senior Tennis Court dance today. The dance will begin at 8:30 p.m. in the Library tennis courts and end at 11:30 p.m.

Joe McDevitt, Champaign, and his seven piece orchestra will play, Chairman Tony Delaurent announced yesterday. Admission is free to all University students upon presentation of identification cards. In case of rain the dance will be canceled.

This is the first mention of the Joe McDevitt Orchestra in the University of Illinois archives. *The Daily Illini* ads below confirm that he had formed his own band that summer and that they performed regularly throughout the summer semester. They just couldn't keep him away from that keyboard!

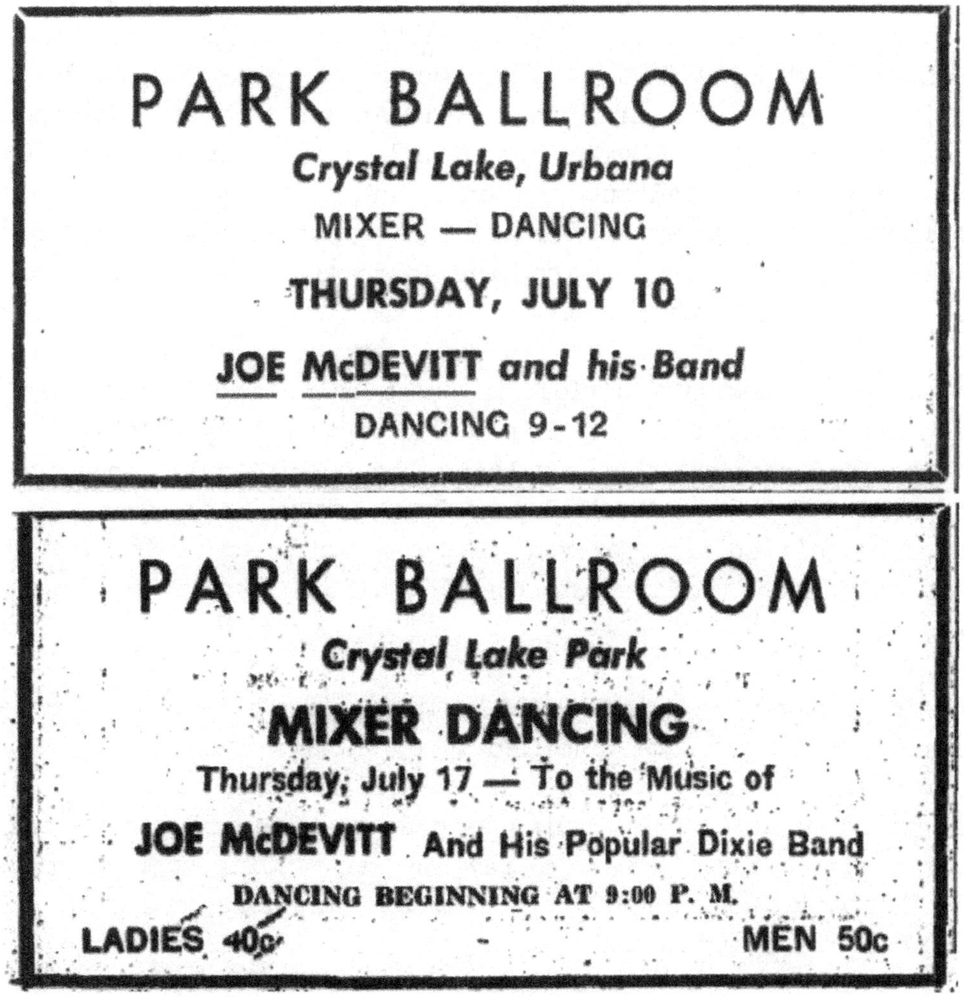

Joe McDevitt Band ads, The Daily Illini, Summer 1941

Champaign, IL   *Early Summer 1941*

Dear Aunt Margaret:

Well, here I am at last writing you a long overdue letter. I know
I promised I'd write, and I should have written just as soon
as I got up here. I've really failed to write the persons that
I should write this Summer. I've written just one post-card
during all this time, and that was in answer to 2 or 3 letters I
received from Dori. I wrote it out while I was eating one noon. I
haven't written to Dad but just once, and that was on the train
on the way up. I guess I have had time to write, but I have so
little time off when I have nothing to do that it's really hard
to sit down and write letters.

I leave the house at 7 o'clock in the morning and I don't get
back until about 11:30 and I'm really tired out by that time,
so that bed is about the only thing I can think of. I took the
afternoon off so that I could come home and write letters. I know
that I didn't do right by you when I was off, but Uncle Mike
kept me so busy that morning that I couldn't get over as I said
I would.

How is Grandma? And how are you getting along? I got your letter
with the premium notice. I mailed it to Chicago this morning.
I hope that it isn't too late. It was due in June, so I don't
imagine that it is. I am living here at the fraternity house this
summer since we don't have to pay any rent during summer school.
The letter was sent to 409 E. Springfield and forwarded here.
Thanks for sending it up.

Dad wasn't getting along so well in his last letter. That
rheumatism just doesn't give him any peace at all, I guess. But
he is determined to stick it out until his pension age is reached.

Did Gertrude come down on her vacation? I really wish I could be
there to see her. I'll bet she looks like a butterball, doesn't
she? How long did she have off?

I really feel like taking a vacation myself - but there's no rest
for the wicked I guess. I'll have about five weeks between the
end of Summer school and the beginning of the first semester
next year. I can't tell what will happen next year yet. From
the looks of things, it looks like I may be in camp, and even
farther than that if we keep getting closer to war. I look for us
to get into it before the next 3 or 4 months, and then nothing
could keep me out of the draft. I'm not afraid of it or anything
like that, but I sure hate the thought of being sent across the
water.

I have a chance to work for those five weeks, or part of them, at
least, in a canning factory up north of here, and I could save
about $150 or $160. I guess I should take something like that,
for it would be a start for next year. It would run into about 15
or 16 hours of work a day. I could take it for a while anyway.

I'm working for my meals and working at night with a band.
Making my expenses but working hard to do it. But am doing
good in school at the same time. I made an A and 5 B's last
semester, which is really good for law school. I was right proud
of those grades.

There are about 100 sisters here in summer school and quite a
few priests. On Sunday they answer the prayers at Mass, and it is
really something to listen to. How is Father Manion doing in the
Army camp -- or do you hear?

Well, Aunt Margaret, I have to go down and wait tables for supper,
and I am playing at the Park tonight. That's the way it always
is -- I don't have time to do a lot of things I would like to
do. But at the same time, when you keep busy you don't have time
to spend money. It's just as well this way, isn't it?

Please answer when you find time, and I'll be more prompt the
next time. Half the trouble is that I can't force myself to sit
down and write. Dori told me she called you. I wish she didn't
have to work like that - it's a hard life, and not good on one's
health, especially a young girl. But she wants to work and make

her own money, and that's all she can do. She's hoping to be able to take a commercial course next year if she can get enough money together. She's a good girl.

Is Ed in summer school? There's one instance that I don't have to be ashamed of myself for not writing. I don't remember when he wrote me last, and every letter that I get from Dad he says that Ed hasn't written him yet. I'll drop him a few lines tomorrow.

Well, I simply must close for this time. Tell Mrs. Edwards and the Kleins hello for me, and write soon. Tell Grandma hello -- she probably won't be able to place me by name. Let me know how you are and if there's anything that I can do.

Love,
Joe

Champaign, IL   *July 17, 1941*

Dear Aunt Margaret:

Just a few lines to let you know what I am going to do now that school is out, and the month of August is before me. I thought I would be coming down tomorrow. I had my application in at the American Can factory up in Hoopeston, Illinois, for a job during the month of August, but it has fallen through. Until this morning I had nothing in mind, and I hated the thought of loafing all this month and not making any money.

But this morning I got a wire from Salem, Illinois, concerning a job down there. So four other fellows and myself, under my leadership, are starting to play at Sam's Place in Salem tomorrow

night. We will be there for 2 weeks, will play 6 nights a week
from 8:30 to 12:30 - so it is easy work. After this 2 weeks, I
will be down 2 weeks until school starts.

Love,
Joe

THIRD YEAR OF LAW CLASSES

By the fall of 1941, Japanese plans for a two-pronged strategy for war with the western powers were nearly complete. The southern plan called for seizure of the economic resources controlled by Britain and the Dutch by invading Hong Kong, Singapore, Malaya, Java, and Sumatra and then isolating Australia and New Zealand. The eastern plan called for attacking the American fleet at Pearl Harbor, invading the Philippines, and cutting off communication lines in the Pacific by capturing Wake and Guam. Thereafter, the Japanese hoped to settle for peace under terms that would assure them hegemony in the Pacific.

While the Japanese planned for war, Joe registered for another heavy course load, six courses totaling fifteen credit hours. Perhaps by then he could see the end of the road ahead, but he must have been a bit frayed at the edges after five straight years of college.

First Semester 1941-1942		
Subject	**Course No.**	**Cr. Hrs.**
Corporations	19	3
Pleading	20	3
Cred. Trans. I	21a	3
Vend. & Purch	29	2
Future Interests	38	4

Champaign, IL   *September 1941*

Dear Aunt Margaret:

I've been so busy getting started that I haven't had time to get started. I guess you've been wondering how I came out.

I am sharing an apartment with a fellow in law school named Paul Stone who married Thelma Jones of Benton. There are four of us: Paul's young brother, Guy, he and his wife, and I. We figure that it won't cost us any more than $25 a month room & board, and it's really quite nice. Thelma teaches about 14 miles from here, but she is home to cook breakfast and supper. For lunch one of us three fellows cooks. We will do our own washing - I'm to iron the shirts. We take a gallon of milk a day, so I drink milk every meal.

I had my tuition deferred, and the first payment of $25 comes due September 28th. Should I write Dad for it? I wrote him a special and explained things to him, but have had no answer. I hope he noticed my new address. I gave it to him. Uncle Mike gave me $40 which bought my books, paid the special fees, a study lamp and other necessities.

And now for a surprise. Felts (Warren) got a job teaching and will probably get married right away. So I get his job playing the chimes - you remember the write up he got in the paper. I have to see for sure about it, because I just went ahead and played them today. I only play four 15 minute programs weekly, & I get $2.50, which is pretty good pie money. Anyway, we're keeping the job in Harrisburg.

Well, I have to get busy, so you let Uncle Mike know I got started OK, and I'll write him about Sunday.

Tell Grandma and Grandpa hello for me - and write soon.

Love,
Joe

P.S. How's Bill? You know who I mean. Tell him hello for me.

We note that fully ten months after his Grandpa died, Joe was still saying "hello" to him in his letters.

The chimes that Joe played on campus were a gift to the University of Illinois from the graduating classes of 1914-1922. The peal of the chimes, fifteen in all, had become a revered symbol for generations of students. A huge affair of weights and chains, the chimes were installed in Altgeld Hall's tower in 1921. The largest chime is ten feet in circumference; the smallest is five feet. When played by hand, they are operated from a keyboard of handles. A long wire extends upwards from each handle to a chime and pulls a hammer which strikes the bell.

Joe didn't know this, of course, but he was joining a tradition that continues today of student musicians playing the U of I chimes. At the time of this writing, the Westminster tune is played electronically at each quarter-hour, and a student plays a concert each weekday at 12:50 p.m. Student musicians may climb the tower on evenings or weekends to play impromptu concerts for friends and family.

Several weeks later, Joan Joiner '43 wrote a Friday column in *The Daily Illini*, October 17, 1941, announcing that there were plans for *forty* dances to compete with hour exams and the football game that weekend. Among the fraternity houses planning parties was Pi Kappa Phi:

> "Paddles and Pledge Buttons" will be the theme of the Pi Kappa Phi pledge dance tomorrow evening. Joe McDevitt's Orchestra will play.

The Thanksgiving break came and went at Champaign, and soon it was December 1941. In <u>An Illini Century</u>, the definitive history of the University of Illinois, Roger Ebert described the mood on the Illini campus that fateful December:

> "On the morning of December 6, 1941 *The Daily Illini* published this confident editorial:
>
> At present the United States is in a most fortunate position - considering it is waging an undeclared war… The United States is in a war on the Atlantic, and it may be soon on the Pacific. Even if war comes on both oceans, it will be 'away from home' and Americans will be relatively secure. Soldiers and sailors may have to travel a thousand miles to die, but they won't clutter up American soil while doing it. The advantage of an offensive war is that the invader can fight on his own terms and times…
>
> Well, hardly. The next morning, Pearl Harbor was bombed. The first reaction was essentially one of relief that the waiting was over. Adele Kaplan wrote in her *Daily Illini* column on December 9, 1941:

At the first mention of the United States declaring war with the Far East, all eyes immediately turned to the men! What was going to become of the reserve officers, draftees, and all capable men between the ages of 17 and 50? They are the ones who are going to 'do or die' for the sake of their country...

Yesterday afternoon as the first reports of war were broadcast over the airwaves, women listened intently... too stunned, too baffled, and too shocked to realize what had really happened...

Independent and sorority houses, as well as other student rooming houses, were quiet, with the exception of news reports over the radios... Men may think they are the only ones who will play an important part in this great show, but don't forget there are wives, sweethearts and relatives who will be living in this war period too...

Studying seems to be an impossibility at this present time. Women can't forget about the war... After a few days things will settle down to almost normal conditions again, and women will go about their duties on campus as always. However, you can bet that every Saturday morning will find the lower parlors of the Women's building filled to capacity with women rolling bandages for the Red Cross..."

"A few students did celebrate, perhaps in relief after the long wait, when Congress finally declared war. But then the campus grimly settled down. The ratio of men to women changed almost overnight from 3-to-1 to 1-to-4. Girls spent Saturday mornings wrapping bandages for the Red Cross. It was a time of waiting, of listening to the war news on the radio, of a University preoccupied with the fact that most of the men who would have been its students were in uniform."[3]

Over the next five months, the Japanese were unstoppable in the Pacific as they executed their eastern and southern campaigns. In addition to Pearl Harbor, they attacked and eventually conquered the Philippines, Guam, and Wake Island from the Americans; East New Guinea and Borneo from the Dutch; and Hong Kong and Singapore from the British. For Americans the world quickly became a terribly threatening place with Germany and Italy battering the British in Europe and eyeing South America, while the Japanese were seizing possessions of all western nations in the Pacific.

Second Semester 1941-1942		
Subject	**Course No.**	**Cr. Hrs.**
Trial Practice	4b	3
Evidence	8	3
Conflicts	31b	2
Contracts II	32	3
Rights in Land	3	2
Military Law	99	2

---

3   Ebert, R. (1967) An Illini Century: 100 Years of Campus Life. Urbana, IL: University of Illinois Press, pp 3-4.

Champaign, IL   *Spring 1942*

Dear Aunt Margaret:

I've certainly been showing my appreciation for this fine stationary, haven't I? Time has been flying by so quickly that it seems just yesterday that I was down to see you and Dad, and see Ed off to the Army. But many things have happened in that seemingly short time. I have really had my hands full this semester or I would have written sooner.

The university is operating on an emergency basis and consequently we are doing work in 1/4 the time it would ordinarily take. We have exams all through the semester in Law School now instead of a single final exam at the end of the semester. The semester will end May 23rd instead of June 2nd this year, and the fact that I have been working quite a bit to make ends meet is the reason I have been so long in writing.

I have been figuring out - rather trying to figure out - a time when I could make a trip down to get certain matters straightened up. I got a letter from the draft board informing me they are still thinking about me and that my deferral expires June 2nd. I'm sure that I will be deferred until the end of June to give me a chance to take the bar exam June 22nd, 23rd, and 24th. But that isn't all the time I need to graduate and not enough to get into the FBI I'm afraid. That's the main reason I want to come down so I can go up and have a talk with the draft board. But I've come to the conclusion that it will be better not to say anything too soon, but rather to wait until near the end of the semester and then make a trip down to talk things over. So don't say anything to anyone about this - and I will make it a point to take enough time off to come down some time in the next two months. I'll let you know when I plan to come. And by the way, I'm liable to bring along a friend I want you to meet. A girl - I guess you get what I mean. But don't worry - I won't do anything rash!

I've written Ed since he is in Camp Robinson, but have had no answer. He seems to like Army life well enough in the one letter that I've had from him - and said that he had it pretty easy since he's not physically as capable as many of the other fellows. I only hope that it continues that way for him.

I've had regular letters from Papa, and he is the only person that I've really had time to write to. I just dash him off a few lines each time, since there's really nothing important I have to tell him usually. When I write you I plan on taking at least 45 minutes to do it - and that's why it doesn't come very often. Papa told me that you had sent him those insurance policies as you had asked him to. He sent me the $50 I had asked for which didn't get very far. I did underestimate what my expenses would be and am pretty pinched at present. But in his last letter he told me he was just about down and out, and that he hadn't heard any word about his pension yet. So I wouldn't think of asking him for any more money.

I've been working more than I really should and will have to discontinue it before long as school work seems to be getting heavier by the day. I've managed to stay pretty well out of debt - but that's about all. I am behind on room & board at present in the amount of $30. Otherwise everything's OK. I've been trying to make the clothes that I have last until June at least - since the prospect of my going into the Army is pretty bright and there's no use buying anything since I would just have to leave it. Except for shoes, I think I'll be able to manage it.

I only hope that my application for the FBI will be accepted before it's too late. That's the one thing I really want to happen and don't think I haven't been praying night and day that it will. Remember me in your prayers, please.

How is Grandma? Write when you have time and let me know how you have been and how Grandma is. I'm sure that I will find some time to come down before long, so don't say anything to the draft board. I think it would be best if I go and talk to them since I know all about it - and what I really need. There's so

much involved that I couldn't get it into a letter. Tell everyone
hello for me and take care of yourself. I'll write again - and
sooner this time. Write when you find time.

Love,
Joe

Champaign, IL   *April 14, 1942*

Dear Aunt Margaret:

That certainly was a sweet letter you wrote me a while back
telling me to bring "?" on down and that you would see that
she had a nice time. I know you would - I wouldn't hesitate to
bring "?" either since I'm positive you would like her very much.
Her name is Virginia Denton - and in my opinion she is a very
nice girl.

School is keeping me so very busy - and I'm working quite a bit
besides that. I'm going to Springfield Thursday to see how my
application for the FBI is coming along. I'll let you know when
I find out. They haven't been investigating me yet that you know
of, have they?

I got a letter from Frances Oberho in Detroit the other day
wanting to know why I haven't been writing. I'll have to drop
her a few lines when I find time.

How is Grandma? You didn't mention her in your letter, so I
suppose that she is feeling OK.

I had a letter from Ed about 2 weeks ago saying that he would
probably be transferred in a short time. I only hope he can keep

out of the troops that are being sent across. He's spent most of
his time in an office and hasn't received any training in the
field at all.

I hate to write such a short letter - but it's 2 a.m. now and
I'm so sleepy I can hardly hold my eyes open. I'll write and let
you know what I find out. You let me know when they start asking
questions about me, please.

Take good care of yourself Aunt Margaret and write and let me
know how you are.

Love,
Joe

In the early months of 1942, the US Navy's Pacific Fleet Command learned that the Japanese had landed on Guadalcanal, largest of the Solomon Islands, located in the Coral Sea. They were building an airstrip from which they could disrupt shipping and communications between America and her Australian and New Zealand allies twelve hundred miles to the Southwest.

War planners considered the loss of the Solomon Islands to be strategically unacceptable. Besides, the Solomons were as good a place as any finally to begin offensive operations in the Pacific. Therefore, in May 1942, Marine Major General Alexander Archer Vandegrift, head of the newly formed 1st Marine Division, was called into the operations office of the US Navy's South Pacific Fleet. His orders were to move his 1st Division to New Zealand and begin plans for an amphibious assault on Guadalcanal.[4]

Code named Operation Watchtower, the objective was to deny the Japanese use of the Solomon Islands to project airpower in the Coral Sea. There was only one problem. General Vandergrift had absolutely no idea where Guadalcanal was.

---

4 Prados, John. (2013) Shadows of Destiny. NAL Caliber

Neither the Japanese nor the Americans understood the full importance of Guadalcanal to the other. As America's first amphibious assault approached, both sides rushed to reinforce troop levels and naval forces. When the assault was launched August 9, 1942, neither side was prepared for the bloody conflict to come.

Prados characterized Guadacanal as a lengthy battle of attrition in which eleven thousand American, Australian, and New Zealander lives would be lost versus eighty thousand Japanese lives. The operation included fierce jungle fighting in "mud, mayhem and misery," with survivors battling dysentery, hunger, and malaria. At sea there were carrier battles and aerial dogfights that offered a hint of what was to come.

Victory was declared complete on February 7, 1943. The long march back in the Pacific had begun.

Champaign, IL   *May 18, 1942*

Dear Aunt Margaret:

Well, the semester is just about over and while I've been busy throughout, I am in the busiest part of all at present. This is final examination week - and I have three of them tomorrow and three on Friday. But I haven't written as often as I should have done, and it is important that I do write now no matter how busy I may be.

School is out next Friday. But I am working Friday and Saturday nights and I have to be back up here on Monday. So as things stand at present I plan to come down for a week or so next Tuesday. Certain things which I will tell you about below may prevent me from doing so.

I need four hours to graduate and can pick them up in six weeks this summer. But my draft deferment expires June 2nd. I have written the draft board and asked them to defer me until next September, so I can finish up this summer and take the September bar exam. I am waiting to hear from them, and I hope it comes this week. However, I'm afraid that it won't. Things are so complicated that I can hardly put it down in writing.

If I don't get a deferment, I will have to take the June bar exam, which means that I will have to start taking the bar review course May 25th, a week from today. That would mean that I wouldn't be down at all, at least until sometime in July.

But for that matter, I don't know how I will be able to just either go to school for six weeks, or take the bar review course, since I don't know where I will get the money for tuition. That's the main reason that I hope to get deferred so I can come down and talk things over.

So you can expect me next Tuesday unless you hear to the contrary.

Love,
Joe

The trip to Harrisburg to visit his local draft board worked out just fine. Joe received permission to complete the administrative law and taxation courses during the summer term and to prepare for the September bar exam in Chicago.

His application for graduation with the law school class of '42 was accepted contingent upon successful completion of the two summer courses. The graduates are pictured in the portrait below. Joe McDevitt is the fifth person from the left in row three. See that little grin? He'd set "a hard goal" indeed for himself, but he'd made it.

SOURCE: COLLEGE OF LAW, UNIVERSITY OF ILLINOIS

Graduation Class of 1942, School of Law, University of Illinois

Champaign, IL   *July 1942*

Dear Aunt Margaret:

Just a few lines to let you know that I received the box you sent
me with the things in it - and I needn't tell you that most of
all I enjoyed the marvelous upside-down cake that you included.
It's the best I've had since the last time I was home.

Well, I'm still waiting for the telephone call from you that will tell me that my letter from the Navy has arrived. I'm expecting it almost any day now - if I'm to go December 1st. They may put me off for a longer time, but I will surely get at least two weeks' notice of when I am to report. Let me know just as soon as you receive it.

I got a letter from Ed. He's still in Florida, although his address has changed. He is now part of a "commando" unit, and claims that he was "roped" into it against his will. Those are the units that go ahead of everyone else - so I hope he succeeds in getting out of it.

I went down to the University after I wrote you the last time and sent you the letter that I mailed to the university. I talked to Mr. Webbers' representative (who is the person who wrote that letter, and who handles that business) and have reached an agreement with him to the effect that I needn't pay anything on my student loan account until I am called into the service. I will go in and see him again immediately before I leave. When I can get $10 ahead I'm going in and pay that graduation fee, which isn't paid as yet.

By the way, I've grown a mustache, and everyone says it looks good - but I'll shave it off before I come down. I guess I should wait about 10 years for that kind of stuff.

Love,
Joe

As his final academic semester wound down, Joe had mentioned applications for two government positions. The first was his application to the Federal Bureau of Investigation.

However, since he had not yet earned his law degree at the time of his application, we may assume that his application never made the Bureau's short list.

The second application was to the US Navy V-7 program. The V-7 had become an immensely successful recruiting program for the Navy, providing a steady supply of mature, highly educated officer candidates for the Pacific Fleet. The program was likewise attractive to college graduates, since it guaranteed an officer's commission as ensign, USNR, upon graduation.

St. Louis, MO   *September 1, 1942*

Joe McDevitt's official Navy medical records report that on Tuesday, September 1, 1942, he reported for his first physical examination with the Navy to establish his fitness for the V-7 program and to earn a commission in the naval reserve. The result:

"Physically qualified for appointment as Ensign, D-V(G), USNR"

Aerial View Showing Ideal Location of ALLERTON HOTEL — 701 N. MICHIGAN AVE. — CHICAGO, ILL.

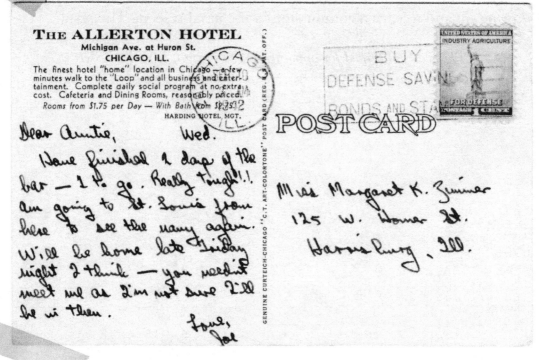

Postcard to Aunt Margaret, September 10, 1942

We have no record of Joe's activities in the fall of 1942. We do know, however, that one day during the first week of December, he boarded a train, most likely in St. Louis, Missouri, bound for New York City. He arrived on December 6 and reported to the Navy on December 7, 1942, as a candidate for the United States Naval Reserve Midshipmen's School at Columbia University.

2

BECOMING A WARRIOR

Upon admission to the V-7 program all candidates were admitted to active duty and were listed as apprentice seamen (AS) in the naval reserve. They then completed a thirty-day introductory program—think "boot camp"—that was long on strenuous physical training, Navy rules and regulations, and "spit and polish" stuff.

Forget that you are going to become an officer because reveille and calisthenics at 5:00 a.m., endless inspections, marching drills, and the works just went to prove that you were in the Navy now!

Midshipman's School, Columbia University, New York, NY   *December 9, 1942*

```
Dear Aunt Margaret:

Just have time for a few lines - to let you know everything is
fine, and to tell you my address.
```

We have very little spare time that I won't get to write you very often - at least for one month. I will be here for about 4 months - if I make good grades. Otherwise would be sent back to the draft board. We get paid only $2.50 per week - the remainder is kept to be applied on the uniforms we will have to purchase at the end of training. I had to pay my transportation but will be reimbursed at some later time. We have only ¼ day - Saturday afternoon - to ourselves, and even then we are restricted to an area immediately adjacent to the "ship." We go to church Sunday A.M. and Sunday evening. The rules are very strict and must be obeyed under penalty of being expelled - but I like it very much. We receive better training than any branch of the service.

I have a room with a fellow from Texas whom I met on the train coming out here. His name is Douglas Johnson, and he's a swell fellow. Our room is on the 9th floor of a twenty story building - and we have to walk up and down the stairs. Whew! Believe me - we are ready for bed when 10:00 P.M. rolls around, and 6:00 A.M. comes pretty quick. The food is very good - and I'm eating like a horse, so will probably gain weight. Monte Foster is on the deck immediately below me (8th) so I will see him quite often. We marched for two hours in the heaviest snow I have ever seen this morning - but it was fun. We are very well clothed. It's time for mess - lunch, so I'd better close. Will write soon. How are you and Grandma.

Address letters exactly like this - not like the return address on the envelope.

Joseph B. McDevitt AS V-7

Midshipman's School

Room 913

Johnson

New York, NY

Love,

Joe

Monte Foster was a high school classmate of Joe's. They had lost touch over the years, so imagine their surprise when they met at Columbia University in New York City! Monte had attended college at Indiana University and must have graduated and been accepted into the V-7 about the same time as Joe. Discussions with members of the Foster family confirm that Monte and Joe reacquainted while at Columbia and that Monte also met a certain New York girl who would play an important role in Joe's future. Monte's name will come up again in a later chapter.

Midshipman's School, Columbia University, New York, NY   *December 28, 1942*

Dear Aunt Margaret:

There really isn't much to write about - but it's been some time since I wrote last & I have a few spare minutes.

How are you & Grandma? Write when you find time. I know what it's like to be busy though - so I understand why you don't write oftener. Your hand is the main reason, of course.

I haven't heard from Ed since I got here. I'm worried about him. Will write him again. I don't think Dad has heard from him either.

Christmas wasn't much this year as you might know. I even got a little homesick - the first time in ages. I mailed a lot of Christmas cards but only received some from Uncle Bill, Dr. Klein, Frances, and Uncle Frank. You're excused, of course, I didn't expect you to send one. Oh well, everyone's pretty busy I guess.

I haven't had any liberty yet. Of course, even when I get some there won't be much doing since we only receive $2.50 per week - as I told you. They save the rest to pay for uniforms, etc. We

have to buy our own toiletry articles, stationary, etc. out of the
$2.50. So I'm learning thrift perfectly.

Not much more to say - and we have inspection this morning.
Those hospital corner beds you taught me really came in handy -
since that's the official bed.

Hope you are both well.

Love,
Joe

P.S. Also get the third typhoid today. The 2nd really made me sick.

Exactly thirty days after joining the Navy reserve, Apprentice Seaman McDevitt completed the AS training and was commissioned a midshipman in the USNR. He immediately entered an intensive three- month training program for junior officers. Joe never mentions in his letters the warning that all V-7 candidates reportedly received during their first company muster. The instructor would bark the famous order. "Look to your left, look to your right. Only one of you guys will still be here in ninety days." The Navy put the fear of God into them immediately.

The initial training included classroom introductions to navigation, ordinance and gunnery, seamanship, and engineering. Sea training followed, typically consisting of three-day cruises in the Atlantic on personal yachts leased to the Navy. The cruise classes included lessons in docking, flag hoisting, anchoring, rules of the road, knots, line handling, and so on.

Whoa! What an eye-opening experience those cruises must have been for the candidates. Many of them had probably never *seen* the ocean, much less sailed on it. As for Joe McDevitt, he knew bean fields and corn fields. He knew about music, including professional dance bands and regimental marching bands. He knew a lot about the law. Now he began learning about the sea.

As Joe began the V-7 program in January 1943, the midshipman's program at Columbia University had already trained and graduated twenty-six hundred junior officers. Other programs at Cornell University, Northwestern University, Notre Dame, Smith College and aboard the Battleship USS *Illinois* had graduated similar numbers. The fleet was growing. The need for reserve officers was insatiable.

Midshipman's School, Columbia University, New York, NY   *January 8, 1943*

Dear Aunt Margaret:

Just a few lines since I only have a minute. We hardly have enough time to turn around.

I told you that I haven't received a card from you - but it did come later and had $2 in it which was a very much appreciated Christmas gift - thanks. Gertrude also sent me $2. I have so little time to write letters - I am really behind.

I am a commissioned "Midshipman." So my address is changed only in one particular - "Midshipman Jos. B. McDevitt". Rest is the same - just drop off the AS, V-7 after my name.

John Benowitz of Harrisburg called the other day but I was at the armory at the time.

Haven't much more to say - just wanted to let you know I'm thinking of you & Grandma. I'll write every time I have a chance. It's pretty tough work. Feeling fine and have probably gained a few pounds. Will send some pictures when we have time to snap them.

Love,
Joe

Midshipman's School, Columbia University, New York, NY   *January 26, 1943*

Dear Auntie: I haven't time to write much - just enough to let
you know that I'm feeling fine, in perfect health, but just about
worked to death and slowly going crazy.

I've never been through such a continual "grind" before in my
life. We have weekends off from 3 P.M. Saturday until 5:30 P.M.
Sunday - but can't go out to have a little relaxation because we
have no money.

I won this War Bond in a Major Bowes Amateur Hour nationwide
radio broadcast last Thursday. I didn't know until Thursday
afternoon that I had been chosen to play on it - so I couldn't
let you know.

I'm sending it to you as a little collateral. We get paid only
$5 every two weeks, and that's only enough to cover toiletry
articles, stationary, and the million-and-one small things that
one needs in a place like this. They are saving the rest of our
pay until we graduate in 2 months. We will receive our back pay,
and will be placed on a salary of $216 per month at that time.

But right now you just have to get out on weekends - away from
this grind, or you get so nervous you can't stand it. All week
long, from 5:30 A.M. to 10:30 P.M. you do nothing but study,
write, study, take tests, etc., and I'm certainly getting tired.
However, I have the best grades in the entire class so far - so I
haven't slipped yet.

So, Aunt Margaret, if you can arrange it, please send me a little
cash now and then. It's all a good investment you can be sure
of that.

I've taken out a $10,000 life insurance policy and named you
principal beneficiary; dad is the contingent beneficiary. It will
be sent to you when it has gone through. Am also arranging
an "allotment" plan with the Navy whereby they will pay my
insurance, etc., give me a small part of my pay check, and send

the remainder to you. We'll arrange a joint bank account later. This is all in preparation to my going on sea duty.

How are you & Grandma? Have heard the weather has been terribly cold which is hard on you I know. Don't care how bad it is though - I'm sure of one thing. I'd rather be there than here.

Cheer up Auntie. I'm making a good sailor and officer so far. I'm band leader and commanding officer of our 6th Battalion which is an honor.

But I need the money even though it will be spent for a few bottles of beer and a show or two. That's the only way the men relax around here, and they all get money from home.

I play the organ at Corpus Christie church for Midshipmen Service, and go to communion every Sunday. It's a wonderful church with a wonderful pastor. Rear Admiral Brady made the sermon last Sunday. Must go to work.

Love,
Joe

"I won this War Bond in a Major Bowes Amateur Hour nationwide radio broadcast last Thursday. I didn't know until Thursday afternoon that I had been chosen to play on it – so I couldn't let you know."

"I have the best grades in the entire class so far…"

"I'm making a good sailor and officer so far."

"I'm band leader and commanding officer of our 6th battalion which is an honor."

"I play the organ at Corpus Christie church for Midshipman's Service…"

Even at this first stage of his Navy career, Joe's initiative, talent, and potential were evident. He may not have known it yet, but surely he had already come to the attention of the Navy command. The fleet didn't need just officers; the fleet needed leaders. Joe fit the profile early on.

The Major Bowes Amateur Hour was American radio's best-known talent show and one of the most popular programs broadcast in America. Edward "Major" Bowes hosted the radio talent show from New York City. "For anyone with bus fare and a harmonica, the show was a grab at the brass ring."

Someone had apparently submitted Joe's name as a contestant… and then forgot to tell him! Nevertheless, he won a war bond and a discount on a big meal from a restaurant across the street from the studio.

Washington DC   *February 1, 1943*

On this date the US Navy redesignated plans for a maritime commission passenger and cargo transport vessel from *Sea Dolphin* AP 93 to USS *Leon* APA 48. Construction work on the *Leon* was to begin immediately.

All present and future attack transports would henceforth be classified **APA** to acknowledge their unique role in the coming amphibious war. Attack transports were designed to carry troops to distant assault sites, to use their boats to land troops and equipment on beaches, and to resupply the troops until the landing beaches were secured.

Midshipman's School, Columbia University, New York, NY *February 2, 1943*

Dear Aunt Margaret:

Will take a little time off and thank you for your swell letter and for the money order. I certainly welcomed both. I went down town Saturday night and saw a small show - and felt like a new man when we started back to work Monday morning.

I received a letter from Dad about 3 weeks ago in which he said he had enclosed $5 - but it wasn't in the envelope. So I wrote and told him that he must have forgotten it. In the next letter he said that since I had so much work to do, I would have no need for money, so there was no need for him to send me any. That's the way he looks at it.

I'm glad to hear that grandma is better. But sorry to hear you've been having so much trouble with your hands. I hope it clears up soon.

I finish up here on March 31st - not on the 14th. I have written Ed to see if he can get his furlough then. I certainly hope so.

Well, I must get to work. I'm going on a three day cruise in the Atlantic Ocean tomorrow.

Love,
Joe

Pascagoula, MS *February 6, 1943*

The keel of the USS *Leon* was laid down as a maritime commission type C3–S-A2 hull on this date at Ingalls Shipyard in Pascagoula, MS. The *Leon* would be a large, Custer (Bayfield) class attack transport. Twenty Custer transports would be completed at the Pascagoula shipyard between 1942 and 1944.

Building times were on the order of one hundred ninety days per vessel. The shipyard was making full use of the mass production technology being rapidly harnessed for the US war effort. The goal of the maritime commission's shipbuilding program was now to build transports and other vessels faster than the enemy was sinking them.

Midshipman's School, Columbia University, New York, NY *March 3, 1943*

```
Dear Aunt Margaret:

I'm pretty tired and sleepy this a.m. having been on watch all
night - but this is the first spare time I've had in quite
a while and must write and thank you for the swell bunch of
cookies that you sent me. I gave all the fellows a sample - and
they all agree that you're a fine baker. I still have some left
in the small can - they keep fresh in it.

Well, Auntie, only 4 weeks to go before we finish up here - and I
can hardly wait. There's so much to be done during the time that
remains that it will probably seem to fly by. We graduate and
receive our commissions as Ensigns on March 31st.
```

These days are filled with worry about how to get things done which must be done. We must have our uniforms ordered within the next two weeks - in order that they may be finished before we leave here. I'm enclosing a copy of the instructions that were given to us.

As you can see, the uniform allowance doesn't come until March 31st, which is after we have finished. We can get a good credit account for our suits and raincoats. But as the instructions say - it is best to pay cash for the other things since you can buy them at the Ship's Service Store at a much smaller price than we would have to pay if we charged them. For example, I can buy my khaki shirts, white Naval shirts, for $1.90 each, whereas if I charge them I will have to pay $3.50 each. That's just one of many examples.

We are allowed to purchase 3 pair of shoes at the Ship's Store for $4.00 a pair. The same shoes cost $11.50 otherwise.

Uniforms will cost about $225 altogether. I get $150 on the day I leave here. But the transportation to wherever I am sent must also be paid out of that. The good thing about all this is that we do get it all back later - I buy a ticket at 3 cents a mile, and the Navy will pay us 8 cents a mile later. But everything comes later and leaves us flat footed when we need it most.

I'm going to order my raincoat and Navy blue suits Saturday on a credit basis. My roommate has connections here in New York whereby we are getting them wholesale through his father. So I will pay his father later. I'm really lucky to have him for a roommate since he is saving me about $50.

I need $75 cash with which to purchase two white uniforms, 2 khaki uniforms, 2 extra khaki pants, 1/4 dozen khaki shirts, 2 black ties, shoes, buttons for uniforms, and insignia, all of which is required - and all of which I can get for less money at the Ship's Service Store. The same items would cost me $125 elsewhere.

I thought maybe that this would be a good time to cash in that insurance policy we almost cashed before - since I have enough besides that one.

I hope to have a few days leave of absence before reporting for active duty - so we can get things worked out. It's so hard to do by correspondence, especially when your hand bothers you so much.

I hate to be writing you about money all the time - but there's no one else I can write to about it. And it _will_ come back eventually to where it came from - with interest. I need it just as soon as possible - but not by Western Union. Within the next two weeks anyway. After March 31st things will begin to clear up. I'll know by March 24th where I'm going to be sent - and will let you know immediately.

Thanks again for the cookies - they really hit the spot!

Love,
Joe

Midshipman's School, Columbia University, New York, NY   _March 3, 1943_

Dear Aunt Margaret:

I received the sad telegram just now - and I mailed the other letter just 10 minutes ago. I wish I had waited because that is not the kind of thing to worry you about under the present circumstances. I'm terribly sorry. Please don't pay any attention to it - I didn't know then.

I feel so helpless - I'd like to come home but can't. All I can do is pray and offer up Communion for Grandma. You hadn't mentioned her being worse off - so it came as a shock. Yet I knew what it was before I opened the telegram.

My prayers are for you just as much as for Grandma. I know that she is better off where she has gone. But a new chapter of your life is opening up before you now - and I want so much that it be a happy one. Everything that I can do is going to make it that way.

I've been worried about Papa too. If he comes up for the funeral please see what condition he's in. I hope he is well.

It's so hard to write a letter when there really isn't anything to say. If Grandma had been a young woman and her death had been unexpected - we would be terribly shocked. But as it was it was bound to happen soon, so we should offer our prayers up for her and also pray that the things which are come to pass as a result of her death will all happen for the best - especially for you who has done so much to make Grandma's last days happy.

Love,
Joe

Joe's Grandma Zimmer died of advanced age and a complication of diseases on Tuesday, March 2, 1943. She was 87 years old. Her body lay in state at the Zimmer residence at 125 West Homer Street where the rosary was said on Wednesday evening. The Reverend George P. Lally conducted a funeral mass on Thursday, and Catherine Zimmer was then buried alongside husband Peter Zimmer and daughter Mary Zimmer at St. Joseph Cemetery in Hardin County.

Personal Journal of Mrs. Rose Vaughan, New York, NY   *March 3, 1943*

> *Kay met Ensign Joe (McDevitt)*

In a brief, five-word journal entry, Rose Vaughan chronicled that somewhere in New York City, her youngest daughter, Kathleen Rita, met Midshipman Joe McDevitt. Kathleen was the second daughter of Martin A. and Rose Vaughan, two immigrants from Ireland.

How to describe Kathleen Vaughan? With help from Rose's journal entries, we'll try.

She was a seventeen year-old youngster who had just recently finished high school.

> *Graduation – June 25, 1942 – lovely day, wonderful to see... class poet and prettiest girl.*

She *was* pretty. She had the classic features of a model in those days. She was slim and willowy with a long neck, a wide mouth and beautiful teeth that made for a big, beautiful smile, large eyes and long, thick dark hair.

> *Kay a College model at Best & Co... 1st job August 11, 1942.*
> *Kay's picture in Mademoiselle March 1943... more to come... very sweet.*

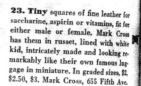
Kathleen Vaughan's first magazine ad, Mademoiselle Magazine, March 1943

According to family lore, Kathleen first saw Joe McDevitt playing the organ at Sunday mass, perhaps at the Midshipman's Service at Corpus Christie Church. She asked Father William Kenealy, a family friend and a chaplain in the Merchant Marines stationed in New York City, to introduce them. There's nothing like a man in uniform, especially one who played a keyboard like that!

As for Joe McDevitt, Kathleen Vaughan caught his eye immediately and captured his heart soon thereafter.

Midshipman's School, Columbia University, New York, NY　　　　　*March 16, 1943*

Dear Aunt Margaret:

Just a line to let you know I received your letter - and thank you so much for your timely help. Lord knows I need it now.

I received a letter from Papa this morning. He certainly puts all his faith in you - he feels so much better when he has been to see you.

Well, hon, the time is drawing near - only two weeks to go now. And while I've been looking forward to the finish - now that it's near I wonder. No telling what will come next - I still don't know what my assignment will be. I should find out some time this week - will let you know then.

I've been attending such a wonderful church - and know the priests so well by now that I hate to leave. They are really swell.

I haven't heard from Ed recently and I don't know whether he will be having a furlough or not. Of course, I don't know if I will get away myself or not. I should wait and write you later

when I know - but I thought I should write and let you know
that I did receive your letter.

Will write the latter part of this week - and let you know
everything.

Take good care of yourself.

Love,
Joe

In Washington DC, the Navy was drawing up orders for the next class of new ensigns from Columbia University. Joe would not receive his orders with his first duty assignment for several weeks. Since our storyline is March 1943, we can share a quick peek at his first duty assignment.

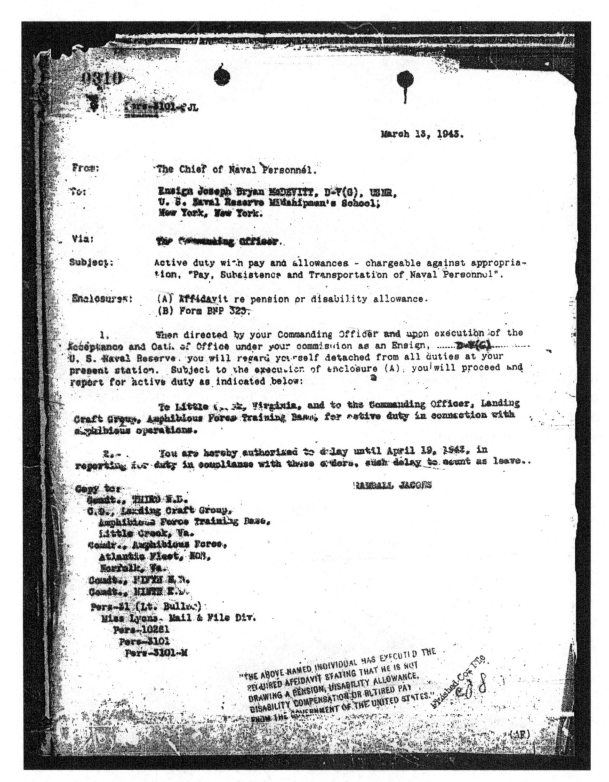

0310

Pers-3101-PJL

March 13, 1943.

From: The Chief of Naval Personnel.

To: Ensign Joseph Bryan McDEVITT, D-V(G), USNR,
          U. S. Naval Reserve Midshipman's School,
          New York, New York.

Via: The Commanding Officer.

Subject: Active duty with pay and allowances - chargeable against appropria-
          tion, "Pay, Subsistence and Transportation of Naval Personnel".

Enclosures: (A) Affidavit re pension or disability allowance.
            (B) Form BNP 323.

     1.   When directed by your Commanding Officer and upon execution of the
Acceptance and Oath of Office under your commission as an Ensign, ...D-V(G).........
U. S. Naval Reserve, you will regard yourself detached from all duties at your
present station. Subject to the execution of enclosure (A), you will proceed and
report for active duty as indicated below:

          To Little Creek, Virginia, and to the Commanding Officer, Landing
Craft Group, Amphibious Force Training Base, for active duty in connection with
amphibious operations.

     2.   You are hereby authorized to delay until April 19, 1943, in
reporting for duty in compliance with these orders, such delay to count as leave..

                                        RANDALL JACOBS

Copy to:
     Comdt., THIRD N.D.
     C.O., Landing Craft Group,
       Amphibious Force Training Base,
       Little Creek, Va.
     Comdr., Amphibious Force,
       Atlantic Fleet, NOB,
       Norfolk, Va.
     Comdt., FIFTH N.D.
     Comdt., NINTH N.D.

     Pers-21 (Lt. Buller)
     Miss Lyons, Mail & File Div.
          Pers-10281
          Pers-3101
          Pers-3101-M

"THE ABOVE NAMED INDIVIDUAL HAS EXECUTED THE
REQUIRED AFFIDAVIT STATING THAT HE IS NOT
DRAWING A PENSION, DISABILITY ALLOWANCE,
DISABILITY COMPENSATION OR RETIRED PAY
FROM THE GOVERNMENT OF THE UNITED STATES."

(AF)

Ensign Joseph Bryan McDevitt, D-V(G), USNR, Active Duty Assignment

Personal Journal of Mrs. Rose Vaughan, New York, NY   *March 1943*

> *A gala time for Kay with Midshipman Joe McDevitt. But Hank appears (surprise) and met Joe at church.*

We know a little about Hank from earlier entries in Rose Vaughan's journal. He was a young man who had dated Kathleen in high school. Kathleen attended her first formal with Hank on June 20, 1942, and Hank spent Kathleen's graduation day, June 25, with Kathleen and the Vaughans.

Hank reported to the Army for boot camp on November 26, 1942. His first furlough was in January 1943; his second furlough was in February; and on his third furlough, March 1943, he met Joe McDevitt at church with Kathleen. Poor Hank—the way their romance was blossoming, he was almost certainly out of the picture by March.

Personal Journal of Mrs. Rose Vaughan, New York, NY   *March 1943*

> *Joe's graduation dance March 29 and graduation from Midshipman School March 31. Joe off to Little Rock – due at Norfolk, Virginia April 19.*

While on leave, Joe sat for portraits at Michael's Studio while in Benton, Illinois.

Ensign Joseph B. McDevitt, USNR, 1943

<u>*Personal Journal*</u> *of Mrs. Rose Vaughan, New York, NY*   *March 1943*

Joe back from Little Rock April 16. Kay had 3 wonderful days. And Sunday Joe came for dinner and left at 11:15 P.M. for Norfolk, Virginia, due April 19.

U.S. Navy Amphibious Training Base, Little Creek, VA   *April 22, 1943*

Dear Aunt Margaret:

Have time for only a few lines, but will write because I know you are looking for a letter.

Nothing unexpected has happened, and while I could probably write a book on what has happened since I left home - I simply don't have the time. Have to let you, Dad, and Ed know what my address is.

Ensign Joseph B. McDevitt
Amphibious Training Base
Little Creek, Virginia

We will probably be here about 6 weeks, so write soon.

Had a wonderful time in New York & Kay says hello. Will write soon.

Love,
Joe

Joe McDevitt, along with many other brand new ensigns, was ordered where the need was great and growing in 1943—amphibious warfare. Neither the scope of training facilities nor the number of training exercises previously conducted matched in size or complexity the Pacific assaults currently being planned for that year. The Navy was developing amphibious doctrine and learning on the fly.

At Little Creek, located in the protected waters of the Chesapeake Bay, amphibious personnel first received classroom instruction in the fundamentals of seamanship, landing craft operation, boat maintenance and control, communications, air support, gunfire control, intelligence, and other skills.

Next they trained on the water, operating LCVPs (**l**anding **c**raft **v**ehicle **p**ersonnel), the workhorse of the amphibious forces, and the larger LCMs (**l**anding **c**raft **m**echanized). These were the two landing craft that would be carried on board the new attack transports being built at shipyards across the country.

SOURCE: WWW.USSORMSBY.COM/GALLERY08.HTM

Landing Craft Vessel Personnel (LCVP):
Workhorse of the attack transport boat groups

At sea they learned:

- To assemble at a rendezvous area and form up under the direction of boat group commanders;
- To circle in formation until receiving the signal to approach an embarkation station at (an imaginary) "transport" vessel;
- To secure their landing craft to the "transport" and receive and make fast the "cargo nets" to be used by "debarking troops;"
- To receive three dozen fully armed (imaginary) troops and to cast off upon command;
- To approach a rendezvous area five hundred to fifteen hundred yards away from the "transport" and to form up and maintain the classic circular formations;
- To deploy to the line of departure and advance under the direction of the boat group commander in his **L**anding **C**raft **C**ontrol vessel (LCC) and the assistant boat group commanders serving as wave guides in LCVPs;
- Finally, to hit the beach! Unload troops! Retract and withdraw! Don't broach that boat!

They practiced in the daytime and at night. They practiced in calm water and rough. They practiced in broiling heat and glaring sunlight that few of them had ever experienced. The sailors complained… and then they practiced some more. None of them had experienced combat, and few of them could imagine it. How did the Navy prepare them? Practice, practice, practice.

Amphibious Training Base, Little Creek, VA   *May 10, 1943*

Dear Aunt Margaret:

Pardon this paper. I am sitting in a classroom where lecture is being given to the men in my crew so will use the time to answer your fat letters which I received OK and enjoyed very much. Was glad to hear that things are OK at home.

Have been working awfully hard here - going to sea all day every day including Sundays. We will be attending classes for about a week or so now which will give my nose some time to get new skin on it. It has peeled about four times now - the sun is so very hot and we're out in it all the time without a hint of shade. But I love it and am in the best of physical shape. The food is plain but is good. And I imagine that I have gained weight although I haven't weighed lately to make sure. Am as black as an Indian. Will send you some snapshots.

This next Friday we have a 72 hour liberty coming to us. From Friday at 10:30 until Monday at 10:30. I am going to New York with Douglas, my roommate in Columbia, and his wife. Kay will meet us at the train. Father Kenealy, who is a chaplain in the Merchant Marines, will be there also. We are certainly looking forward to getting away from this place for a change, even though it will only be a short time. It's the last freedom we will have most likely. We expect to be here for three more weeks most likely.

In re. the settlement of Grandpa's estate - I'm glad things are being done. As far as my part is concerned - it is all yours and if papers are to be signed, they will be signed to that effect.

By May 15-16, I will start mailing the money for Dr. Klein - about $50 every two weeks, and will also pay interest. That's only fair. I will send it to you & you take care of it. Will be sending you money all along now. I may well need a little myself - for reasons which I will tell you - although you surely know by now.

I have been intending to buy Kay a diamond. However, I haven't asked her yet. So nothing has been done. You needn't worry about things going any further for some time. It will really be an engagement ring. And I have no intentions of getting married before I go overseas. But if she wants - then I shall buy a ring if I can find a decent one for a reasonable price. Maybe she will say "No" - so I wouldn't count on anything.

I received the 2nd highest mark in the Officer's Class here at the base. Just found out this morning. Don't suppose this means very much around this place however.

I sent the Easter cards a little late, as you know. Had been at sea and had no opportunity to mail them on time.

Am enclosing $14 which is the amount my pictures cost at Michael's Studio in Benton. He has already sent Kay's to her - but I want you to take the one you want, Aunt Esther to take the one she wants, and then send the other two to me so I can mail one to Aunt Bernice. Will send $25 which should cover all the charges.

Take care of yourself - I will write again soon.

Love,
Joe

"I received the 2nd highest mark in the Officer's Class here at the base. Just found out this morning. Don't suppose this means very much around this place however."

Wrong, ensign! Joe McDevitt had already caught the eye of the command staff at amphibious forces in Little Creek. He soon would be designated an assistant boat group commander, the first supervisory position for new amphibious force officers.

Personal Journal of Mrs. Rose Vaughan, New York, NY　　　　　*May 1943*

> Kay went down to Norfolk, Virginia, over Decorations (Memorial) Day weekend to visit Joe. A wonderful time.

Amphibious Training Base , Little Creek, VA　　　　　*June 2, 1943*

Dear Aunt Margaret:

Received your letter and was so glad to hear from you. I was especially glad to hear that Uncle Steve has heard from Bernard and that he was well and fine. He will probably be exchanged before long and be able to come home for a while.

It's so hot down here we can hardly stand it. We're out in the sun without any shade all day long. I came about as close to passing out yesterday as I ever have. The perspiration is just rolling off me right now.

We've had very little spare time and expect to be sent out from this base almost anytime. When we do start moving I will promptly send you a wire as to change of address. You asked for the names of my friends here so you could write them and keep in touch with me. I have plenty of friends but they all leave here at the same time I do. I will keep you well posted - and if there is anyone to whom you could write,

"Little Creek, May '43. Joe was so sun tanned in these photos that you can't see his face very well."

I'll send his or her address. I went to New York as I told you I was going to and had a perfectly wonderful time. Doug and Betty (my roommate and his wife) went up with me and met Kay's folks. Kay and Betty became very good friends and Betty invited Kay to come down to Norfolk on a visit. So the last weekend saw Kay down here in Virginia. I was lucky enough to be off a little while to see her. We took several snapshots both here and in New York. As soon as Kay sends them to me, I will send them to you. She's ordering an extra set made for you.

Remember I told you that I was going to offer her an engagement ring. Well, I didn't do so - not because she refused or anything like that, but because it just isn't the right time. That will just have to wait - and no telling how long.

How are things going in regard to the settling up of the estate? You asked me whether you should file a claim and whether you are eligible to do so. Now you'll just have to accept the advice of the attorney since I don't know all the facts and I don't have any Illinois law books to consult. However, on the basis of what I do know, I would say that you can and should do so. Let me say this much - whatever my share may be will go to you.

To tell you the truth the life I am now living has changed all my thoughts. Law is far from my mind - I just think thoughts of the sea and war. I know now that it will be very difficult to adapt myself to civilian ways of life again. Wish that there was some way of passing the Bar without having to go back to school again. That will be hard to do.

I'm enclosing the negatives of the snapshots you asked for. And by the way - you mentioned that you were sending those other two portraits that Michaels of Benton made of me. I haven't received them as yet. And did you get the ones of Ed and I together which Metcalf of Harrisburg made? If you will just tell him, he will send one to Papa. Maybe you have already sent them.

I sent Ed a birthday card and $25 for a present. Kay bought the card and sent it to me - and reminded me that May 30th was his birthday or I'd probably forgotten. She sure has a remarkable memory. I must not forget that hers is on July 28th. I received a box of Sander's chocolates from Frances this week. I don't know what to do. Also had a long letter from Gertrude. Had a nice letter from Aunt Helene in reply to a letter I wrote her. Hear from Dad regularly. Also heard from Dori wanting that picture I promised her. I have no time to answer most of them – yet I ought to.

Enclosed money to be used any way you want to.

Write real soon. Hello to everyone.

Love,
Joe

This is another especially revealing letter. After seven months of intensive training, the Navy had utterly and completely changed Joe McDevitt. Their training had redirected all of his thoughts, along with his motivations and energies, from becoming a lawyer to becoming a warrior:

> *"To tell you the truth, the life that I am living has changed all my thoughts. Law is far from my mind – I just think thoughts of the sea and war."*

These two sentences evidence the total transformation that the Navy sought in all of its reservists, officers, and enlisted men alike. Joe's university mindset, a preoccupation with balancing work and studies, was gone. Front and center was a reserve line officer, preoccupied with matters of command, leadership, and the well-being of his crew.

Only two sentences, but Aunt Margaret would not have missed their significance. Surely after reading those lines, Margaret Zimmer, spinster aunt who raised Joe McDevitt from age eight, put her letter down and thought to herself, "Oh my."

Amphibious Training Base , Little Creek, VA   *June 16, 1943*

Dear Aunt Margaret:

Many things have happened since I last wrote to you both in the line of duty and along other lines also. So I shall take a little time out to explain everything - and ask your opinion on one thing in particular.

First and foremost something about which you will be as happy as I am. I was in New York last weekend and Kay and I became engaged. We announced it at her home last Sunday for dinner. Mr. and Mrs. Vaughan, Kay's sister Rosemary, and husband Budd Christie, and their little son Stephen and Father Kenealy were there at the time. I only wished all the time that you could have been there too - and Kay was wishing the same thing. Now I know that I told you I was going to forget it for the time being - but it wasn't that simple - it couldn't be forgotten that easily. Besides, I'm very happy about it - and I know Kay is too. And I also know that you are assured that she is everything I've told you she is - and that you have enough faith in me to know that I wouldn't make a mistake. All the problems involved with other girls I've known before are absent in this case, and her parents and sister are tickled to death - they treated me royally. Mrs. Vaughan said that she had two fine sons as well as two fine daughters. I know that the future looks dull and filled with uncertainties but the past has also been just as troubled and has worked out OK so far. I'm not worried that the future won't work out the same way. If anyone has reason to worry it's Kay - she can't be certain where she would live, or on what income, she doesn't know my Father, brother, or you, etc. - and yet she isn't worried because she trusts in me - and she <u>knows</u> that she will like you. And I'm certain that you will think the world and all of her. Enclosed are some pictures that were taken of her when she was down here. They also include some of my friends and their wives. Doug and Betty are in there too. I don't have the ones of Father Kenealy yet - will send them as soon as I get them.

Aunt Margaret, she's looking forward to having a letter from you in the near future, so won't you please take a little time out and write her a nice letter. She will certainly enjoy it and I can assure you that you will receive a very nice letter in the near future. I sent you her address but there is a small change. Here it is:

Miss Kathleen R. Vaughan
524 West 22nd Street
New York (27), NY

Kathleen visiting at
Little Creek, VA, June 1943

The way I feel I could go on writing on this subject indefinitely, but there are some other things to tell you about.

On the enclosed typewritten sheet is a short memorandum concerning me. I had a wonderful time at the luncheon - the Admiral is a wonderful person. As a result of the honor, I received a promotion and was also recommended for an increase in rank. But the letter probably won't come through for some time. However, as a result of all this I will be retained at this base indefinitely, at least for three more months as an instructor of new officers. Whether to be happy or not I don't know. I'm pretty disgusted with the place. But it is a step upward.

I've been expecting Ed to drop in this week. He wrote that he was going to try to come up here for three days. Sure would be glad to see him.

I haven't bought the ring as yet because most of these places seem to want too much. I suppose a lot of people will be surprised, Frances for one. But I've given her no encouragement whatever. And I don't know what Dad will think. He has surely expected something like this before now, however. Of one thing I'm sure - all the folks on our side of the family will be more than pleased when they get to know Kay.

Now please write her soon - she's just dying to be sure that you approve of what we've done - and I know that you do. And just drop me a short line to let me know what you think. I promise that you will be present, and that we will ask your consent before anything else is done.

By the way, Auntie, when do you think you would be able to come out on that visit you mentioned. It would be a small trip for you and I'm sure you would enjoy it.

I received the pictures OK but Kay liked the one she has best. I'll probably send them back to you with the rest of my things.

Must close now so I can get your letter in the mail. It's an important one!!!

Love,
Joe

P. S. You can tell the glad things to anyone you care to - I'm proud of it.

"On the enclosed typewritten sheet is a short memorandum concerning me. I had a wonderful time at the luncheon – the Admiral is a wonderful person. As a result of the honor, I received a promotion and was also recommended for an increase in rank."

We made every possible effort to obtain a copy of that "short memorandum" and to identify the honor that Joe mentioned here. Regrettably, all efforts failed. Nevertheless, the honor confirmed that the Navy saw the potential in this young amphibious officer. Details about his promotion and increase in rank follow in letters to come.

Pascagoula, MS   *June 19, 1943*

On this date, the USS *Leon* APA 48 was launched at Ingalls Shipbuilding, Pascagoula, Mississippi.

Amphibious Training Base , Little Creek, VA   *July 28, 1943*

Dear Aunt Margaret:

What hectic days these are - I never know what is going to happen next. We have been expecting to ship out for the past week but something always delays it. We have been terribly busy completing our last minute training and have been out at sea on practice maneuvers about every day. I've been trying to write this letter ever since I got your telegram and letter. And my goodness, auntie, it was sure a sweet letter and I just love you to pieces for the things you said. And I'm sure that Kay will enjoy your letter too - you've probably written her by this time. Oh of course you have since I remember now that she told me so in one of her letters. I'll have more to say about this later on although I probably won't have time to finish all I have today. There are so many things to be said - about so many things.

Ed was down last weekend for 3 days and we were certainly glad to see each other. It's lucky that he could get off because I can't. He stayed with me here on the base and ate out here also. I took him out to sea with me on a maneuver which he enjoyed immensely since it was the first time he had ever been to sea.

Now that you're back in Harrisburg (and I'm sure glad your stay in the hospital's over and that you are feeling better. Here's hoping that your feet will be better very soon.) There's something I want you to do. I want you to go to the bank and find out just what has to be done to make out a joint bank account in your and my name. I know they will want both our signatures - you can give yours easily enough and the bank can send me the papers to sign. I intend to make out an allotment of $100 a month which will be sent directly to the bank and deposited in the account. It will be a checking account of course. After it reaches a pretty good sum you can buy some war bonds with part of it so there will be interest coming in. Just now I'm trying to pay some of my debts off - and after I leave the country you can continue to do the same. Later on, if possible, I'll try to increase the allotment. Anyway, you check up at the bank and let me know <u>right away</u> just what has to be done or have the bank get busy and have it done.

I'm expecting Kay to come down here on her vacation - arriving the first part of this week. Should receive a wire tonight letting me know. She was going to rush down last Thursday when it appeared that we were going to ship outright but I wired "no hurry" as soon as plans were changed.

Tuesday

Well to continue what I was talking about last Sunday. I met Kay at the train yesterday morning. She will be here for a week at least. She and Lt. Richard's fiancée, who lives in Philadelphia, came down along with her mother (the girl from Philadelphia) and they are staying at a very nice home so she should have a wonderful time - even though I won't get into town so very often. But she knew that before she came down. And I also warned her about the mosquitoes - they are bad, but not so bad as they have been. She showed me an awfully nice letter she received from Aunt Helene and Uncle Frank. And I believe she wrote you yesterday or today so you should hear from her by the time you receive this letter. Today is her birthday and I have a big cake for her.

Hon, I'm afraid I'm going to have to cut this letter short again - or better still just finish up and mail it since I want you to get to the bank as soon as you can. It will be time for the leaving before long. Let me know what is happening.

I'm in perfect health and happy about things in general so don't ever worry about me. I go to Communion every Sunday and served mass for the first time in years Sunday.

If you have any clippings or news about anyone I know send them here to me.

I'll call you up before we leave from this base and will write again soon. You write when you have time.

Love,
Joe

No hurry, the Navy changed its mind again. After completing their training at Little Creek, Joe and the officers and enlisted men in his battalion were transferred to Ft. Pierce, FL, for advanced training.

They soon realized that training at Ft. Pierce was different. It was ocean training, with strong, variable currents and unpredictable squalls that could capsize landing craft. Hitting the beaches in Florida was more challenging than at Little Creek. It demanded superior seamanship; it demanded greater discipline at virtually every stage of their maneuvers; and the heat was unbearable… worse even than Little Creek. By then, however, they understood that the heat might be worse still where they were going. Practice, practice, practice.

Advanced Amphibious Training Base , Ft. Pierce, FL   *August 7, 1943*

Dear Aunt Margy:

So much has been happening since I received your warm letter of congratulations upon our engagement. It might seem that I had put off answering without sufficient reason but that's hardly true.

First since you mentioned that you were waiting to hear from Joe, I thought perhaps he had not told you that he had been transferred to Ft. Pierce. I knew he was worried about you being sick and concluded that he'd rather not upset you any more until you were feeling better. He answered back - "No, Katie, I don't keep secrets from anybody. Aunt Margy knows I'm here by now."

I had planned to spend my vacation with him in Little Creek, and it temporarily shattered all my plans to learn that he was going to be shipped further south. I had my ticket bought and was wishing the days off the calendar, when he called me and said they were leaving there. Then I postponed everything so that I could come down here to Ft. Pierce for the first two weeks in August. Plans were again upset when he informed me that the latest information was they would be shipped out to sea by that time, so in desperation I just packed up and came the next day. I've been here since last Monday and will leave within the next few days - as much as I hate to.

We've been having a glorious time being small town folks. Joe gets off the base nearly every day at 4:30 and we either go to a movie and stop for a soda on the way home or spend the evening with some other Navy couples who have their homes down here. We went to the Officer's Club to celebrate the first night when Joe gave me my ring. His friends cooked up a little party and it was a nice surprise for me and a good way to meet all these people he mentions in his letters. As a rule though we enjoy coming back here to the house where I'm staying and playing the piano. The couples who live here are all very friendly and we sing our heads off while Joe tries to keep us in tune. It probably sounds awful to the rest of the people around here but we like the sounds of our own voices even if they don't. Too, that way we have lots of time to talk and try to figure out some plans for the future. Believe me it sounds easy - but the Navy keeps us busy - changing its mind so often. For some reason, Joe's orders to ship out will be delayed now - for how long nobody knows, not even the men themselves.

I guess you're wondering - and rightly so - just what we've decided as far as being married is concerned. Well, it looks like we'll have to wait for a while anyway, since neither one of us wants a hurry-up affair. We'd like to have Fr. Kenealy marry us since he's the one who first introduced Joe and I, and have it in New York with both families present. We could never go ahead without having you there to "give Joe away" as he puts it. I wouldn't consider it under any other circumstances and I know he wouldn't either. So, until such time as we can accomplish all this, we'll just have to be content to talk about it. And hope that it won't be too long before it will be a reality.

We're going to try to see Ed before I go back. I'd love to have this opportunity to meet Joe's brother but it's a case of "so near but yet so far." It stands to reason that Ed can't get off whenever he wants to and whenever it's convenient for us to meet him, but we're trying hard and I hope we can work something out. I got a grand letter from him as soon as he heard the news - also one from Helene and Frank. I told Joe that his folks certainly had been wonderful as far as making me feel welcomed into the family is concerned, and I do appreciate it so much.

I know it's hard for you since we've never met but be assured that I'll try my very best to be the kind of girl that you'd want for him to have as his wife. Harrisburg is a long way from New York but maybe someday I can take advantage of your invitation to come out for a visit, but until then I guess letters will have to serve as a means for introduction.

It goes almost without saying that my people have nothing but the highest regard for Joe and repeat again and again that they couldn't hope for a finer son-in-law.

Thank you for your birthday card - I hope to hear from you again soon. We'll have to compare notes on Joe's activities from time to time, and to get together on the latest happenings.

Sincerely, Kathleen

P.S. Enclosed is a picture of the house I'm staying at down here. We're taking some pictures so I'll be able to enclose a few snaps next letter. Please excuse this company paper - it's all I have with me.

Kathleen and Joe at Ft. Pierce, FL, August 1943

Advanced Amphibious Training Base , Ft. Pierce, FL   *August 23, 1943*

Dear Aunt Margaret:

I've had no chance whatsoever to get into town to a Notary Public hence the delay. I hope to do so tomorrow so I'm writing a few lines today to put in the letter as soon as I can get the Power of Attorney notarized.

We will be leaving here within three weeks at the very least and will go back to Norfolk to board a transport. We may not leave there at once but that remains to be seen. Kay is coming down there to see me off. I wish I could get home first but that will be impossible I'm afraid. However I will call you long distance before we shove off.

I was planning on going up to see Ed today but my liberty was canceled. It has been raining hard now for two days and we are practically under water. Our clothes are all mildewed. I'll hang mine in the sun when it finally comes out again.

What has happened in regard to the will. Let me know when you change your address so I can get in touch with you in a hurry.

Well, there's nothing more to be said. We've been working very hard and long hours. I feel like sleeping most of my spare time.

Write soon - and I'll write you often from now on. Take good care of yourself.

Love,
Joe

P.S. Don't make any remarks about when you received this.

Pascagoula, MS   *September 11, 1943*

On this date, the US Navy accepted the USS *Leon* and placed her in partial commission through September 27, 1943, for transit by an auxiliary vessel ferry crew to Brooklyn, NY. There the Bethlehem Steel Shipyard would complete her conversion to final specifications for the Navy's new generation of large attack transport.

Advanced Amphibious Training Base, Ft. Pierce, FL   *September 15, 1943*

Dear Aunt Margaret:

We're leaving tonight and time is short so I'm just going to write the important things.

We are due in New York City this weekend, but are stopping at Little Creek, Virginia on the way. Some of us will be at sea by the first of next week- we don't know just who it will be yet.

I will call you some time this weekend. I'll reverse the charges because the call will have a better chance of going through that way.

Before I call I want you to find out all about the bank account and be ready to tell me. You've never told me whether it was all arranged or not. I signed the card you sent - but the bank has never sent a check book or anything. What is the full name of the bank? I must know so the money will go to the right place.

Be sure to leave a forwarding address at the Post Office if you move.

I'd love to see you but I'm afraid I'll have no free time whatever, and there probably isn't enough time left.

I'll write more on the train. We're just about to leave now.

Don't fail to arrange the bank account. I'll get the call through just as soon as I can.

Love,
Joe

P.S. Send my letters to Kay until I notify you of my address. Since she is in New York City - I'll get mail quicker that way. She has moved - here is her new address:

Miss Kathleen R. Vaughan
454 Ft. Washington Avenue
New York (33), NY

New York, NY   *September 24, 1943*

Dear Aunt Margaret:

Well, dear, this phone call probably brought you a big relief. You'd probably decided I had already left the country. And by rights I should have done so by now. I don't mind telling you that I'm disappointed to have to remain behind while all the friends I've been working with for the past 6 months go to England to take part in the invasion of France. While I am receiving an advance in rank which I wouldn't receive otherwise

- nevertheless there's no war in this country and I certainly
haven't been doing any fighting so far. And the thought of
having to spend three more months in Norfolk and then three
more months in Florida is most disgusting. However, orders are
orders and I must do what I am told.

I came to New York with my outfit to aid in getting them ready to
go across. We got here yesterday and Lt. Enweiler (my commanding
officer) and I are returning to Norfolk tomorrow after the boys
have left. There isn't much that I can do though so I've had
some time to spend with Kay and her family. I'm at her home now
and am going to spend the night here. They are wonderful people
- you'll like them when you meet them.

I didn't write Dad and tell him I was leaving like I did you
- and it's good that I didn't. While he hasn't heard from me
- at least he isn't worried with the thought that I've left the
country. I can write him now and tell him that I'll be around
for a while - and he will be happy about it.

I will now have the position of Boat Group Commander and will
have the rank of Lt. (junior grade). When my new outfit has
finished training, we will ship out, I hope, and I will advance
to full Lieutenant. So it's a promotion all the way around. But
I'll miss all my old friends.

I've tried to call you every night for the past week - ever since
I came back from Florida. But it has just been impossible to do.
That (Little Creek) is the world's most crowded place right now.
I'm sorry you've had to wait Auntie. The operator told me to
reverse the charges since there was a better chance of getting
you that way. And, too, I haven't the money just now. We haven't
been paid for two months since our pay accounts have been "closed
out" preparatory to going across.

The allotment to the bank account will start next month if the
Navy supply department gets things straight for once. $100 per
month as it stands now - when my rank increases I may be able
to increase it. But that's one of the reasons again why I want

to go overseas. The pay is more and one doesn't have to spend anything. As long as I'm here on shore I have to pay the Navy $60 a month for rent and $21 a month for food. So it's hard to save any money.

My address will be the old one:

Amphibious Training Base
Little Creek, Virginia

Kay has had engagement announcements made and we are going down to pick them up now. You'll be getting one soon.

What is Father Lally's full name - we want to send him one. And what is Uncle Steve's address - I guess she wants to send them to the whole family, and I want them all to know. This thing is going to be done right the whole way around.

If the opportunity presents itself that you can come to Norfolk for a visit, be sure to let me know well in advance so Kay can arrange to come down at the same time. I'll have more free time now to see you at nights if you can come & you and Kay can spend the days together. I'm afraid I'll never get enough time to get home.

Well, I must close now. I'll write when I get back to Norfolk. And I'm going to call you tonight. Be good and write often.

Love,
Joe

Boat group commander... a *very big* promotion. The boat group commander was a division commander, responsible aboard ship for all administrative and operational activities of one hundred forty sailors and officers in the boat division. (The term *ship* referred to the attack transport; the term *boat* referred to the landing craft.) Further, the boat group commander was wholly responsible for the boat group's performance out on the water, i.e., for putting the boots on the beach. This was the core mission for the new attack transports.

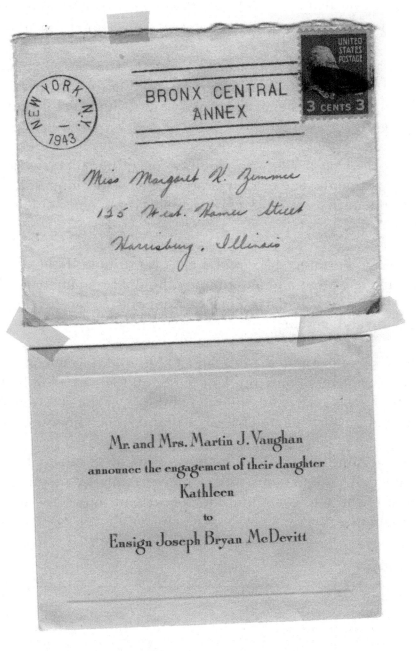

Joe and Kathleen's engagement announcement, September 1943

Brooklyn, NY   *September 27, 1943*

The USS *Leon* arrived at the Bethlehem Steel Shipyard on September 27, 1943, and was temporarily decommissioned for final conversion to an attack transport.

Shipyard workers immediately swarmed aboard the ship and got to work. On the other side of the world, the Pacific Fleet was waiting for the arrival of the large attack transports and the new, fast attack carriers with which to launch their island-hopping strategy.

The *Leon's* conversion began with modification of her superstructure and her interior compartments. The reconfiguration of deck machinery and rigging to a configuration known as "yard and stay rigging," came next. This was the fastest way to move cargo at that time.

Hold #1 became berthing space and a light cargo hold, hold #2 was to berth troops and limited cargo and ammunition, hold #3 remained as a large cargo hold, hold #4 became an enlarged sick bay, and hold #5 was re-equipped to handle heavy cargo and gasoline.

The yard workers next added a built-in CO_2 firefighting system and enlarged fire mains, rearranged booms and king posts, and added a jumbo boom at #5 hatch to lift her two LCMs and Sherman tanks. Next she received three sets of triple Welin davits which allowed her to carry and launch her twenty-four LCVPs.

Her armament came next in the form of two 5 inch/38 cal. dual purpose guns, four twin 40mm AA gun mounts, and eighteen 20mm AA gun mounts. She also received top of the line communications gear and top secret air and surface radar installations.

Kathleen R. Vaughan, New York, NY   *October 15, 1943*

Dear Aunt Marg:

I do hope you're not sick again - it's been so long since I've heard from you. I guess you've been busy closing up the house - Joe said you were going to.

We've moved just recently so I know what a job you have ahead of you - a house entails so much more effort than an apartment.

It was so nice to talk to you on the telephone the night Joe called you from here. I felt very selfish taking him away from you for even a minute, but it was lovely to talk with you for a few seconds anyway.

I guess you're just as happy as I am that Joe is going to be in the country for a few months more. I know he is disappointed - he wants to see "action" very much. But as far as I am concerned the longer he is kept here the better. I am going down to Norfolk to see him next weekend and I'm looking forward to the trip very much. I'll travel at night and be there for two days - Saturday and Sunday. It takes about 10 hours from New York - a very short distance when I think back to the 36 hour trip down to Florida on my vacation. That was a terrible train but reservations are very hard to obtain unless you apply weeks in advance, and I wasn't sure I could go until the last minute. It was worth it though once I got there.

That's all for this time. Keep well and let me hear from you when you have a few minutes.

Sincerely, Kathleen

Amphibious Training Base , Little Creek, VA   *November 1, 1943*

Dear Aunt Margaret:

It has been so long since I heard from you - I'm wondering if
you have my current address or if you have moved and I don't
have your current address. I'm going to try and call you tonight
and here's hoping I succeed at getting a call through this time.
I have tried three times without success - and I have not had an
answer to the last two letters I have written you.

I certainly hope you receive either this letter or the phone call
tonight because they will both contain big news - which will
probably not be a big surprise to you.

Kay and I plan to get married November 27th at Corpus Christie
Church in New York City. Fr. Kenealy will perform the ceremony.
Since I have been retained at this base as a training instructor,
and will be going back to Florida for another several months, I
can no longer see any reason for waiting. Of course, I've thought
the entire situation out from top to bottom as also has Kay, and
while we have both been of the opinion that it might be better to
wait until after the war, nevertheless the end of the war is too
far to put off what is, at present, the most important thing in
the world for me.

Kay is a most wonderful person and I need someone like her. I'm
absolutely positive that you will be proud of her - and proud of
me for picking such a wonderful person. I'll be proud of her
forever.

Now for the important part. I don't want to get married unless
you can be present at the ceremony. Ed is going to be best man,
and Kay's sister, Rosemary, will be the bridal maid. Dad is going
to be here also. He's been writing Kay regularly wanting to know
when the wedding date would be so he could have time to get a
Pullman reservation. He couldn't stand the trip by coach. I wrote
him just before I started your letter and told him to write you

in order to see if you could come out to New York City together
and make the trip nicer for both of you.

I want you to accept all the war bonds that I have sent you as
a gift and use them to come out on. You needn't feel bad about
cashing them since it's for just such a purpose that they were
purchased.

November 27th is on Saturday. I will probably arrive in New York
on Friday night and won't get to stay very long. I'm trying to
arrange it so I can get there by Wednesday or Thursday and have
a longer visit with you and Dad and Ed. But the Navy may not
agree. Kay will return to Norfolk with me after the wedding where
we will live in a married officer's community.

Marriage will solve many problems for me in addition to happiness.
I will be making more money and Kay is the type of person who
knows how to save it. She will take care of my debts - I can't
seem to make any headway. By the time I've paid my insurance, my
war bond, my laundry and cleaning, my wardroom fee, my mess bill
and about a dozen other bachelor's office expenses I have just a
little to salt away for just such a thing as getting married.

But I'm not going to worry about that now - I know things will
be taken care of.

I'm due for an increase in rank to Lt. (jg) soon. It should have
been through already but it will date back to September when it
does come which is the same as having it now.

I've been on watch all night and it is now 4 a.m. - I'll be
relieved at 7 a.m. I have two out of every three nights off which
I will be able to spend at home. In Florida I have 5 out of every
six nights off.

Now, Aunt Margaret, I know you have trouble writing because
of your fingers, but won't you please take time out for a few
minutes right now and drop me a few lines. And you should write
Kay a line also don't you think. She wants you present at the

wedding almost more than anyone else. It won't be such a big affair - just the relatives and a few of her friends. There aren't many who can get off on Saturday morning - and none of my Naval officer friends will be able to get off to go up to New York. I only hope that Ed will be able to make it OK.

Drop Dad a line and see what he is planning. He will probably write you right away.

Tell me how you have been and what has happened.

I asked you to send me my bridge coat (the heavy coat) and my other Navy blue suit and the two extra pairs of Navy blue trousers in my last letter. It must not have reached you although it has not been returned as yet. I included a money order in it so I can check up in that way. It's getting pretty cold here and I do need them so I hope you receive this letter. I shouldn't take any chances sending cash but the P.O. is closed for remodeling and won't be open until the day after tomorrow. The mail is being handled by the Ship Service Store but they can't send money orders - so I do hope you receive this letter. Please send them as soon as you have time so I can get the coat cleaned in time for that big event.

Hello to everyone. I'll call you tonight and write you very soon.

You must come!

All my love,
Joe

Amphibious Training Base, Little Creek, VA   *November 8, 1943*

Dear Aunt Margaret:

Just a few lines tonight. I'm worried because I haven't heard
from you in such a long time. I don't know whether you have
received my letters or not - but they have never been returned.

I won't repeat what I said in my last letter, Auntie, since you
may not have had time to answer as yet. And what I said in
it probably surprised you so that you haven't regained your
self-composure.

I said that Kay and I are to be married at Corpus Christie
church. But that has been changed. The ceremony will take place
in The Lady's Chapel of St. Patrick's Cathedral - a beautiful
chapel in the largest church in New York City. It is right across
the street from Radio City Rockefeller Center, downtown New York.

But I have problems - some which you knew would arise sooner
or later. I have to have (1) a Baptism certificate, (2) a record
of my confirmation, and (3) a birth certificate. You can get the
confirmation record from Fr. Lally - it should be in the church
records. But I don't know how to get the baptismal record - I
guess Dad will have to try to get it. And he can swear to an
affidavit of my birth as he did when I came into the Navy. So,
Auntie, will you please obtain a certificate of my confirmation
from the church, and ask Fr. Lally if there is any way he can
attest to my baptism - I'm afraid Papa can't get it in time. For
that matter you could also make out an affidavit of my birth Dec.
22, 1918 at McGehee, Arkansas. It's only right since you have
played the biggest part in bringing me up that you should also
play a big part in getting me married.

Kay has written you by now - she wanted to let me write first.
And you will receive the wedding invitation just as soon as she
can mail them. Oh I'm hoping so hard that you will be able to
come. You will have a wonderful time - and I'd give the world to
see you, and have you meet Kay's folks.

Don't think that Ed is going to be able to make it. He is being transferred to North Carolina and it isn't certain that he can get off. I sure hope he can - I don't know who I'd get for best man besides him.

I must write Uncle Frank and Aunt Helene. And all the folks. Kay will not forget anyone. She's the most capable person I've ever met - you will think so too.

One more thing. Being married will bring me more money. And Kay will have control of the purse strings. She will make certain that my debts get paid - and it won't take very long. Also I'm to become a Lt. (jg) before long and when we go to sea I'll become a full Lieutenant. So Dr. Klein will be taken care of shortly. The truth of the matter is that I'm so confounded busy that I never have time to take care of my personal affairs. I've been making $171 a month and spending it. But I never do anything. I never go off the base. It just goes for my mess bill, laundry, wardroom fees, clothes, and necessities. I had my wallet stolen 2 weeks ago right after pay day with $85 in it. But at the same time I know that I'm a bad manager. The only thing I have done is buy war bonds and that will be coming to you.

Kay will change all that. She is very efficient and will play her duty as my wife. She won't be content to allow things to go on as they have in the past.

I'm enclosing a little note to elaborate on as you see fit and put in the paper. I want everyone to know about it. Now please hurry with the birth affidavit. Kay can get the marriage license by herself if she has it. I've already had my Vasserman test - and we should get everything completed as soon as possible. I may not get there until the day before so I want you to plan on being there on November 25th. Kay will meet you. You and dad and Ed will probably stay at a hotel. People in New York usually live in apartments which just fit the size of the families - and that's true of the Vaughans. You'll like it better with your own room and bath anyway won't you.

My but it's getting late. I could write on forever but I didn't get any sleep last night and was at sea all day today. So I must close to get some sleep.

Please write soon and "puleeze" take care of the records for me.

Love,
Joe

Encl.

For The Paper

The marriage of Ensign Joseph B. McDevitt, nephew of Miss Margaret K. Zimmer, 125 West Homer Street, Harrisburg, and Miss Kathleen R. Vaughan, daughter of Mr. And Mrs. Martin A. Vaughan, 454 Ft. Washington Avenue, New York City, will take place Saturday, November 27th in the Lady's Chapel of St. Patrick's Cathedral, New York City. Ensign McDevitt attended the Harrisburg City Schools and graduated from Harrisburg Township High School in 1936. He attended SIU for the next two years then transferred to the University of Illinois where he obtained the A.B. and LL.B. degrees, graduating in 1942. Immediately thereafter he was called into the Navy, having enlisted in the V-7 program, and was sent to the United States Naval Reserve Midshipman's School, Columbia University. After receiving his commission in the Naval Reserve, Ensign McDevitt was assigned to active duty as a division officer in the United States Amphibious Force base at Little Creek, Virginia. Sometime later, he was made an Assistant Boat Group Commander and was sent to the Advanced Training Base at Fort Pierce, Florida. He has recently been appointed a Boat Group Commander and is training an amphibious unit at Little Creek. The engagement was announced last April. Miss Vaughan, a native New Yorker, is at present a model with Best & Company, Fifth Avenue. The ceremony will be performed by Lt. William Kenealy, Chaplain, United States Merchant Marine, a close friend of Ensign McDevitt and Miss Vaughan.

Amphibious Training Base, Little Creek, VA   *November 11, 1943*

Dear Aunt Margaret:

Well, it isn't taking me quite so long to answer your letter this time, is it, Aunt Margaret.

I just came in from being at sea since 5 o'clock this morning and it is now 11:30 p.m. I have the watch tonight and will not go to bed at all. This is the way things have been going for the past five months so I'm not completely to blame for not writing more letters. I am dragging half the time but I will admit I do more work than I would necessarily have to. However, it hasn't done me any harm since I will be getting a spot promotion to Lieutenant (jg) any day now - it should have been through a month ago but it has been delayed in the Bureau of Personnel in Washington, D.C.

Your letter wasn't quite what I had hoped it would be, Aunt Margaret. I usually send all the letters I receive from anyone to Kay - you see we have no secrets from each other even before we are married. But I am not going to send her your letter because I know that she would worry with the thought that you are not behind us. I myself have not the slightest thought that I am not doing the right thing and that you will realize one day it was the right thing. You will realize that there is not another girl in the world who is the equal of Kay and that she will do more to help me and keep things running smoothly than anyone else could. She is a wonderful person - everyone who has known or met her agrees and congratulates me on having such a grand person in love with me.

As to my reason for not waiting: we had decided to wait until the war is over. We had talked it over with Fr. Kenealy and with Chaplain McCauley (the Chaplain here on this base) and they had told us that we should be firmly convinced in our own minds before deciding to do otherwise. Well, there was a time when I thought the war was going to be over in another year - but that opinion has changed. I think that the war will last until at least 1945. And that is a long time to wait - to leave not knowing what you would be coming back to. I will not be in the country for many more months - but they will be happy ones. And when I leave I will know that there is someone thinking of me constantly - someone who will be waiting for the day I return - someone whose every act while I am away will be for the betterment of our future. All the faith and trust in the world can be placed in Kay and she knows that she can believe and trust in me to the same extent. Now if that isn't for perfect harmony then what is.

You asked me why we didn't wait at least until Easter. Easter is a long way off - I may not be here then. I realize that it seems rather sudden, Aunt Margaret. But I'm sure that you realize that things always happen suddenly these days - at least as far as the Navy is concerned. I cannot say that I will be able to do a certain thing as much as a month in the future. Even now I am not absolutely certain that I will be able to get to New York on November 27th. But I'll do my level best - and I know I will succeed. It's just about the most important thing that ever happened to me - and certainly the most looked forward to event.

Aunt Margaret I didn't say - at least I didn't mean to say - that I didn't have the money to get married on. I have. I have been saving to that extent. I meant to say that it has taken a great deal of what I make to live on due to the high cost for officers here in the Norfolk area. There are so many Navy men here that businessmen can ask almost any price and get it. But I will be very capable of getting started adequately. Being married will save a lot of money, and I will make more money because of additional allowances. When I leave the country Kay will go back to her job, and her savings will be added to mine. Don't worry, I have thought of the future as well as the present. When I go to sea I will be sending approximately $200 a month to Kay - and she will have the list of everything that I owe and will take care of it. When I return everything will be clear and we can start with a clean slate. And you are figured in the whole deal.

Now as to you're coming to the wedding. I'm almost certain that Dad will be coming. I can safely say he is probably happier than he has ever been since Mother was alive. He writes almost every day and he writes Kay more than he writes me. Ed said that Kay has done more to cheer him up than anyone he had ever seen. She likes him immensely - just from his letters, and likewise. And he will not be disappointed. He knows that he won't get to see me for long - but that thought hasn't deterred him from his plans. He is getting a sleeper through Pen Dixon so the trip won't be hard on him. I'm not sure about Ed yet - he's in the same boat as I am. He has been transferred to North Carolina so it won't take him nearly as long to get to New York if he can get off.

If you think you can get off to come, I will send you the money to make the trip and will have your room all ready for you when you arrive. Kay will take care of that end of it. We were so hoping you could make it so please try, Aunt Margaret, and let me know soon whether you can make it.

Please try to feel as I do, Aunt Margaret. It makes my heart sad to think that I am doing something that you don't want me to do. But I'm doing it because I know it is the right thing to do. And that it will make for the future happiness of two people who have all the faith in the world in each other.

I know that I have been very irresponsible in the past in many ways and that I haven't shown the proper consideration for you. I have so many things on my mind all of which pertain to the Navy and I have quite a big job at present with 569 to take care of as well as supervise the work of 55 officers. But I also am positive that marrying Kay will do away with all of the past negligences - believe me.

Write just as soon as possible, Aunt Margaret.

Love,
Joe

"I have quite a big job at present with 569 to take care of as well as supervise the work of 55 officers."

In addition to serving as boat group commander at Little Creek, Joe McDevitt had also been designated executive officer (XO) of his boat group, Flotilla 19. This position carried heavy administrative responsibilities and required strong leadership and communications skills.

Bill Janega, who trained under Joe at Ft. Pierce and served in his command in the Pacific, remarked during the research phase of this book:

"Your Dad really had a way of working with his men. He was an officer but he really had a way of talking to the men. He treated them all right. And for that reason we tried harder to run those boats exactly the way they were supposed to be run. He worked us hard, of course, and we were always complaining about that. Practice, practice, practice. But we learned our jobs. We were good. One of the reasons we all came home from the war was all that hard work he put us through."

Kathleen R. Vaughan, New York, NY   *November 14, 1943*

My Dear Aunt Margy:

I know that by now you've heard from Joe about the plans we've
been making for the wedding - I intended to write you shortly
after he did but I've been very busy during the last week trying
to make arrangements for everything after I came home from work
in the evening. It takes up all my spare time and left nothing
except a few minutes to write Joe before I hopped into bed.

In the letter I received from him today he said not to count too
much on your coming East. He was extremely disappointed and I am
myself. I know that we picked a very difficult time for you and
I'm really sorry it had to be that way. You certainly have more
than enough to take care of at this particular time trying to
settle the legal matter of the estate and know you haven't been
feeling entirely well either. I hope that arthritis in your hand
is somewhat improved. Ed wrote to me recently and he said that
it seems a little better when he saw you recently but that it was
still a bother.   I was sorry to hear it. Such things can be very
trying - I know because my Father suffers at times from neuralgia
headaches which last for days and weeks sometimes. He can't seem
to get any cure for the trouble either.

I feel I do not have the right to urge you too much about
coming to New York, for you might think I am being selfish
in the matter and not trying to understand that there are
good reasons to keep you at home. I know how important Joe's
marriage is to you and that if it was at all possible you will
be right there to "see him through." However it is mainly for
your own sake that I wish you could be here, so that you could
meet Fr. Kenealy who introduced Joe and I, my mother and father,
Rosemary my sister and your future daughter-in-law. You've
probably formed an idea in your mind of what we're like, but
meeting us personally would give you a definite idea of us. We
aren't a bit fancy Aunt Margy - just plain people like yourself.
I think that people from out-of-town usually think of New
Yorkers as very unfriendly and inconsiderate and I've never been

able to figure out the reason, because most of them are just as neighborly as people from smaller towns and like everyone else they think that their city is the best in the world.

I'm looking forward to meeting Joe's Dad and Ed but the picture won't be complete if you aren't there too. You are Joe's mother in the fullest sense of the word - I never think of you as anything else and I want you to approve of me just as I would if his mother were alive. I think that you two are closer than Mother and son because you share the affection and love that is usually spread out among the other members of a family. I don't want you to ever feel that after Joe and I are married his devotion to you will lessen, because the feeling he has for you is entirely different from the feeling he has for me. The love you gave him as a child and the guidance when he grew older is something that can never be replaced by another person. I can only hope to do half as well in helping him in the years to come and I will try my very best to measure up to the standard you have set for me. I could never hope for a finer person to go through life with than Joe, but it is not to his credit that he is the man he is today, it is all due to you and I thank you from the bottom of my heart for giving me such an admirable husband. I am so proud of him just as I know you must be. I want you to believe that we are sincerely and honestly in love with each other and we felt almost from the beginning that we were "right" for one another. After what is considered by most people a very short courtship and engagement, it might seem that we are flying head over heels into a flimsy war marriage with no thought to the future, but we are both old enough to realize the responsibilities we are taking on. Too, we are both good Catholics and we know that we are marrying for life - not for a few short years. We intended to wait until after the war but we also realized that neither of us was happy being so far apart and seeing each other so seldom, so we decided to get married now and be together for the rest of the time Joe will be in the country. It will be hard to get started again in civilian life after all this is over but we won't be just beginning. We will have the foundation of our marriage and we will know what to expect of each other. I have no doubt that we are doing the right thing and that we will be happier in the long run for getting married now.

I guess I've rambled on here for quite a spell but I wanted you to know for certain just what motive prompted us towards this decision. These are hard times in which to consider matrimony for there are so many obstacles not present when there is no war. I'm sure Joe and I never dreamed we would be planning these things a year ago. But obstacles or not, we both have a clear picture of what we are doing and a definite idea of what we want in life.

I hope very much to see you the weekend of the 27th but if you can't come Joe and I will be thinking of you every minute and missing your presence. Best regards and fondest love from your future "daughter".

Kathleen

Kathleen Vaughn, New York, NY   *November 14, 1943*

My Dear loving husband-to-be in 269 1/4 hrs.:

Guess who I was just speaking to on the telephone please. Your Aunt Margy! Put the call through and reached her all in the space of about fifteen minutes. I took a chance and called station to station and I got her before she went to church - she was just getting ready she said. She was very sweet.

I didn't ask her why she wasn't coming or anything like that. I just said, after we had spoken a few words, that you had told me not to count on her making the trip and that I hoped she would be able to work out a solution and could get away even for

the weekend and go right back. She was cute - said that she
wanted to come very much but that right now she had a lot of
expense and wasn't certain if she could manage it financially.
Heck, Joe, it's the most understandable thing in the world -
you're not marrying a wealthy gal and situations like that have
come up in our own family at some time or another. It usually
happens that way - expenses come all at once seemingly and you
have to sit down with a pencil and paper and figure out just
what can be done. If that's the only reason do you think you
could manage to send her a railroad ticket? Maybe I am over-
stepping the line of discretion in making such a suggestion
because after all whatever you do is between Aunt Margy and
yourself, and I'm in no position to offer solutions - perhaps
there are other reasons besides. I don't want to decide anything
for you that you can ably decide for yourself knowing all the
facts. However this is the point: I know it will cost a lot for
us to travel - you a rd. trip and me one way and the Florida
jaunt will follow pretty soon after we get back to L.O. I know
too that you want to have enough to cover the few things for
the wedding and our stay however short or long in New York,
without having to worry. But, don't think I am hoping for a very
expensive round of merrymaking in New York, and that if you sent
the ticket I'd be disappointed in having to settle for a more
conservative time on your leave and afterwards in L.O. I haven't
planned anything for us to do - I think it's unimportant just
that we'll be together is the main thing. We'll both be glad
to have a rest I think and not have one single thing that has
to be looked after. So if you're using that as a consideration
just forget it. We'll have fun whatever we do. Gee whiz honey
please don't feel I'm trying to interfere - I just thought you'd
be disappointed if Aunt Margy isn't present and if money is the
only drawback forget it altogether because we can get along on
very little. Your expenses for the wedding are few 1) the church
fees 2) flowers for everyone except Rosemary (the bride buys the
flowers for the attendants). That's all as far as the wedding
itself is concerned - after it's over you take on a life-time job
of supporting a wife.

I wrote to Helene and Frank Zimmer tonight so you can skip them if you want. You ought to take care of Uncle Mike and Aunt Esther - I don't correspond with them freely so it would seem odd if I was the one to let them know our plans. The Zimmers are different - I write to them pretty often and feel I know them well. I feel like an old school mistress sometimes the way I ramble on and tell you all the things you should do, but we want to do things right, don't we? Yes we do. Oh honey I love you so much - I wish I could do everything for you starting now, but there are some details you just have to take care of yourself. Knowing how busy you are I feel like a slave driver at times but you'll be able to relax after it's over.

Aunt Margy said she was sending me your confirmation papers tonight. She said the mail delivery was getting very slow - it took five days for her to receive the letter you wrote Monday. She got it Friday or Saturday.

Peg and Les are here tonight - Peg's staying over tonight. It's fun to have them around - don't have to treat 'em as company. We just do whatever we want and leave them in the living room. They have so much to settle and they're so funny - in a complete daze. But happy as sin. Peg and I made a pact tonight - we're both going to go to bed early tonight. We were so sleepy this morning - last time we looked at the clock it was 6:30 and getting bright. I slept in with her in my single bed last night because it was so late I didn't want to wake R. and gee it was funny. I always sleep right in the middle and I have a slope in the mattress - it curves in in the middle. With two of us it was worse - made the thing slope even more and we were hanging on to the sides and sleeping uphill. Mom and R. think we're a riot cause we talk so much don't even stop when we're eating. They tell us we'll bore each other - fat chance.

Well, sweetheart, your Katie is going to brush her hair now and go to bed. I love you ever so muchly and want these days to hurry oh so fast. Goodnight Joe darling.

Your Katie

"My Dear loving husband-to-be in 269 1/4 hrs.:"

This will be an especially emotional letter for the McDevitt family to read. The fire destroyed all of the letters Kathleen and Joe exchanged after he went overseas. This single letter provides the briefest notion of Kathleen's love for Joe. No wonder he looked forward to mail call!

On November 15, 1943, Joe McDevitt received another physical examination from the Navy. The result:

> Examined this date and found physically qualified
> for promotion to Lt. (jg), D-V(G), USNR

Amphibious Training Base, Little Creek, VA   *November 18, 1943*

Dear Aunt Margaret,

Your prodigal son back again and barely able to keep his eyes open. Sitting in the office on duty drinking black coffee but nodding just the same.

I'm sorry I was late getting that waiver of appearance back to you - it just fell aside on my desk and didn't come to my attention soon enough. That's why I want you to go ahead and sign anything that comes up. Of course, when Kay is my wife she wouldn't let such a thing happen and would see that it was signed on time. I'm not telling you any fib when I say we're busy. Today was the first chance I had to pick up the insured packages you sent me although I've had notice of their arrival for four days. All I had time to do was pick them up and take them to my room - didn't even get to open them. But I know what they contain - I'll get to it sometime tonight.

Well, I had a letter from Kay today telling me that she had
called you. She leaves no stone unturned. I'm sending you
her letter - you can see by it just what kind of a girl she is.
Common sense! I'll bet you were surprised at that call weren't
you.

Of course, I had already planned on doing what she suggested.
Now here's what you do: I'll send the money for your ticket
right away and will have your hotel room arranged for you. In
the meantime, you cash the war bond, or bonds, which have
arrived and buy yourself a new dress, hat, etc. - whatever you
want. Don't feel backward about cashing them - it was for just
such an occasion that they were bought. And there will be more
to take their place. You will have a nice vacation and I know
you will like New York City and all of Kay's folks. Dad will be
there also.

I still am trying to get a call through to you - I'm not as
lucky as Kay was. This region is filled with servicemen all
trying to make long distance calls.

I just hope that if Dad gives us a wedding present it will be
money because you know how he is in his selection of gifts.
There isn't much of anything he could give since we will be
living out of suitcases for the first month and can't very well
set up housekeeping. I'm letting you know right now that I don't
expect a present from you and I'll skin you if you do it! Get
me!

The wedding invitations will be out soon. They should be nice
since Kay has good taste.

Did you put the article in the paper? And will Fr. Lally
announce the banns next Sunday? Bring a note with you from him
saying that they were announced. I'm telling Kay to send him a
wedding invitation.

And by the way I am now a Lieutenant jg - (junior grade that
means) so have him call me that. And the paper also.

I'm so sleepy I can hardly write but I'll be on duty until 8 a.m. so I'd better wake up.

Still don't know about Ed and don't know who I'll get in his place. It may have to be Dad. It would be funny having him for best man wouldn't it!

You should arrive at least by the 26th. The wedding is at 11 o'clock the 27th, Saturday.

I'll call tomorrow if possible and see if you think you can make it.

Kay is the only one of her kind I'm sure you will agree.

Do some fast planning or we will be terribly disappointed!

Love,
Joe

Lt. (jg) and Mrs. Joseph B. McDevitt,
Married in The Lady's Chapel of St. Patrick's Cathedral,
New York City, November 27, 1943

Amphibious Training Base , Little Creek, VA   *December 5, 1943*

My Dear Aunt Margy:

Joe and I received your lovely letter today and we were extremely glad to hear from you. I understand perfectly that you are somewhat handicapped with your hand, and that you can't write as often as you perhaps would like to, so you don't ever need to apologize to me about the length of time between letters. I've rather suspected you haven't been feeling well lately - it's a shame to have to suffer so. Arthritis is an agonizing thing and many people don't realize how painful it can actually be. I used to work in hospitals in my free time before I came down here and I've seen some bad cases of it and I can readily sympathize with anyone who suffers with it.

I know you were very, very disappointed not to be able to attend the wedding and Joe and I are sincerely sorry that things worked out as they did. As Joe told you over the telephone, he was out on the beaches for 4 days and nights recovering boats that had been stranded on the beaches after the terrible storm they had here. They had no sleep and the only food they ate was some cold sandwiches and coffee that they brought out to them. He couldn't leave there to attend to writing a note and enclosing your ticket, and the Telegraph Office no longer carries the service of wiring money. He very nearly didn't get off in time to catch the ferry boat that would take him to the train so it was just a miracle at all that he arrived in time for the wedding itself. He was really exhausted when he got to New York and he very nearly came down with a cold that would have laid him up but he warded it off fortunately.

He felt <u>so</u> badly about the mess he had made of everything but he really couldn't have done any better under the circumstances. When there is an emergency down here at the Base they don't give a hoot what matters you have to attend to - orders are orders and they cannot be disobeyed. We thought about you all that day and Joe remarked 3 or 4 times "There is only one person missing now to make this wedding complete." He felt as though he had "let you down" and it bothered him more than a little bit. Joe loves you very much and I don't want you to think that in all the excitement he forgot all about you. We missed your presence more than you think and were extremely sorry we couldn't have arranged matters in a better way.

I want to thank you most heartily for sending us such a beautiful gift for the wedding - it is something that will be very useful when we have our own place. Pretty lace doilies make a room look so much more attractive - I have always wanted some nice ones for myself. I will write Mrs. Edwards very soon and thank her also. I nearly went wild about the pictures you enclosed of Joe as a child - weren't you unselfish to part with those snapshots! I will be more than satisfied if our children look like that! He certainly was a sweet looking youngster and I can't help wishing I knew him then and that we had grown up together. I wish you would send me the ones you mentioned in your letter of yourself and the house - I certainly am interested and would love to see them. I only have one picture of you from the set taken in Harrisburg when Joe was home in April but I would be glad to have as many as you want to send me. We'll be able to send you some pretty soon - they take so long to develop film down here. I won't get them before next Monday but I'll send along any that are good and clear.

We are living at the Pine Crest Hotel here and it is pretty nice. The housing situation is very bad and not in the least exaggerated so we consider ourselves lucky to have gotten this. It must have been a lovely place at one time but they've let it run down now to some degree - they can be very independent because if you don't like it the way it is someone else will be glad to take it. The biggest disadvantage at the moment is the lack of heat. They are conserving coal and don't send up a scrap of warmth during the day so the rooms are very chilly and drafty as a result. I'm trying to shake off a cold now but this situation doesn't help very much. We hope things will improve since it's getting colder now and they will be forced to do something about it.

We are really very happy being together like this though - the surroundings are unimportant when we can see each other. Joe has to be on the Base 3 nights a week but he can come home every other evening unless he has the duty or they go out to sea and stay out real late. There are some nice couples staying here too so we enjoy ourselves on our free evenings. Joe will be writing first chance he gets and you will be hearing from me regularly. Don't worry about writing yourself. We understand about that. Just take care of yourself and we will be content.

Love from your "daughter" Kathleen

Amphibious Training Base, Little Creek, VA   *December 12, 1943*

Dear Aunt Margaret,

A beautiful Sunday afternoon "at home" with my wife - and no call to worry about the sordid affairs of everyday work. And so there is finally time for me to write you a letter and tell you in my own words just what has been happening and what a wonderful change has come into my life since the 27th of November.

Kay has written you and so you've already heard about the wonderful wedding that we had - and all about Papa being the best man, and, of course, Papa has been to visit you and probably kept you awake nights telling you all about it. So it should be enough for me to merely say that the whole ceremony and the reception which followed were just as nice and beautiful as I had ever hoped they would be. Only one thing was missing and that was your presence. I know you were just as disappointed as Kay and I and Dad were that you couldn't be there. I tried to get to town to wire you the money but it was absolutely impossible. I just did get to the wedding myself. We spent 4 days starting on the Monday before the wedding on the beach due to a big storm which came up and I just got back in time to jump on the boat to New York in my working clothes without a shave or a bath for a week.

We spent our "honeymoon" in a very beautiful suburb of New York called Bronxville and I caught up on the sleep which I've been missing for weeks past.

We are now living in a hotel at Oceanview, Virginia, which is just 10 minutes by automobile from my base. One of my assistants also lives here and since he has a car, it is very handy. We come home every night - and "home" with Kay is such a wonderful place to come home to. Believe it or not, I've gained 10 pounds since we were married and I'm happier than I've ever been. I'm sure glad that I waited - that I never went ahead with plans which I had in the past. They would have been a mistake. Kay is everything any man could want.

We are leaving for Florida next Sunday or Monday and will have no time to come home in the meantime. The Navy is really speeding up the Amphibious Training Program - we will be in Florida 6-7 weeks and will then be ready to go across. There's a possibility that I will remain behind again which would please me now that I'm married. But everything that comes along will be taken in stride by Kay and I.

So let's plan on this: since we probably won't have a chance to come home to you - we will plan on you coming "home" to us in Florida as soon as we are settled down there. I'll send your ticket and you can come down and teach Katie a few of the tricks of pleasing her husband. Is it a bargain? Florida is swell in the winter time!

Love,
Joe

On January 7, 1944, Joe received his first fitness report as boat group commander. His commanding officer rated his overall performance "Excellent" and commented that:

"Performance of duty while under observation in Attack Boats was excellent. A very dependable and well qualified Boat Group Commander. Qualified for promotion with contemporaries."

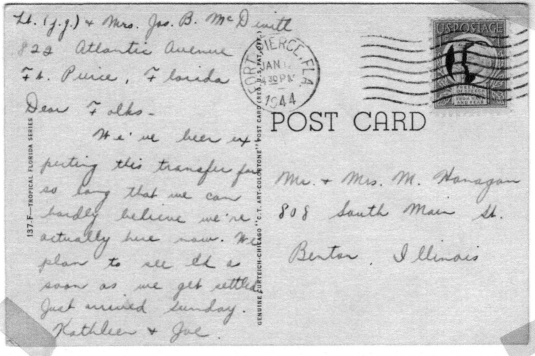

Postcard to the Hanagan's, January 12, 1944

Advanced Amphibious Training Base, Ft. Pierce, FL   *January 16, 1944*

Dear Aunt Margy,

As you see from the post mark we have finally arrived in Ft. Pierce. We've been here exactly a week, and you know how it is getting settled in a new place. It does take time, so I had to put off writing for a few days.

We are living in a room in a private home and it is a very nice homey atmosphere. We were hoping to get a house or an apartment but so far we haven't had any luck. I wish we could find a place of our own, because I think it would be grand to have you come down to Florida and visit Joe and I. Maybe we will be able to work out something later on - at the present all the apartments seem to be filled. I expect there might be some vacancies if one or two groups are transferred up to Norfolk - when that will be I have no idea, but I imagine some of the boys should be moving out soon. I really hope we can arrange it though - I believe a little vacation would make you feel a great deal better. We've been wondering how your hand is - I hope you've not been bothered too much lately.

Well, now, Aunt Margy, I'm really anxious to tell you this bit of news, and I don't feel that I can wait any longer. Joe and I have decided that "three" is a family and I am quite sure we are going to have a baby! Isn't that the most wonderful thing - we are so thrilled about it. I went to the Doctor just after I arrived here in Florida mainly to ask him for relief of some sort. I have not been at all well the last few weeks - my meals give me considerable trouble - especially breakfast. He gave me an injection and I'm to go back in another three weeks. Joe is just as pleased as he can be and wants to tell everybody right away. I am just as happy about it too - I really think God is good to us.

Joe has been working very hard since we've come down here. He had to stay at the Base night before last-he came home last night but he won't be in again this evening. They have a good many of these night maneuvers and by the time they are finished it's too late to get in.

We've had a letter from Ed already - I wrote him just as soon as we got here because he's been so anxious about seeing Joe and I. He can get to Ft. Pierce on a weekend pass (he's in Gainesville, Florida now you know) but the problem is I don't know where we're going to put him. We just have the one room and I don't think the lady we live with has a spare bed she could put to use. This town is so overcrowded that I don't even think there are any hotel rooms available. I wouldn't like for Ed to have to stay in a hotel though anyway - we'd want him right close. We'll just have to figure something out when the time comes. We're going to call Ed tomorrow night when Joe is home.

Well, I do hope you will be feeling better and that you can write soon and tell us what you think of the idea of having a grandchild. I've told my family and they are so elated over it - I know you will be too. Do take care of yourself Aunt Margy and when you feel like writing don't forget to send those pictures of yourself that you mentioned. I want to see them very much.

All my love and Joe's too, Kathleen

Advanced Amphibious Training Base, Ft. Pierce, FL   *February 6, 1944*

My dear Aunt Margy,

Well Joe and I both enjoyed your lovely long letter and we were very glad to hear that your hand had improved a bit so that you could write us. I hope the relief continues and that you will continue to improve even more.

I sent the wedding pictures to you about a week ago and I suppose you have them by now. They went to your house at Harrisburg since I did not have Esther and Mike's address on hand when I addressed the package. I know you drive over to pick up your mail though, so you undoubtedly received Joe's letter also. Perhaps he sent his to Benton - I'm not certain now since he mailed it himself.

I'm glad you liked the slip we sent you and I want to explain about the address on the package. You see it was sent from Norfolk, Virginia - we were still there at the time, but we weren't sure how long it would be before we would be in Ft. Pierce, so we put a Florida address on the return label. We expected to leave a few days after I sent the package and in case there was any mixup in the mails we did not want it returned to us at Norfolk. As it turned out however we were delayed and delayed, and did not arrive here in Florida till the 9th of January. I wrote you soon after we got here, but you evidently had not received my letter when you wrote to us. You traced our route very correctly - we took Route 17 till we got to Jacksonville (I believe it was anyway) and then we switched over to Route 1. It was a very nice trip and we had good weather most of the way.

We enjoyed having Ed for a visit two weeks ago. He had a weekend pass and came down and stayed here at the house with us. We rigged up an Army cot and he slept out on the sun porch. He and Joe were so glad to see one another, and I was delighted that this long awaited meeting finally came through. Ed and I have written each other ever since Joe and I were engaged, and we've been trying to manage a way to become actually acquainted for so long but there have always been difficulties. I think Ed is really a grand person and I'm very fond of him already.

I think it was lovely of you to make us those lovely feather pillows - and the blanket too. It is really something to look forward to. Joe is always telling me about the feather mattresses he used to sleep on when he was in Harrisburg. You are really too nice to us - you'll have us both spoiled altogether.

Joe enjoyed the clippings from the newspaper that you enclosed and I wish we could have heard that broadcast. Seeing your name in print though was the next best thing and I am returning it to you so you can keep it.

Joe isn't home tonight or I would have him add a few lines to this. I think I'll go to bed early this evening so I'll end up right here and say good night. Let us hear from you again when your hand is in good condition. I intend to write Dottie Hanagan a note very soon in answer to the nice letter we received from her. Tell her to be patient for a bit longer.

Good bye for now and much love from Kathleen and Joe

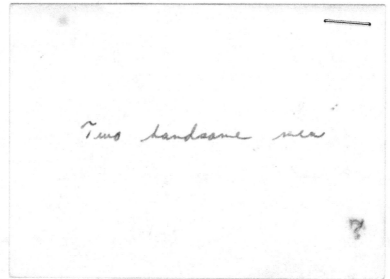

Two handsome men

Brothers Joe and Ed McDevitt,
Ft. Pierce, FL, January 1944

Bethlehem Steel Shipyard, New York, NY   *February 12, 1944*

While Joe was training in Florida, the USS *Leon* was recommissioned in full on February 12, 1944, Captain Bruce B. Adell in command. Most of the crew had not yet arrived aboard, but the commissioning ceremony was described by Lieutenant A. A. Smyser, USNR, in <u>A War History of the USS LEON (APA 48)</u> (hereafter, <u>A War History</u>):

> *"February 12, 1944, was a bright, cold and icy day at the Bethlehem Steel Shipyard in Brooklyn. The wind off the bay was so cutting not many of the guests could stand the weather long enough to hear the commissioning speech.*
>
> *But the new skipper, Capt. Bruce B. Adell, USN, said Ponce de Leon had been an adventurer and a fighting man and the ship that bore his name was going to be an adventurer and a fighter*

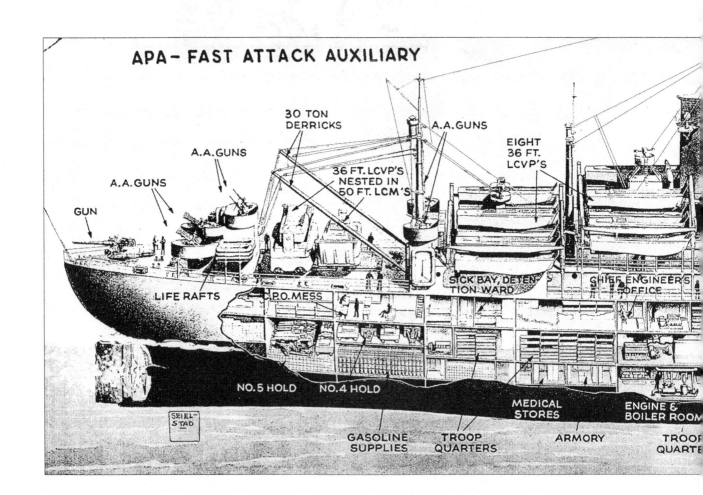

too. As he spoke, troops 8,000 miles away in the Marshall Islands were winning Eniwetok Atoll from the Japs, foot by foot. The new fleet was flexing its muscles.

The Leon is not one of those sleek, trim ships with polished, accusing guns glistening for the newsreel cameras. She's a bulky, hulky pile of steel, top-heavy with landing boats and invasion gear – an assault transport.

If you have an April 1945 issue of "Fortune" at hand you can see her plans, she's that secret.

She's beautiful only if you happen to see her so after all the trouble and boredom she put you through. Her bow comes out of the water like a big three-story building and fans out over your head and then stretches back 492 feet to the fantail.

All that's in between is for moving men and guns and trucks and food and ammunition, carrying them for weeks if need be, and supplying all their needs in a crowded, sweaty, dirty sort of fashion.

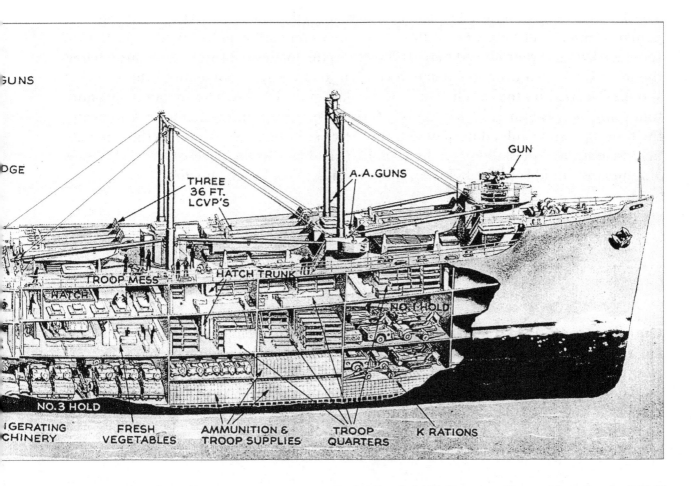

Combat Loaded APA Transport, Fortune Magazine, April 1945

Where other transports were made for rear areas, this one was designed to stick her nose into the very foremost areas, to take American troops where American troops had never been before, land them and give them supplies for the very first days of fighting, to fight herself if need be.

Most transports can only unload along docks. The Leon loaded and unloaded anywhere there was a sandy beach and sometimes coral reefs.

From the time she was commissioned, her sights were pointed at Tokyo Bay, beaches toward which she constantly prodded but never reached while the war lasted."

The Fortune Magazine article cited in the first section of <u>A War History</u> above contained a superb cut-away view of the Navy's new combat-loaded APA transport. That two-page layout is reproduced here. It illustrates the loading of troops and cargo below the main deck according to a detailed combat loading plan that assured the very first supplies needed on the beach would be the last items loaded. The diagram also illustrates how twenty-four LCVPs and two LCMs were stowed on the main deck to assure the fastest possible unloading. These transports were America's answer to the Japanese defensive strategy of island strongholds and airfields across the Pacific Ocean. The new amphibians would land the boots on those islands… any beach, any time.

On February 19, 1944, Lieutenant (jg) Joe McDevitt, accompanied by fifteen ensigns and one hundred twenty-five enlisted men of the boat group division, arrived at Pier 33, New York Navy yard. Did they pause and stare at this brand new ship of theirs? Perhaps so. Then, Joe and his division climbed the gangplank and boarded the USS *Leon* to report for duty.

New York, NY   *February 29, 1944*

Dear Aunt Margy,

I hope you don't mind getting a letter that is brief but right at
this minute I can't write a lot. I just wanted you to know that
Joe and I are in New York again. I am living at home, and Joe
is at a Port of Embarkation. He hasn't left as yet and I hope to
see him again before he does. I will give you his new address so
that you can write him.

Lt. (jg) Joseph B. McDevitt
USS Leon
c/o Fleet Post Office
New York, New York

I hope you received the wedding pictures and enjoyed them. I
sent you a basket of fruit before we left Florida but it went to
Harrisburg to your house. The smooth oranges are for juice and
the ones with the rough skins are for eating. I wasn't sure if
you were still at Esther and Mike's - I couldn't remember their
address at the time anyway.

If there are any papers that I must sign over to you, in regard
to the sale of the house, send them along and I will gladly
attend to it promptly. You mentioned having sent papers to Joe
in your last letter - we never received them. If he has to sign
anything more I think you better send it to him right away to
avoid delay. I hope you are well - please write when you can and
let us know all the news.

Much love, from Kathleen

Once Joe McDevitt and the *Leon* commenced sea duty, we can chronicle Joe's work through the *Leon's* log entries which tell the story of the ship and its crew. Immediately following the cover page of each monthly log was a list of officers and their duties followed by a section entitled Administrative Remarks. These remarks provided details about notable events on each four-hour watch. Selected excerpts from the Administrative Remarks section begin here.

The *Leon's* first log, dated February 1944, noted that Joe McDevitt went to sea with multiple duties. He was a watch officer, which qualified him to serve four-hour watches on the bridge and to assist the captain or the senior officer of the deck (OOD). He was a division commander, responsible for administering L Division, the boat group personnel. He was also the boat group commander, responsible for planning, organizing, and leading *Leon's* landing craft during amphibious assaults.

A War History (cont.)

"In Long Island Sound off the shores of New York and Connecticut and in frigid weather Leon put on all the steam the engine could give and found out her top speed, then ordered full astern and found out how quickly she could stop.

She turned full circles and figured the diameter, tried out her new equipment, measured her strength and documented it.

Her crew was learning, too. Down in Hampton Roads in sight of the green countryside and cozy homes of Newport News and Norfolk she got her landing boats and steamed up Chesapeake Bay to try them.

She tried her guns up there too – she and the carrier Franklin, which was also getting ready for the Pacific war. Yard time then. All the kinks that had popped up were ironed out – winches fixed, rigging changed, equipment overhauled."

Log entries confirm that Joe McDevitt was busy outfitting the *Leon's* boat group division.

DECK LOG USS Leon: Administrative Remarks   *Thursday, 9 March, 1944, 08-12 hours*

Moored port side to Pier No. 4, Berth 26, Norfolk Naval Yard, Portsmouth, Virginia in 7 fathoms of water with the following lines out: Bow and stern lines, 8" manila, double up. Held quarters for muster. 0800-1200 Navy yard personnel from Shop No. 56 were on board. 0935 Amphibious Board of Inspection, Capt. Hutchison and 13 officer members came aboard to conduct inspection. 0945 Ensign Johnson and three men left the ship with secret radar equipment under armed guard. 0945 Lt. (jg) McDevitt left ship with party in LCM to obtain landing boat ordinance. 1116 Inspection party left the ship. 1130 Commenced embarking beach party. 1135 Received on board for use in the general mess from Embassy Dairy, 30 gallons of fresh milk. Inspected as to quality by Lt. Commander Pearse USNR and as to quantity by Lt. Ritter USNR. 1150 Ensign Johnson returned to the ship. 1159 The workmen left the ship for lunch hour. Made daily inspection of magazines, ready boxes and smokeless powder samples. Conditions normal. Completed embarkation of beach party.

(Signed) W. P. WILKINSON, Lt., USNR

The log entry below is the *first* entry posted by Lieutenant (jg) Joseph B. McDevitt as watch officer.

DECK LOG USS Leon: Administrative Remarks   *Thursday, 16 March, 1944, 16-20 hours*

```
Moored starboard side to Pier 2, Berth 21, NOB, Norfolk,
Virginia, in six fathoms of water with the following lines: Bow
and stern, 8" manila; Fore and aft bow spring 1" wire; Fore
and aft quarter spring and waist breast, all lines doubled up.
1702 Ship breasted into dock. 1823 While loading cargo a load
accidentally swung into lifeline, breaking two stanchions and
bending one, starboard side, No. 3 hatch. 1830 A cargo load hit
and damaged a piano sitting on dock. 1855 The fire main and
flushing system was secured for repairs. They were replaced back
in service at 1917.

(Signed) J.B. MCDEVITT, Lt. (jg) USNR
```

An event-filled first watch is NOT what a brand new watch officer fancied. This particular entry suggests a brand new crew operating brand new loading equipment on board a brand new ship. And what did they strike with a cargo load at 1830 hours? A piano!

Every day for the new crew and ship was an important event, but March 17, 1944, was especially significant for all. The *Leon* began loading her first shipment of provisions and cargo and embarking her first replacement troops. The troops just came and came and came: 1288 Marines with 59 officers of the 47th Replacement Battalion plus 45 prisoners.

Such a site! Could there possibly be enough room to hold all those men and their equipment? Already aboard were the *Leon's* crew of 575 enlisted men and officers. All these men aboard a 492 ft. ship sailing for a tropical climate. The crew quickly learned an early lesson of how to live in crowded quarters.

DECK LOG USS Leon: Administrative Remarks   *Friday, 17 March, 1944, 08-12 hours*

Moored starboard side to Pier 2, Berth 21, NOB, Norfolk, Virginia, in six fathoms of water with the following lines: Bow and stern, 8" manila; Fore and aft bow spring 1" wire; Fore and aft quarter spring and waist breast, all lines doubled up. 0800 Mustered crew on stations. 0802 First check on Marine troops which came aboard on previous watch shows 1288 troops, 59 officers, 45 prisoners included. 0805 Daily inspection of magazines and smokeless powder samples showed normal conditions. 0835 ship's draft forward 17' aft 26'. 0850 Commenced loading provisions in numbers 3 and 5 holds, and cargo in number 1 hold. 0945 Commenced embarking Seabea troops. AUGUSTIN, E.J. OOM, USNR, in charge, 193 enlisted Seabeas reported aboard from the Norfolk, Virginia Receiving Station. 1013 Completed embarkation of Seabeas. 1100 Fire Alarm System was secured to be repaired. 1125 Fire alarm system was placed back in proper working order. 1126 Ceased loading provisions in 3 and 5 holds.

(Signed) J.B. MCDEVITT, Lt. (jg), USNR

Then, the big day arrived.

A War History (cont.)

"Capt. Adell got his orders... At 0715 on March 18, 1944, she cast off her lines and set out for Pearl Harbor with the destroyer escort Blackwood DE 219.

In the open sea between Norfolk and Panama and then on the 12-day run from Panama to Pearl Harbor, the little escort and the big transport practiced the maneuvers invasion convoys would use, frivolously, with only the horizon to bound them in.

For many officers and men it was the first time out. They got the feel of the ship and the feel of the sea. They also got the feel of foreign liberty in Panama and never forgot it – because for 14 months there was never another liberty like it.

Panama had whatever men wanted and all it asked in exchange was money. Savings disappeared, savings for which there would be no use for 14 months, and nobody forgot Panama."

During this first cruise, crew members assigned to deck watch duty, including Joe McDevitt, served their first of many night watches on a combat loaded transport. Seaman 1/c Paul Prentice never forgot his first night watch aboard USS *Fremont* APA 44. His description, taken from the ship's history, follows:

"I bet no sailor ever forgot his first night-watch and the enormous responsibility he felt while many of the crew and 1200 troops slept. Before going on watch, there was the eye-conditioning in the red light. Then reporting to the Watch station on deck, the Watch began. Except for an occasional voice in the head set, I felt like I was completely alone yet I was honored to be so entrusted. I also remember the moon was not up yet when I began my first night-watch and the ship was in total blackout. The sky was full of stars that just disappeared off the edge of the earth. As time went by, the moon came up and the horizon was once again clearly defined.

When relieved from the Watch, it was down to the galley for a quick cup of coffee and sometimes a cookie or donut was waiting for those going off Watch. Then it was hit the sack because there was always the eight bells muster."[5]

---

5   Retrieved from www.ussfremont.org.

A War History (cont.)

"A soon as they passed through the canal, the Leon's address changed from Fleet Post Office, New York, to Fleet Post Office, San Francisco. Fleet Post Office, New York, had meant gay times in New York, Norfolk and in Panama. The Pacific held no such promise."

New York, NY   *March 21, 1944*

Dear Aunt Margy,

I've just returned to New York a few days ago, after being with Joe in Norfolk, Virginia for a week. When his ship pulled into port down there, he wired me at home and I took the first train I could get out of New York. The ship was there loading on supplies and I saw Joe every other night when he had liberty and was free to come home. We had a small apartment - the upstairs part of a tiny bungalow and it was located near enough so that Joe was only about 45 minutes from the ship. The last time I saw him was Thursday night when we had dinner together. He had to be back on the ship at ten o'clock so it was rather a brief goodbye - perhaps it was just as well that way. I haven't had any news from him yet, but I expect it will be some time before I start getting his letters, so I'll have to be patient. He particularly asked me to write to you before anyone else, because he is aware of how long it is since he has been able to write himself. Before I was married and living with Joe I never fully realized how few spare moments he actually had. I scold him sometimes when he asks me to write for him, because I know how much more you would rather hear from him directly, but he does the best he can and I guess we can't expect any more than that. Once they get away from port and really get out to sea, I think he'll have more time to himself and then you can expect to hear more often.

As for me, I feel much better than I ever have since my pregnancy began. Of course, I knew that after the first 3 months were over I would be more comfortable, but it seemed so long to wait. I'm beginning to take an interest in food again so I guess the worst part of it is behind. I expect to be delivered around the first week in September - maybe Labor Day (wouldn't that be a lark!). I've made an appointment with the doctor I'm going to have, for next Tuesday and I'm making my first trip to the dentist tomorrow. I went to the Doctor for a few times while we were in Florida, but haven't been to one since then. I'm going to attend a Maternity Class which starts Monday. Rosemary attended it before she had her baby and I'm all enthused about going. There are ten lessons in all - the first few explain the anatomy of the body and show the positions of the baby at different months - they have slides for that. One lesson is on Labor and Delivery, one on what to buy for the baby and another on giving the bath. I don't recall what the rest are about, but all in all, when you are finished with the course, you have a lot more confidence because you know what to expect. It keeps me busy at any rate and that's what I want to do most.

Well, I have so many others to write to that I'd better ring off. I've owed Helene and Frank Zimmer a letter for weeks and I want to take care of them today. You know though, when you travel around as much as I have been in the last month, it's very difficult to keep up with everyone. It's a good day for writing letters, however, for New York is buried under six inches of snow (imagine that - when we all thought spring was just around the corner). They are clearing it off the sidewalks but in places it is still nasty underfoot.

Well, Aunt Margy, dear, I hope you won't get yourself all upset over Joe's having left the country. I know it is foolish to say, "don't worry" about him for you can't help but do that now and then - I do myself. But I have a great deal of faith in prayers, and every night I ask God to protect Joe and bring him back safely and soon. I know he is always remembered in your prayers too, and I can't help but feel that everything will be all right.

Please do take care of yourself and when your hand is feeling good enough to write, let me hear from you.

Very best love from your daughter, Kathleen

The crew of the *Leon* conducted convoy maneuvers with the *Blackwood* as they steamed across the Pacific Ocean. The crew began to learn the type of life they would lead aboard the *Leon*, the ways of the Navy and the sea. They learned that the Navy had lost some good ships and many men due to inadequate training and carelessness. They learned that every man had to do his part, from the captain handling the ship to the newest man and lowest rating on lookout or on guns.

Taking a sextant reading

They practiced relentlessly the gamut of on board ship drills that would soon be vital to the ship's survival: fire, collision, gas, man overboard, damage control, fire and rescue. The slightest slip on the part of any man at the wrong time could mean the loss of the ship, which could mean the loss of a beach, which could mean the failure of an operation.

One drill in particular must have given everyone aboard pause, sailors and troops alike—abandon ship. The Pacific Ocean is a very large body of water, and the thought of going over the side must have been terribly intimidating. A copy of the memo "WHAT TO DO IN THE CASE OF ABANDON SHIP" written by the chief executive officer of USS *Ormsby* APA 49 follows. It conveys the substance of what the crew was told and how they were trained for this worst case scenario.

WHAT TO DO IN THE CASE OF ABANDON SHIP

USS Ormsby APA 49

The coming operation is going to be a tough one, and no doubt some ships are going to go down. It is well within the realm of possibility that this ship may be one of those to go down. With this in mind, the following hints are brought to your attention so that you may study them, think them over and profit by them if and when the occasion arises.

Bear one thing in mind, this ship will not be abandoned while there is the slightest chance in the world of keeping her afloat. We expect to fight the "Mighty O" just as long as the guns are above water, there is a man left to load a gun or a shell to shoot out of it. If we do find out that the ship cannot be saved, then we shall try to give all hands time to get over the side and clear of the ship.

"Life Raft Stations" will be given first followed by "Abandon Ship", if and when that becomes necessary. WE WILL NOT USE THE WORDS ABANDON SHIP UNLESS WE MEAN IT.

All men whose life raft stations are at the rafts are to be sure that they know how to cut them adrift when so ordered. Carry a knife and see that you have something handy with which to slip the pelican hook. As many boats as possible will be launched and all others are to have their lashings cut adrift.

As there is a possibility that the loudspeakers will be out of commission, all bosn's mates are to take up and pass any word that is given by competent authority.

If you have to go over the side, wear what you have on at the time, but try to be fully clothed. Clothes will protect your body from many things and if you have your life belt or jacket the additional weight means nothing.

Do not jump unless you have to. If time permits, go down a net, ladder or line. If gloves are handy, they will save you some skin if you have to slide down the line. Keep your shoes on until the last minute as they will protect your feet while on the nets or ladders or climbing down the side of a capsized ship. They will also protect your feet if you have to jump, especially if there is debris in the water.

Wear a knife and take it with you when you go. It can come in handy for many things, from cutting a line to opening a can of rations, not to speak of playing games with sharks.

Try and learn the names of your shipmates who aren't swimmers and keep an eye on them. Be on the lookout for men who have neither life belts nor jackets and assist others to blow up their belts if they haven't done so. Do not blow up your belt unless you are in the water. If you can swim, get over and put as much distance between the ship and you as possible, then blow up the belt.

If destroyers are dropping depth charges, blow up your belt and shift it to the small of your back, raising your midship section as clear from the water as possible and thereby lessening the shock to your spinal cord and nervous system. If there is debris floating around, grab a piece and raise your midship section clear of the water.

Do not go over the lee side, as the ship will drift down on you.

Don't jump unless there is no other alternative. If you have to, keep your clothes on, cross your legs, protect your chin, hold your nose and jumped as far out as possible.

Before going over try and locate the nearest boat, raft or anything else liable to support your weight. Do not attempt to climb in at once, hold on to the raft until you recover your breath and then move carefully. If there are a large number of men, put the weakest or those without belts in the raft, all others hold on. By doing so you can handle many more men.

If the nets and ladders are crowded, grab yourself a fire hose, secure the inboard end and go down that. Do not slide unless you are wearing gloves, but go down hand over hand. Whether on a net or ladder or sliding down a line or hose, watch out for the man below you. If you are jumping be careful that you do not jump on anyone.

If you have to jump, get as close to the water as possible, but do not jump from the bridge or boat decks.

On an operation such as this the chances are that you will be picked up within a reasonable length of time. Follow the instructions of the ship's officers of any ship which might pick you up. And don't forget that even if this ship is sunk, her organization still continues. While you are subject to the disciplinary jurisdiction of the ship that picks you up you are still a member of this ship's company and your regular officers and petty officers have the same status in relation to you as they had aboard the vessel when she was afloat.

Efficient lookouts and snappy gun crews can keep us from being sunk, but if that does occur don't lose your heads. Other ships have gone down and their crews picked up. Do everything in your power to save the ship and when that fails do everything that you can to save yourself. But look out for the injured, the non-swimmers and the boys who lose their heads.

Know what to do, how to do it and when to do it. When the time comes, make a good job of it.

G. W. MCCORMICK
Commander, USNR

With Permission

New York, NY   *March 25, 1944*

My dear Aunt Margaret,

It seems we don't have much luck with our letters - they are
always crossing in the mail. I just received yours this morning
and mine must have reached you a day or two after you mailed
your own.

The information I gave you regarding Joe was not much but is
all I know at present. I left Norfolk on March 17th and whether
or not Joe sailed then or not I can't tell. I wouldn't have
been able to see him after that or contact him anymore so there
was no point in staying longer. He and all the men were to be
restricted to the ship and the exact date of their departure was
kept secret even from them. His address from now on will be
Lt. (jg) Joseph B. McDevitt, USS Leon, c/o Fleet Post Office, New
York, New York. I haven't heard from him since I left there and
I guess it will be some weeks before I get any mail. It will
come in bunches when it does arrive, so I guess we'll just have
to be patient. I think it would be a very nice idea to have his
picture and a short write up about him in the paper, so that his
friends will know all about his activities. As soon as I hear
from him, I'll send you a Special Delivery and tell you what he
says but you'll probably get some mail about the same time. My
telephone number is Wadsworth 3-5343 if you ever want to call
me. Yes, Joe and I were married in St. Patrick's Cathedral -
must be the same one you were speaking of. It is the largest
Catholic Church in New York and a very beautiful one. What does
Father Lally mean when he says we aren't very Irish in the way
we spell Vaughan? Most people spell it without the A at the end
like this Vaughn-and that is not the Irish way. At any rate my
father brought it over from Ireland and kept the spelling they
use there on the other side and Vaughan it has always been. You
tell him I think the Irish are all right too, and I wouldn't try
to hide my nationality by changing the spelling of my name. I
would like to meet him - I know what a grand person he must be.
Joe speaks of him so much.

I was thrilled to receive the pictures you sent and I am going
to keep them a bit longer so I can get to know the people better.
Mother and Rosemary saw them too and thought they were lovely.
If you have the proof of the picture of Joe and Gertrude together
at the back entrance of the house, please let me know. I'd like
to keep that one especially-you know I've never seen Joe in
anything but a uniform and it seems funny to see him in civilian
clothes. I think that the house looks lovely from the snaps -
you should be very proud of it and I can understand why you are
anxious to get the property business settled.

Well, dear, this is all the news I have for you for the present.
Oh, no - there is something I forgot to tell you last time I
wrote and that is the names we have picked out for the baby. If
it is a boy we are going to call it Jeffrey Lee, and if it is a
girl, Marianne after Joe's mother. I hope you don't mind that
we changed the spelling of Mary Ann so that it is all one name.
I'd like it to be a boy (that looks just like Joe) but we'll
be happy whatever it is. Now it's goodbye for a little while - I
hope you are feeling well. This is such a nice time of the year
and it's a shame not to feel like yourself.

My very best love to you from your daughter, Kathleen

P.S. You know I would never be offended with you and that was not
my reason for delaying in writing. I enjoy your letters ever so
much - write soon again when you feel up to it.

DECK LOG USS Leon: Administrative Remarks   _30 March, 1944, 16-20 hours_

Steaming in convoy T.G. en route from Panama, C.Z., O.T.C. in
USS _LEON_ in company with USS _D. J. BLACKWOOD_ (DE 219), escort
commander. Course 284 (T), 284 (PGC), 270° (PSC). Convoy speed

```
16.5 knots.  (85 r.p.m.).  1900 clocks were retarded one-half
(1/2) hour to conform with zone plus 6.5.  Average r.p.m. 86.6,
Average steam 450.


(Signed) J.B. MODEVITT, Lt. (jg) USNR
```

Joe mastered the responsibilities of deck watch duty and ship handling quickly. In his first fitness report Captain Adell noted that Joe had qualified as OOD underway (Senior Officer of the Deck while underway at sea). The OOD is normally stationed on the bridge and, in the absence of the captain, is his direct representative, with full responsibility for the ship.

The on board ship drills continued for twelve days. Over and over and over, until crew responses for each drill were automatic. The drills continued until Captain Adell was satisfied with the stopwatch readings. Speed saves lives. Slowly the crew learned… tightened up on the drills, smoothed off the rough edges. One wonders how often a sailor or an officer paused to look out over the vast, lonely Pacific Ocean during this period and wondered, "How did I ever end up here?"

Taking a break on the main deck

The challenge of preparing mentally and emotionally for combat was never far removed, especially with a ship full of Marines and seabees. How does one prepare for an enemy who will try his best to kill you, to destroy your ship, and to send a full combat team to the bottom of the ocean?

The Navy's response was drill, drill, drill. To become the very best fighting vessel that you can be. To create a bond with your fellow crew members and your officers was vitally important. To become so proficient in your mission that failure is unthinkable. Aboard every ship in the new and growing Pacific Fleet the training was underway. The fleet's confidence was growing.

454 Fort Washington Ave., New York, 33, NY   *April 5, 1944*

My dear Aunt Margy,

I received my first letter from Joe today and it came as a
complete surprise - I expected to have a much longer wait.
However the only reason I did get it, was because the ship was in
port en route to its destination. I believe he was in Panama City
- of course he wasn't able to state his location but from various
hints he gave me I can usually tell where he is. He managed to
get ashore and see some of the sights. He says he is getting a
nice tan. They have probably left there by now since the letter
was written about two weeks ago - however maybe it's best not
to mention it around too much, just to insure his own personal
safety and also those who are with him. I always feel that the
less said about the location of our ships the better, don't you?

I hope you are well - write when you can.

Much love from Kathleen

A War History   (cont.)

*"On Good Friday, April 7, 1944, the Leon steered down the narrow neck of magnificently colored
water that marks the entrance to Pearl Harbor and reported to the Administrative Commander,
Amphibious Forces, Pacific Fleet, for duty."*

3

OPERATION FORAGER: SAIPAN

Duty came soon enough. An operation was in the books and everyone was training.

The Navy's leapfrogging strategy sought to bypass heavily defended Japanese positions and concentrate the Allies' limited resources on islands that weren't well defended but were capable of supporting the drive to the Japanese home islands. The first assault had been Guadalcanal in the Solomon Islands. The amphibious assaults on Makin and Tarawa in the Gilbert Islands came next. Following that was the Marshall Islands. Navy planners bypassed the heavily defended islands Wotje and Maloelap and targeted Kwajalein, the largest atoll in the world, and then Eniwetok Atoll, the western-most island in the Marshall Islands.

Eniwetok's conquest came when the *Leon* was being refitted and commissioned back in Brooklyn. The atoll provided a vast Pacific anchorage for the fleet, a new home base closer to the Japanese home islands than Pearl Harbor twenty-five hundred miles away.

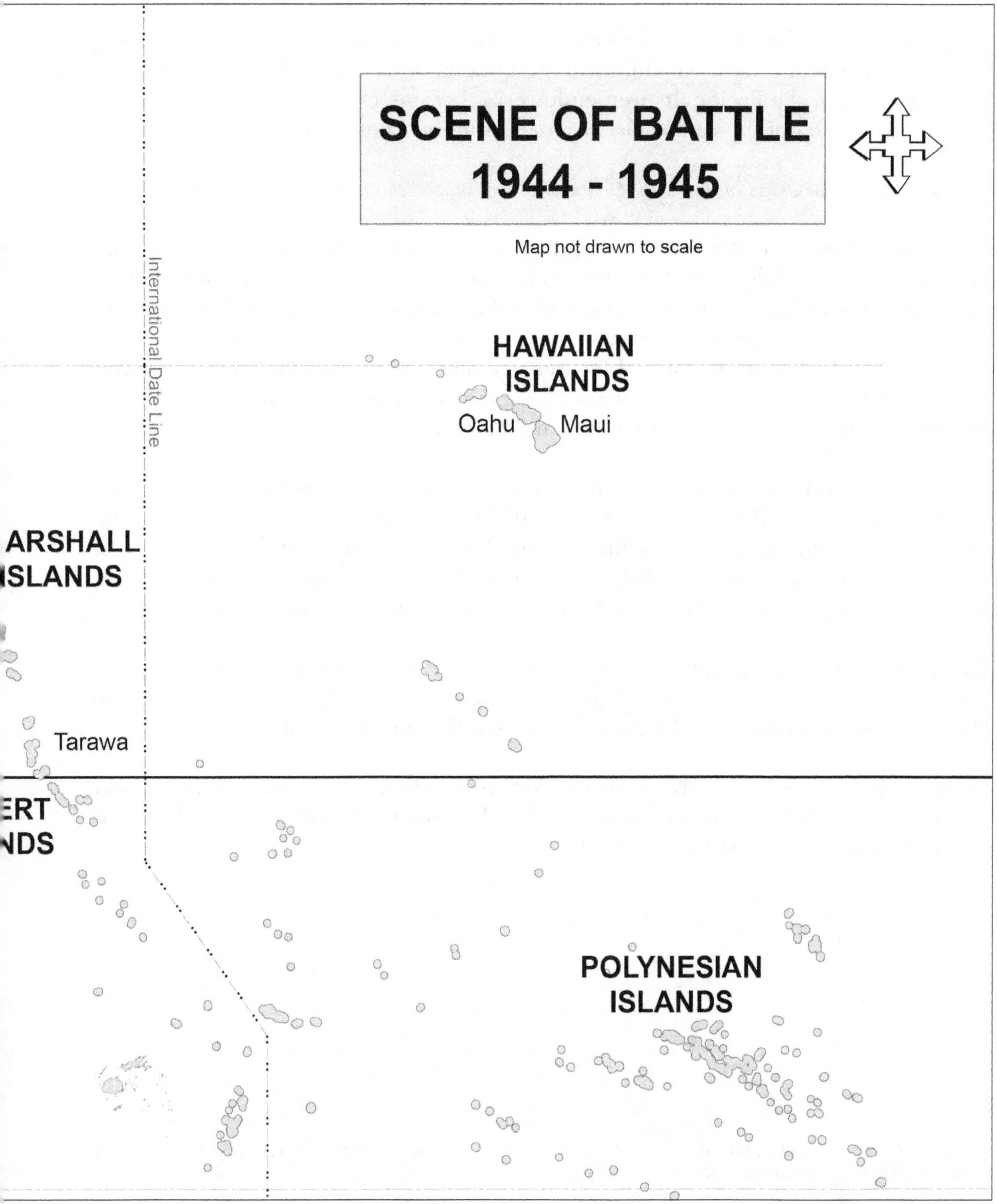

SCENE OF BATTLE
1944 - 1945

Map not drawn to scale

HAWAIIAN
ISLANDS

Oahu   Maui

International Date Line

ARSHALL
ISLANDS

Tarawa

ERT
NDS

POLYNESIAN
ISLANDS

Few people knew the objective of Operation Forager: the Mariana Islands, including Saipan, Tinian, and Guam. Saipan, the largest island, would be the largest amphibious assault to date in the Pacific. Its tremendous size became clear to everyone when the Navy's commander of the Pacific Ocean Areas, Admiral Chester Nimitz, directed:

"All major Commanders in the Pacific Ocean Areas will support this operation."[6]

For months planners had scoured the Pacific for ships and landing craft, then for more ships and more landing craft. As early as February 1, 1944, all attack transports, attack cargo vessels, and landing ships and craft *in or destined to report to* the Pacific Ocean had been assigned to Operation Forager. Thus, before the *Leon* was even commissioned in Brooklyn, she had been earmarked for her first amphibious assault. The importance and scheduling of this operation probably explained the extraordinary intensity and pace of Joe's training at both Little Creek and Ft. Pierce.

Whereas all previous assaults had landed a single division, Operation Forager envisioned landing two full divisions of Marines, the 2nd and the 4th Divisions, on eleven adjacent beaches. It proposed a coordinated, simultaneous assault over a protective coral reef several hundred yards wide. Saipan would be a major challenge—both in planning and execution—for the Marines and for the Navy's new amphibious forces.

The number of attack transports needed to land two divisions was so large that Forager's master plan called for two transport groups, Able and Baker. This was a "first" in amphibious assault planning, and it greatly increased the complexity of everything.

Group Able included three transport divisions of three transports each, which would land the 2nd division over the northernmost Red Beaches ONE, TWO, and THREE and Green Beaches ONE, TWO and THREE.

---

6 Dyer, G.C. (1969) The Amphibians Came to Conquer: The Story of Admiral Richmond Turner, p. 874. Retrieved from www.Ibiblio.org/hyperwar/USN.

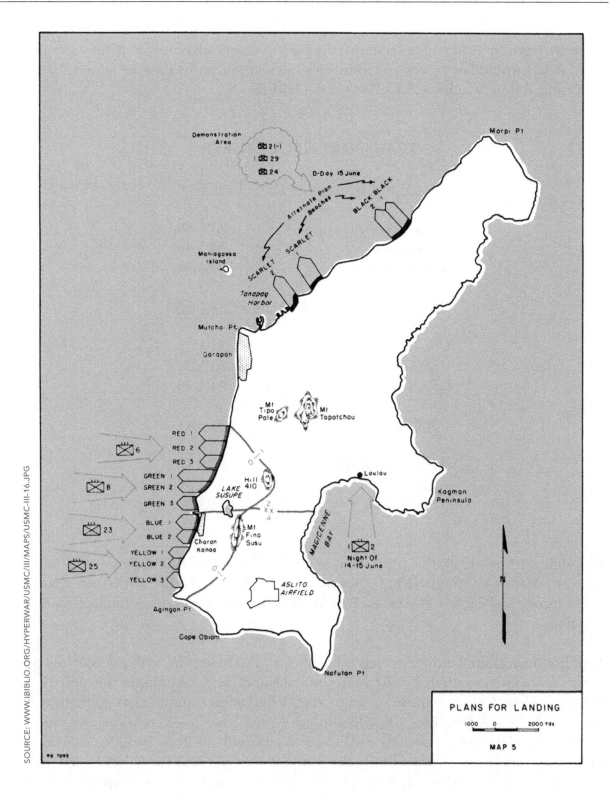

Saipan Landing Plan

Transport group Baker also contained three transport divisions of three transports each. Baker would land the 4ᵗʰ division over the southernmost Blue Beaches ONE and TWO and Yellow Beaches ONE, TWO and THREE.

TRANSPORT GROUP BAKER

Transport Division 26 (Blue Beaches)

USS *Callaway*	APA 35
USS *Leon*	APA 48
USS *Sumter*	APA 52

Transport Division 30 (Yellow Beaches)

USS *Fuller*	APA 7
USS *Calvert*	APA 32
USS *Knox*	APA 46

Transport Division 20 (Reserve Force)

USS *Leonard Wood*	APA 12
USS *Pierce*	APA 50
USS *O'Hara*	APA 90

Throughout April 1944, the *Leon*, often in convoy formation with *Callaway* and *Sumter*, sailed to Maui one hundred miles southeast of Oahu to practice drills and simulate landings on the beaches at Maalaea Bay, Maui. She made four cruises in all to Maui for practice.

Training during the landing exercises began with the basics for both the Marines and the sailors. The essentials for the Marines: pack and carry assault gear for debarking; form up below decks and move to the correct debarkation stations; start going over the side (left leg leads); use the *vertical* handholds to climb safely—in daytime and night—down three floors of cargo nets with thirty-five pounds of gear, banging against the ship every step of the way; and time the jump aboard the LCVPs as they tossed about in rough seas. Oh, and yes, how to quickly unfasten your backpack straps and helmet straps in case the unthinkable happens.

The transport crews practiced a growing repertoire of assault drills. They included embarking and debarking the beach parties; embarking and debarking the landing craft control (LCC) vessels of the boat group commanders and LCVPs for assistant commanders; embarking and debarking the ships' landing forces; loading and unloading cargo from all holds; convoy sailing with multiple formations; gunnery drills; aircraft recognition drills for deck officers, watch hands and gunners; general quarters, general quarters, general quarters. The pace and intensity of the training picked up throughout April.

USS Leon, c/o F.P.O., San Francisco, CA   *May 1, 1944*

Dear Aunt Margaret,

I've just finished writing you a V-mail letter since it should reach you much quicker than this one. It's so hard to write an interesting letter since censorship regulations are so strict. And as you can well see my handwriting has not improved a bit.

I'm ashamed of myself for having waited so long to write. I promised Kay that I would write you at once and in each of her letters she reminds me of it. It seems that I just can't write a good letter these days - I start one and something interferes and when I get back to it again it just seems no good.

The main reason is that in the past we have always included all the news in our letters and now I can't include any of the news. So I just have to "shoot the bull."

I hope Kay has been writing you often since she can probably tell you more about me than I can. She writes every day but of course I only receive them when we are in port and can pick up the mail. Then I get all my mail at once. So far I've had letters only from Kay and one from Papa which is all I can expect since I haven't written any myself.

I can tell you this much at least. That I'm well and contented with my work, and brown as an Indian from life in the open air. We have a very nice ship - as Kay probably told you and I'm kept as busy as the devil which helps a lot - one has less time to think that way. When I go to bed at night I sleep rather than be awake and think. Of course, I'm always lonesome - who isn't. For the people we love and things back home - and most of all for our wives. I have such a wonderful wife, Auntie. Oh, how I do wish you two could get together soon. I know you would make a wonderful pair. She must be getting to the "plump" stage for sure by now. She's so cute - she writes that the Doctor says about the last of August but that she may as well say Labor Day and be technical. In her last letter she says it "kicked" for the first time - in the middle of the night of course. Guess I don't know what I'm missing by not being with her now. Yet, I'm so glad it's as it is since Kay is so very happy and her mind is so occupied that she hasn't much time to spend worrying. I only hope and pray that God will be good to us and let everything be perfect for her sake.

But I do think a lot - about the future. Sometimes my future doesn't seem at all bright because of what has happened in the past and what yet remains to be done. And there isn't a lot that I can do about it from where I am now. But I am just cocky enough to know that I can get along no matter what comes. And I do know that my wife will be the greatest help I've ever had. Whether I will go into law or not remains to be seen - it seems so far away even after I return.

Write soon and give me all the news about yourself Aunt Margaret. And don't forget the newspaper clippings you always send. Send your letters Air Mail to

USS Leon
c/o F.P.O
San Francisco, CA

```
I shall send you V-mails often.  You will understand if I don't
have much to say.
```

```
Love,
Joe
```

A War History: (cont.)

"Aboard, the censorship was objectionable. And, with troops embarked, the chow line was impossible. Men had to wait in sweltering lines that stretched past the appetizing smells of the incinerator and garbage grinder and had to stand up to eat. "Feed 'em stew" became a famous phrase.

Newspapers and magazines were continually writing about the Navy's new air conditioned transports, but the living compartments were continually so hot men usually slept on deck where they were subject to the whimsies of the rain.

With troops aboard and 2,000 men living in tropical temperatures on a 492 foot ship, water had to be rationed. The food wasn't as good. Moving down the decks was like elbowing through the crowd at a sideshow.

When the men understood that those things had to be, they tolerated them with rare good humor. What these civilian sailors couldn't tolerate were the hardships that didn't have to be, the difficulties and snafu that grew from people not knowing their jobs.

Gradually these lessened. Knot after knot was ironed out. The beach party was recognized at inspection as the best beach party of any ship in the division.

Soon the Leon was unloading faster than any other ship. Her guns were hitting the sleeves that planes towed overhead in target practice. And a pride in the Leon was growing."

On May 5, the *Leon* sailed from Pearl Harbor for Kahului Harbor, Maui. On May 8, they loaded the assault troops of Battalion Landing Team 2-23, 4th Marine Division, and all of their vehicles and cargo. Then, in full convoy formation Transport Division 26 went to sea and honed their war skills again: damage control, man overboard, gunnery, abandon ship, fire and collision, aircraft recognition, new convoy formations. Aboard the crowded transports, the work was especially demanding. Standing room only was the order of the day, every day.

A War History (cont.)

"On May 14, 1944, Transport Group Baker went through a full dress rehearsal, point by point, just as it would occur only a few weeks later on an island whose name was still known only to a handful of officers: Saipan, fourteen hundred miles from Tokyo, and 600 miles beyond the once-feared redoubt of Truk.

During the practices some ships had tragic accidents, dropped boats, injured and killed men. One of the bombardment battleships went aground. The LSTs carrying the first wave troops were caught in an explosion at the West Loch ammunition depot at Pearl and had tens of men killed and hundreds injured.

On the Leon no one was seriously hurt. Landing boats weighing 27 tons were swung on end and off the ship as safely as the precious little sacks of mail. And Captain Adell gave her the nickname she was to earn many times over in the months to come – "The Lucky Leon."

But lucky didn't mean that everything was fine. Liberty at Pearl Harbor was allowed only every fourth day and there was little to do when you did get off. The girls and the liquor and the cars were for shore-based personnel and officers. There was just enough to make a man homesick and angry. And he had to fight the crowd to be back on the ship by 1800 (Navy for 6 p.m.) or get in trouble."

On May 16, a coordinated landing with transport groups Able and Baker was simulated on assigned beaches in the Maalaea Bay area. Debarkation and preliminary launch of troops, artillery, and tanks were conducted. All boat control officers and boat crews were exercised in their duties, with practice approaches to the beaches during simulated landings. All troops were reembarked prior to darkness.

On May 17, groups Able and Baker launched another full, coordinated landing at Maalaea Bay. This time naval gunfire and air support units participated, *simulating* all scheduled and call gun fires. Initial supplies and troops only were landed on the beach. Reembarkation was completed on May 18, and a critique was held on board USS *Leonard Wood* during the afternoon. With the exception of minor adjustments, the rehearsal had indicated that the plans for the operation were sound and complete.

Operational Plan, Amphibious Forces: Operation Forager

1. Transports arrive and anchor in outer transport areas eight thousand yards from Saipan beaches. At "Land the Landing Force" command, Marines debark into LCVPs.

2. LCVPs proceed to tractor transfer line for troop transfer to LVTs (landing **ve**hi-cle **t**racked—assault craft with steel tracks for crossing reefs).

3. LVTs form up in waves and proceed to the line of departure four thousand yards from beaches.

4. LVTAs (landing **ve**hicle **t**racked **a**rmored—armored tracked vehicles with a 75-mm gun turret and heavy machine gun instead of troops) arrive from LSTs (landing **s**hip **t**anks) and form the first wave at line of departure.

5. All waves form up on control vessels and wave guides and await order to commence run to the beaches.

The schedule for the final exercise of May 19 comprised a complete coordinated ship to shore assault from the surrounding seas against Kahoolawe Island. For the first time, the approach was supported by naval gunfire and air support using *live* ammunition. The final assault was launched after landing craft had reached and deployed at a line of departure three hundred yards from the beach. All units were reembarked prior to darkness and all vessels returned to their assigned ports.

Upon return to Pearl Harbor, Captain Adell met with all the *Leon's* boat group officers. Together they reviewed and critiqued in detail every aspect of their performance.

New York, NY   *May 24, 1944*

Dear Aunt Margy,

Such a long time with no news from you and I'm beginning to
think you must be sick or else very busy. I hope it's the latter.

I just received a letter from Joe's father this afternoon and he
says he has heard from Joe. I was glad to hear of it - have
you gotten any mail from him (Joe) recently? I have been getting
a few letters about once a month - sometimes after a three week
interval they arrive. Joe's letters can't leave the ship until
it gets into port and they usually stay out for periods of a few
weeks or more at a time. Might as well be thankful for it as it
comes I suppose - There isn't much point in wishing it were any
different. It gets lonesome sometimes though, waiting for the mail
to come - I suppose you often feel that way too. I seem to miss
Joe more and more as the time draws near for the baby to come.
Of course I'm very fortunate to have my family here and I try to
keep busy. I've been knitting a lot lately.

I had a nice letter from Monte Foster recently. Thanking me for
sending him Joe's address. Monte used to write to us while we
were in Florida, and I knew Joe wouldn't get around to it right
away, so I let Monte know Joe was gone over. Maybe they will meet
up somewhere. Monte says he expects a leave in the States soon
- I hope so for his sake. He's been gone a long time and is
looking forward to a trip home.

How is the sale of the house going? I wish it could be settled
quickly so you wouldn't have it on your mind. If you don't buy
it yourself have you decided where you will live or what plans
you will make? I suppose you are kept busy with the legal end
of it - it's always such a long drawn-out affair isn't it?

Ed has been moved out of Florida to a new Field in Louisiana.
He got home to Little Rock once on a very short pass and hopes
he will be able to do it more often. He seems to think he will
be there for a few months anyway - he hasn't had any orders

so far. Maybe he will get to Benton again before he does go overseas. How are Esther and Mike - have you seen them lately?

It's a very nasty day here in New York - rainy and raw outside. We've been having very warm weather right along - the very hot, sticky kind that isn't very comfortable. Maybe this rain will clear the humidity out of the air - we're hoping so.

No more news for now. Hope everything is all right with you. Did the floods do any damage to your part of town? Keep well and let me hear from you when you can get to writing.

Much love from Kathleen

On May 26, 1944, the *Leon's* crew began embarking the men of the 2–23 Assault Battalion, 4th Division, and combat loading all of their vehicles and equipment. Three days later she left Pearl Harbor in company with all assault forces comprising the northern attack force, TF (Task Force) 52.

Altogether the task force included thirty-seven attack transports and auxiliary ships jammed with troops and equipment. Beg, borrow or steal, the Navy had mustered and trained the greatest amphibious assault force ever seen in the Pacific Ocean.

The convoy steamed westward under constant vigilance. Japanese airpower in the Gilberts had been neutralized, but submarines were on the prowl. Routine general quarters sounded at dawn and dusk, but there was no evidence of the enemy.

Almost literally, tons of sealed documents marked "Top Secret" had come aboard the transports before leaving Pearl. These contained superbly rendered beach maps and submarine reconnaissance photographs of the landing areas on Saipan. Boat officers and beach teams pored over the maps. Each day there were formal briefings in the wardroom aboard *Leon* and other transports. The weather was stifling hot, but the sea was calm. Nights brought a blessed cool breeze and the decks were crowded with cots.

The assault group reached Eniwetok Atoll, Marshall Islands, on June 8. For the next three days they conducted maneuvers and practiced gunnery. Finally, the last elements of the invasion force arrived and refueled: the bombardment groups, the carrier groups, the minesweeping and hydrographic survey group, and the fueling group. The armada was ready. On June 11, TF 52 departed Eniwetok to arrive at Saipan and Tinian at H-Hour 0830 on D-Day 15 June. The task force was led by one of America's top naval leaders, Admiral Kelly Turner.

Once again the *Leon's* wardroom hosted intensive briefings, devoted not only to beach landings but also to identification of enemy aircraft—Zekes, Judys, Bettys, Kates, Vals, and Haps. Everything on the ship was secured. Life aboard was intensely, uncomfortably burdened with security precautions. There were sentries on deck. On every side, stretching almost out of site to the horizon steamed the mightiest armada ever seen on the Pacific Ocean… battle wagons, carriers, cruisers, destroyers, transports and countless other vessels. The site stirred emotions and an overwhelming sense of pride. Yet, much later, the production was to be outdone and upstaged by a still more magnificently stirring spectacle.

Rear Admiral Waldron L. "Pug" Ainsworth, commander of the bombardment group, sent this message to his ships:

> "Today a large United States Naval Force of which your ship is a part is on its way to take the Islands of Saipan and Tinian away from the Japs, and make them give up Guam to its rightful owners… I promise you days and nights of hard fighting, as we must make the seas safe for our transports and pave the way for our Marines with plenty of shells and bombs. We are trained; we are ready; and we are going into close action. I have the utmost confidence in your ability to put the Japs where all good ones are…"[7]

---

7 Morison, Samuel. E. (1968) History of the United States Naval Operations in World War II: New Guinea and the Marianas Islands. V. 8. Boston: Little, Brown and Company, p. 173

USS Leon, c/o F.P.O, San Francisco, CA   *June 7, 1944*

Dear Aunt Margaret,

Won't have time to write a long letter this time, but I do want
to drop you a few lines this evening since we will be able to
mail letters tomorrow - and it will probably be the last chance
for quite some time. I've written twice before and haven't had
an answer as yet - you're undoubtedly finding it hard to get
around to writing. I only hope that you aren't ill - or that
your finger is causing trouble again. Perhaps your letter is
waiting for me at our next mail port - I will certainly enjoy
hearing from you and all the news from home.

In every letter Kay reminds me to be sure to write you. She's
afraid that you will be jealous since she hears from me so often
and writes you telling the news. And you write back and say that
you haven't heard from me yourself. Well, I'm not going to have
that happen.

These are history-making days with the invasion of Europe now in
full swing and a big movement under way in Italy. In addition
things are happening in other parts of the world which you folks
at home aren't hearing about as soon as they happen. At any
rate, it will go down in history as a very busy month.

There is no news which I can tell you naturally. The heat has
been a big nuisance - making sleeping difficult. It's probably
beginning to get pretty warm at home by now isn't it?

Write just as soon as you can and give me all the news. Perhaps
you can find some interesting newspaper clippings like you
usually do. And perhaps when I write you again I will have an
interesting story to tell - after it has happened.

Love,
Joe

War History (cont.)

"Two days before the landing when we were deep in so-called enemy waters, a Liberator bomber came over the convoy, circled and dropped a sack of mail in the water – letters from home. A destroyer fished it out and made the deliveries. We'd still like to thank the very human admiral who planned that event. And so on that memorable day there was an evening summons over the P.A. system, and not a summons to General Quarters: "Now hear this… now hear this. All mail Petty Officers lay down to the Post Office on the double!" It was a call that periodically would make cheers ring out all over the ship and gladden all hearts in the Pacific Theater, breaking the crushing boredom and bringing relief, joy, and alas sometimes tears."

One day before the landing, the PA system announced another call: "Now hear this… now hear this. Last call for fresh water. Last call for fresh water." Lines of Marines formed at fresh water stations on all the transports as assault troops topped of their canteens.

The night of June 14 was ominously still aboard the *Leon*. Officers and crew reviewed their objectives for the operation:

1. Provide assault beach party for Blue Beach TWO;

2. Debark troops in LCVPs and proceed to the tractor transfer line for transfer to LVTs;

3. Provide control vessels and wave guides for escorting assault waves to line of departure;

4. Provide control vessels and wave guides for leading assault waves to Blue Beach TWO, the assault waves to consist of LVTAs followed by LVTs;

5. Transfer artillery units to LSTs;

6. Unload supplies and vehicles to support assault units;

7. Treat casualties as received.

Off-duty officers and crew, Navy and Marines alike, slept fitfully, if at all.

Naval historian Samuel Eliot Morison, an observer aboard the USS *Honolulu*, tried to imagine what the Japanese defenders on Saipan must have felt on the morning of June 15, 1944:

> "At sunrise the inhabitants looked out on the greatest display of shipping ever beheld in the Marianas. Admiral Nagumo and General Saito, the Japanese commanders, may have been astonished, but they were not dismayed. They had every confidence in the ability of their ground troops to delay and harass the Yankee invasion until Admiral Ozawa and the Mobile Fleet, now hastening north from Tawi Tawi, could smash up this arrogant array of amphibious power. The enemy might take unconsidered atolls like Tarawa and Eniwetok; but Saipan - never!"[8]

---

8 Morison, Samuel. E. (1968) History of the United States Naval Operations in World War II: New Guinea and the Marianas Islands. V. 8. Boston: Little, Brown and Company, p. 185.

U. S. S. LEON (APA-48)

PLAN OF THE DAY

Thursday, 15 June 1944.

0300 - Reveille.

0315 - Breakfast. ← ⟨⟨⟨⟨⟨ NOTE:

0430 - Synchronize all watches.
Commence the Battle of Saipan.

0530 - Set Condition 1-A.
All troops lay below to your troop compartments.

0535 - Up all gripes.

0545 - Lower all davit head boats to the rail.

0547 - Sunrise. Light ship.

0550 - Synchronize all watches.

0600 - Or when directed commence debarkation.
Lower all boats as directed.
1st and 2nd divisions open all hatches as directed and unload cargo
as directed.
2nd division be prepared to hoist casualties aboard.

1832 - Make preparations for darken ship.

1847 - Sunset. Darken ship.

NOTE 1. TO THE TROOPS.

Best of luck. Shoot straight and give the yellow B——ds hell.

NOTE 2. TO SHIP'S COMPANY

For many of you this will be the first time in action. Every man
has a job to do and every job is vitally important in an operation
of this kind. It is expected that all hands do their job in an
efficient and seamanlike manner.

NOTE 3. All hands on gun stations are reminded to have their gas masks,
steel helmits and life jackets with them at all times.

S. W. CARR.

USS Leon Plan of the Day Thursday, June 15, 1944

Transport Division 26 approached the outer transport area ten miles off the BLUE Beaches of Saipan. The bombardment was underway… it had been underway for two days. It was deafening. At 0450, the *Leon* set condition 1-A and commenced lowering her LCVPs and debarking her boat group: Boat Group Commander Joe McDevitt, assistant boat group commanders serving as wave guides, and the *Leon's* full complement of four-man LCVP boat crews and five- man LCM crews. Below decks, the Marines trundled up from compartments and filed to their assigned debarkation stations, preparing to climb over the sides and down the nets to LCVPs, thirty-six men per boat.

Debarkation was scheduled for 0530, but was postponed until 0540. At 0542, the order came: "Land the landing force." The Marines of the 2nd and 4th Divisions began debarking along a four mile stretch of sea. LCVPs approached individually to load their assigned troops, circled in formation until all boats were loaded, and then followed the control boats to the inner transport area and the tractor transfer line. There, assault troops transferred into LVTs and followed control boats and wave guides to the line of departure. They were four thousand yards from the beach.

Then the Navy played its last card. Carrier based fighters strafed the beaches and twelve bombers dropped twelve hundred 100-pound bombs. On schedule, the first assault wave composed of the amphibious tanks, LVTAs, arrived and formed up on their wave guides. When the order was given, all assault waves followed the control boats along eleven beaches for the estimated twenty-seven-minute run to shore.

The first waves didn't receive any resistance until they approached the reefs off the beaches. Then suddenly the water seemed to explode everywhere. In every direction and in the lagoon between the reef and beaches great geysers of water arose from exploding artillery and mortar shells. Then small-arms fire, rifles and machine guns, joined the fire. The LVTAs and LVTs ground toward shore taking heavy casualties.

The landing plan called for the more heavily armed and armored LVTAs to cross the reef, climb up the beaches and clear the way through enemy defenses, which planners expected to be greatly weakened by the preparatory bombardment. The LVTs were then to penetrate eight hundred yards inland before unloading the Marines. But the deluge of Japanese fire and natural obstacles strewn on the beaches—including debris, tree stumps, shell holes, and ditches—foiled the plan. Instead, some of the LVTs unloaded their troops a scant two hundred yards from the water, badly congesting the landing zone. Those troops came under fire immediately by snipers on the beach and by heavy weapons fire called in by spotters.

Marine First Lieutenant John C. Chapin described clearly in his history, "Breaching the Marianas," the extraordinary beach scene when he landed on D-Day:

> "All around us was the chaotic debris of bitter combat: Jap and Marine bodies lying in mangled and grotesque positions; blasted and burnt-out pillboxes; the burning wrecks of LVTs that had been knocked out by Jap high velocity fire; the acrid smell of high explosives; the shattered trees; and the churned up sand littered with discarded equipment."

Chapin's unit formed up and moved inland, but they could not escape the precision of the Japanese artillery fire.

> "Suddenly WHAM! A shell hit right on top of us. I was too surprised to think, but instinctively all of us hit the deck and began to spread out. Then the shells really began to pour down on us: ahead, behind, on both sides, right in our midst. They would come rocketing down with a freight-train roar and then explode with a deafening cataclysm that is beyond description.
>
> It finally dawned on me that the first shell bursts we'd heard had been ranging shots, and now that the Japs were "zeroed in" on us, we were caught in a full-fledged barrage. The fire was hitting us with pin-point accuracy, and it was not hard to see why-- towering 1500 feet above us was Mt. Tapochau, with Jap observation posts honeycombing its crest."[9]

Naval gunfire eventually suppressed the observation posts on Mt. Tapochau. The Marines then discovered spotters hidden above them in chimneys of nearby factories and in camouflaged hammocks in the trees, and then behind them in "sunken" Japanese gunboats lying on the shore. Spotters and snipers were everywhere. The Japanese defensive strategy quickly became clear. They needed to stop them on the beaches... not

---

9   Chapin, John C. (1994). Breaching the Marianas: The Battle for Saipan, p. 3. Retrieved from www. Ibibio.org/ hyperwar/USMC-C-Saipan.

with defenders *stationed* on the beaches who would be vulnerable to naval firepower, but rather with spotters and snipers on the beaches calling in fire from heavy weapons cleverly deployed and hidden further onshore.

A coast guard photographer who landed with the early waves captured an all-too-familiar image of that day—two Marines shot by Japanese snipers as their group rose to move off the beach. The snipers, who were hiding in the hedges at the right, moved down the beach as soon as their targets dropped to the sand.

SOURCE: NATIONAL ARCHIVE

Two Marines hit by snipers on Saipan beach

In the water, the defensive fire was no less deadly. The Japanese had marked the reef and approach channels with small flags used to call in fire on the amphibious forces. Fire was directed first at the command vessels which were easily identifiable by colored flags they used to communicate with the beach, the wave guides, and the landing craft.

Joe McDevitt's control vessel was hit three times by mortar fire as he led the assault wave toward the reef. He was wounded by shrapnel from the last round while standing exposed at the rear of his boat. The blast blew him overboard. In a picture taken several operations later in the war (p. 280), he identified Ensign Francis W. "Red" Toon, one of his assistant boat group commanders, as the man who "pulled me to safety when I was hit at Saipan."

Four decades later, whenever Red Toon and Joe McDevitt met at *Leon's* ship reunions, Red Toon hugged Joe and wept. Strong bonds formed between shipmates in combat.

The following picture, believed taken by a shipmate aboard the *Leon*, shows Joe McDevitt being lifted to a boat from the beach to be taken to the *Leon* for treatment. The *Leon's* surgeon extracted multiple mortar fragments, mostly from his back. Several fragments were lodged so near to his spine that the surgeon left them in, fearing that extraction might cause paralysis. Following the surgeon's advice, Joe performed exercises each morning for the rest of his life to strengthen his back.

Joe McDevitt being transferred to the Leon for medical treatment

For two full days the intensity and accuracy of the fire on boat approaches and beaches of Saipan remained devastating, first to the assault troops and then to reinforcements. The bombardment punished Marine artillery units setting up on the beaches; it punished medical aid station personnel, beach party teams, and command post personnel. The Marines lost all four of their battalion commanders and two thousand casualties on D-Day.

But boats crammed with battle-tested Marines kept coming ashore. The assault wasn't perfect, but it was working. The first wave reported they had landed at 0850; the second wave at 0851; the third wave at 0854; the fourth wave at 0856. Eight thousand Marines landed in the first twenty minutes along eleven assault beaches. Twenty thousand men with tanks and artillery were dug in by nightfall and ready to fight. The landing that the Japanese didn't believe the Americans could accomplish had succeeded.

Morison witnessed the assault and marveled that,

> "To a superficial observer, the scene might have appeared completely mad, and the shouting and swearing over voice radio circuits at times did sound like bedlam let loose; but to anyone familiar with amphibious assault technique the landing was a magnificent demonstration of planned and courageous activity. Commodore Theiss and his control officers in the PCs and LCCs had the thing in hand every minute of the day."[10]

As unloading of troops and cargo progressed on D-Day, the *Leon* was becoming a hospital ship. While the hatch booms swung out ammunition, gasoline, jeeps, tanks, and all the other stuff of war, at 0955 the davits lifted aboard forty-one wounded and dead men. The wounded stretched on litters along the main deck, awaiting entry to the dressing stations and operating rooms aft. There was no room for the dead. Their bodies were wrapped in blankets and ponchos and sent back to the beach.

At 1549 on D-Day, the crew of the *Leon* completed the debarkation of all assault troops, artillery, and shore parties.

---

10 Morison, Samuel. E. (1968) History of the United States Naval Operations in World War II: New Guinea and the Marianas Islands. V. 8. Boston: Little, Brown and Company, p. 196.

At 1832, *Leon* went to general quarters, and at 1840 she got underway to retire from the area. All transports except those with priority cargo were ordered away from Saipan to avoid night attacks by enemy aircraft. They cruised around in great circles one hundred miles to the east, returning the next morning.

A War History (cont.)

"At 0315 while underway to Saipan, enemy planes were reported. The crew went to General Quarters at 0316 and secured at 0345. No planes were sighted. At 0415 enemy planes were reported at six miles. The Leon went to General Quarters again and executed tight turns. Several planes were sighted in the clouds and some ships fired. The Leon did not fire. TBS afterward reported that all planes in the vicinity were friendlies.

At 0655 Leon set Condition 1-A, entered the transport area, lowered her boats, and began unloading scheduled cargo. The crew soon learned that the Japs had attacked in force throughout the night on the beaches. Boats arrived immediately and throughout the day carrying approximately 250 casualties from the beach and from other ships. They came so rapidly and in such numbers that it was impossible to keep records or do anything except treat the most seriously wounded.

The Leon's Dental Officer did an excellent job supervising the receiving ward set up in the troop officers' mess. Ambulatory patients were directed to and treated at the forward battle dressing station. Wards for the serious patients were set up in the chief petty officers' quarters and in the troop officers' quarters. The ship's four doctors labored around the clock, perspiring endlessly, wearing only their shorts, conducting surgeries on the dinner tables in the troop officers' wardroom.

At 1746 the Leon got underway for night retirement in company with other transports in Task Force 52.4."

At 0500 17 June, 1944 D plus 2 day, *Leon* went to general quarters, set condition 1-A, and proceeded to the transport area, anchoring at 0722. All boats were lowered and the ship's crew spent the entire day toiling in the heat and the sun unloading cargo, while the boat crews ferried their precious cargo to the beaches and returned for more.

Tanks, bulldozers, jeep and trailers, ammo, water, rations, gasoline, flame thrower fuel, twenty-five hundred gallon and five thousand gallon water distillation units. Whatever the Marines needed to fight their way off the beaches, the *Leon's* crew and their mighty thirty-ton boom lifted out of her holds, swung over the side, and lowered into boats for delivery to Blue Beach TWO.

A War History (cont.)

"The Leon's hands were happy to receive the ship's Beach Party back aboard at 1400 on D plus 2 day. The beach crew had been pinned down by mortar fire and sniper fire on the beach since D-Day. After a minimal rest, the beach party doctor and eight corpsmen turned to, making it possible to run two operating rooms simultaneously.

LST (landing ship tank) 275 pulled alongside at 1222 with more casualties, and the medical team fell further behind. Most of the patients had been injured on the beaches by fragments of mortar shells.

At 1805 the Leon completed unloading for the day and got underway with Task Force 52.4. She would spend the next five days convoying in the Central Pacific and refueling at sea while the Great Marianas Turkey Shoot played out.

Down in the Philippines, the Japanese fleet had sortied through the San Bernardino Strait, steaming for Saipan and the invasion fleet. The Japanese were hell bent to save Saipan. To protect the invasion fleet, Admiral Spruance's attack carrier Task Force 58 moved out for battle west of Guam. Word that a great battle had been joined was passed to all hands over the public address system. Lookouts watched the sky earnestly. Radio-men bustled about with coded, secret messages."

While the *Leon* cruised and waited for five days, six of the wounded aboard the ship died. George Gibb, USS *Sumter* APA 52, described the Navy's burial party protocol in his <u>Battle Star History</u>:

> "Officers and crew not on duty gathered aft. A solemn cortege from Sick Bay appeared, bearing a litter on which was a body, shrouded in a cocoon of carefully stitched canvas. Nestled coldly beside the corpse, inside the canvas, was a 5-inch shell… solemn and appropriate convoy to Deep Six. The Chaplain said prayers, scarcely audible on the windswept deck. Taps sounded, via a record thoughtfully provided in advance by USN. Pharmacist Mates lifted the inboard end of the litter and the body slowly and with dignity slid off and splashed into the sea below. Gunners Mates armed with Garrands sent three volleys crashing into the air. Padre would raise his arm and all present joined in singing that stirring old hymn:
>
> *Eternal Father, strong to save,*
> *Whose arm hath bound the restless wave,*
> *Who bidd'st the mighty ocean deep,*
> *Its own appointed limits keep;*
> *Oh hear us when we cry to thee*
> *For those in peril on the sea.*
>
> The National anthem then blared forth from the P.A. system. Nobody spoke much afterwards."[11]

The *Leon's* four doctors and the corpsmen stayed up night and day, and the other 300 wounded survived.

When the great Marianas Turkey Shoot was over and the Jap fleet routed, the *Leon* went back to Saipan and finished unloading on 24 June, D plus 9 day. She transferred 44 ambulatory patients ashore and 167 casualties to a hospital ship. She then embarked the U.S. Army 347th Working Battalion and got underway in company with Task Force 52.18.15 bound for Eniwetok.

---

11   Retrieved from www.oocities.org/uss_sumter/georgegibb.htm.

Immediately upon departing Saipan, Captain Adell began preparing the ship's <u>ACTION REPORT</u>. Every US Navy vessel involved in an operation between 1942 and 1945 prepared and submitted to fleet command an <u>ACTION REPORT</u>. It contained a detailed description of battle action, an assessment of ship performance, and recommendations for improvement. Action reports are available to researchers at the National Archives.

Selected, verbatim excerpts from Captain Adell's <u>ACTION REPORT</u> follow.

USS LEON (APA 48)
<u>ACTION REPORT - OCCUPATION OF SAIPAN</u>

July 1, 1944

C-O-N-F-I-D-E-N-T-I-A-L

From Part VI:

1. Performance by all hands during this operation was satisfactory to the Commanding Officer.

2. There were no casualties to personnel aboard ship. The following members of ship's company were injured during performance of their duties on or near Blue Beach:

Lt. (jg) J. B. McDevitt - shrapnel wounds

Ensign J. A. Prather - smoke inhalation

S1c W. B. Lilze - shrapnel wounds

S1c V. C. Queer - crushed foot

<u>Report Conclusion:</u>

The USS Leon received all plans and orders and attempted to carry them out as scheduled. All hands were thoroughly instructed and briefed. Troops, vehicles, ammunition, cargo and operational gear were unloaded as planned and ordered and were transported to the line of departure on time. In view of the fact that all hands and gear worked smoothly and efficiently the Commanding Officer would have difficulty in singling out any one department, officer or man whose performance of duty was outstanding in comparison of the others. During the operation there were no casualties on board ship to personnel or the ship's gear.

Separate reports by The Medical Officer, the Beachmaster, and the Boat Group Commander were included in the *Leon's* <u>ACTION REPORT</u>. The verbatim content of Lieutenant (jg) Joe McDevitt's report follows.

USS LEON (APA 48)

June 28, 1944

C-O-N-F-I-D-E-N-T-I-A-L

From: Boat Group Commander

To: Commanding Officer

Subject: Saipan Operation, Observations

1. Operational events on Blue Beach TWO continued as planned until the dispatch of the first assault wave. During the final run from the Line of Departure to the beach there was a marked tendency for the first wave on Blue Beach ONE to give way to its right, which, coupled with the fact that the first wave on Yellow Beach ONE maintained a steady course, produced a decidedly narrow frontage for the seventeen LVT's of the first wave of Blue Beach TWO. By the time waves were approximately one hundred yards from the reef the assault frontage of Blue Beach TWO waves had been reduced to three hundred yards maximum thereby diminishing the interval between LVT's on that beach to twenty yards and less (whereas the correct interval had been established as forty yards) making an excellent target for the enemy.

2. To alleviate this situation the Blue Beach TWO LVT's slowed down producing a sag in the overall assault front and delaying perhaps a minute the H-Hour on Blue Beach TWO. A further result was the disunity of organization and command which occurs when the wave cannot be maintained in scheduled formation. This disunity was probably more noticeable when the waves hit the beach and can be described by Commander Duesendorf, USMC, the Commanding Officer of "E" Assault Company, BLT 3, 23rd Regimental Combat Team, 4th Marines who was returned to LEON with shrapnel wounds.

3. I further observed the definite absence of heavy bombardment of the right half of Blue Beach TWO and the left half of Yellow Beach ONE. Heavy fire was concentrated on the town of Chara Kanoa, and a dense pall covered the island both to the north and to the south of our beach which itself remained clear and sunny. The only shells which we observed fall on this beach were the rocket salvos fired by the LCI(G)'s. The strafing of planes which approached the beach from seaward appeared ineffective because of that approach.

4. Enemy mortar fire was evidently present to cover all areas of the water within one hundred yards seaward of the reef. The LCO on which I was operating received three hits within the space of a minute at the point of our maximum advance approximately fifty to seventy yards seaward of the reef, and LVT's were advancing in the face of heavy fire from the beach as well. I saw at least

three Japanese barges, the so-called "gunboats", in the reef area and witnessed the blasting of two of them by LCI(G)'s. I could not ascertain whether they were firing although they seemed to be underway. A pillbox on the right flank of Blue Beach TWO was active.

5. I was injured when the LCC received the hits previously described

CONCLUSIONS AND RECOMMENDATIONS

1. Too much confusion in traffic control, especially at Blue Beach channel. Poor coordination from beach master to primary and group control down through LCC and BCG boats. Subordinate officers are not well enough trained for this job. Procedure improved after first four or five days, but could be improved much further. In any future operation in which landing boats hit the beach directly this matter should be thoroughly worked out. In particular, there should be better coordination between primary and LCC control boats during assault phase. Neither point can control beach-bound traffic alone; they must work together to handle traffic, especially transfers, efficiently.

2. No adequate plans for handling small boats at night when the beaches were secured. Rarely was much night unloading accomplished with small boats. Consequently they were anchored and tied up all over the area. It was very difficult to communicate with them, once dispersed. If the enemy had been successful in getting his own small boats in this area he could have created great confusion and possibly caused great damage. In future operations of this sort every effort should be made to get boats back aboard parent ships for the night. If ships returned to the transport area early in the morning little or no delay in unloading would result, with the additional advantage of rest for boat crews and opportunity to repair boats. Boats which cannot possibly be brought aboard transports should be sent to definite areas adequately patrolled and protected for the night. This would make it much easier to contact boats during the night if necessary.

3. Much careless loading of boats was observed. Responsibility for this rests on both the ship and the boat crew. Numerous boats with

overloads and dangerously unbalanced loads were observed. Many of these swamped because they could not be beached, necessitating much extra work by salvage boats, obstructing the beach, and sometimes seriously damaging the boat engines and putting it out of operation.

4. Operation plans were too complex. Careful revision would have greatly reduced the bulk of non-essential material which had to be thumbed through to obtain any desired piece of information. Tabulation or indexing would have helped greatly.

5. LVT drivers had difficulty in finding and remaining in the assembly areas of the various beaches on their return trip. Much of this trouble was due to strong drift, from south to north which was present on D-Day. They should have some plainly marked boat or buoy at which to assemble when they return from the beach.

6. Boat lanes were not adequately marked especially on D-Day. Some waves hit the wrong beaches and later during the transfer of boat waves and cargo there was much interference between the boats and LVTs of adjacent beaches. The first wave should mark the approximate limits of the beaches with buoys or other devices. These waves have the best facilities for locating the correct areas. If because of enemy action or for other reason this is not possible, the second and third wave guides or flank tractors should be equipped to mark the boundaries of the beach. These markers would provide a reference point for all craft standing by off the beach as well as those landing on it.

7. LVT drivers have been trained to obey only the orders of their own company commanders. Their signals have not been coordinated with those used by the Naval Amphibious Forces. Control of LVT's can be greatly simplified if drivers are trained to obey the commanders and signals of Naval Wave Guides so far as such commands have a direct bearing on the maneuvering of the waves. A great amount of time was wasted at the Line of Departure because LVT's failed to obey orders of Wave Guides during the "forming up" stage, and several waves hit the wrong beach because they did not follow their wave guides.

8. It is believed that best results can be obtained by Wave Guides
   if they lead from the center front of the wave and not from the
   flanks.

                              Respectfully Submitted,

                              Joseph B. McDevitt
                              Lt. (jg) USNR

Joe McDevitt's contribution to the Action Report was written from bed aboard the *Leon* while he was being treated for his wounds. Two letters which follow, June 22, 1944, and July 3, 1944, were written during his recuperation.

A verbatim copy of the medical record of his diagnosis, treatment, recovery, and discharge for wounds received is presented below.

NAVMED H-8

(1943)

                    MEDICAL HISTORY

                    MCDEVITT Joseph Bryan

                    Name of Place: USS LEON

A 6-15-44

DIAG: WOUND, FRAGMENT, SHELL, MULTIPLE.

2584   KEY LETTER "K"

1. Within Command

2. Work

3. Negligence not apparent

4. While leading first wave approaching Saipan on 15 June 1944, a shell exploded
at 0845 astern of the LCVP on which he was standing. He was evacuated to the ship and arrived at 1030.

PE: Multiple small fragment wounds (0.2 to 0.5 cm) in diameter, 2 thoracic vertebra, 6 thoracic vertebra, right subscapular region, left and right upper arms, left buttock, left calf and right submandibular region.

RX: Tetanus toxoid. Sulfathiazole 2.0 gms stat, then 1.0 gm q4h. X-rays show all fragments to be small and superficial.

6-15: B.P. 100/60. Condition satisfactory.

6-17: Some slough around wound at level
of spinous process of 2nd thoracic vertebra. All wounds healing.

6-19: Progress satisfactory.

6-21: All wounds dry except one on buttock and over. Sulfathiazole discontinued.

6-23: Progress satisfactory.

6-31: Up and about.

7-5-44: Discharged. All wounds completely healed except one on level of spinous process of 2nd thoracic. To return for dressings.

Day 21: To duty, under treatment.

RICHARD L. PEARSE
LT. COMDR. (MC) USNR

USS LEON (APA 48)   15 July 1944:

All wounds clean and well healed. No discharge. No limitation of motion of neck, spine or extremities. Other than minute foreign bodies in soft tissue, chest negative. To duty, fit for same.

R.L. PEARSE
LT. COMDR. (MC) USNR

USS Leon, c/o F.P.O. San Francisco, CA   *June 22, 1944*

Dear Aunt Margaret,

This will be a short letter since there is little to say and because the things which one sees and does these days are not the best inspiration for letters home. But I have time on my hands while the others are all busy which must be spent some way. I spend as much time reading as possible and find that it does much to brighten one's spirit. And then when feeling thus I write letters.

You must have a lot of trouble with your finger these days since I haven't had an answer to any of the letters I've written you.

It could be that the letters may never have reached you at all. I hope they have since I wouldn't want you to think that I'd completely forgotten you.

I suppose you're keeping up with the news of Europe and the Pacific these days aren't you. I hope you are since they are telling you more than I can state in a letter home, and you can bet your bottom dollar that we are right in the middle of it.

We have no idea when we will return to the states. I'd give anything in the world to be there by September 1st.

I'm so anxious to know what is happening at home and how things have turned out so won't you please write soon Aunt Margaret.

Don't worry - I'm "in the pink" though a little sore in the muscles.

Your loving nephew,
Joe

USS Leon, c/o F.P.O., San Francisco, CA   *July 3, 1944*

Dear Aunt Margaret,

Well, Auntie, ours has been rather a one-sided conversation so far, hasn't it? Do you know that I haven't heard a single word from you during all this time and it worries me no end because I know you must have a good reason for not writing. Have you not been receiving my letters? Or is your hand causing you that much trouble?

Anyway, I enjoy sending you a few lines now and then and so hope you enjoy receiving them.

There was quite a spell when I didn't write anyone, first because I was too busy, and then because I couldn't. But that's all in the past now. In fact at present I'm having a so-called "rest" period and have nothing to do besides write letters, read books, see the movies, get out in the sun and regain the tan I had before, play bridge, and other such pastimes which all grow very boring. Letters are hard to write because there's so little to say. However, I'll soon go back to "duty" again and be wishing I still had all this spare time.

At any rate we have been seeing our share of this war, and I have been doing my part. You have a very lucky nephew - just say a prayer that he doesn't win any more rest periods. The price of such periods is too great in most instances - mine was an exception.

At present I'm in the best of health and in as good spirits as can be expected of a man who is thousands of miles from the people and things symbolic of home. Nor do the prospects of an early homecoming seem particularly bright. There's a slight possibility that October will find us in the states - let's hope so.

So it begins to appear that I will not be present to play the role of anxious and nervous Papa when our first child is born. Certainly I will be very worried way out here - anxiously awaiting a cablegram from New York City. I have all the faith and confidence in the world that things will go right - Kay has never mentioned any troubles or troubles expected. But the best things go wrong sometimes and that's what worries me. I don't suppose my presence would matter so very much since a woman in the pains of childbirth undoubtedly doesn't have much time for any male besides the doctor. But just the same it would be great to be there to see the little tyke.

Did you see Ed and Dad when he had his furlough? I haven't
heard from either of them since they were at home. Ed expects
to be sent back to Florida soon - and how he hates it! But
confidentially the longer he is kept right in the USA the better
I like it. We had some of his outfit with us and I'd hate to see
him going where we took them. That's where I got it!

Auntie, I am so looking forward to hearing from you. One of your
typical letters with the newspaper clippings in it. And news of
everyone at home. And news of how you've been and how things
are going. I'm so worried about you - so please write soon. Have
you heard from Kay lately?

Love, your nephew,
Joe

Saipan fell July 9, 1945. After detailed assessment, the amphibious campaign against Saipan was judged a model operation and became the template for all further assaults in the Pacific.

Sometime in late August 1944 Kathleen received an always-unwelcome letter from the Navy confirming Joe's injury. Although by then she would have received numerous reassuring letters from Joe since D-Day, any formal communication from the Navy received by any American household was a frightening experience.

In reply address not the signer of this
letter, but Bureau of Naval Personnel,
Navy Department, Washington, D. C.
Refer to No:

226094
p-53231-1d

25 August 1944

NAVY DEPARTMENT

BUREAU OF NAVAL PERSONNEL

WASHINGTON 25, D. C.

Mrs. Kathleen Rita McDevitt
454 Ft. Washington Avenue
New York, New York

Dear Mrs. McDevitt:

The Bureau regrets to inform you that your husband, Lieutenant
junior grade, Joseph Bryan McDevitt, United States Naval Reserve,
was wounded in action on 15 June 1944, while in the performance
of his duty and in the service of his country.

Due to the great volume of communications now required for essen-
tial fleet operations the dispatch received concerning your husband was necessarily brief. You may be assured that the best
medical care is provided for injured naval personnel.

It is hoped that your husband will communicate with you in the near
future advising you of his welfare, if he has not already done so.

Your anxiety is fully understood.

By direction of the Chief of Naval Personnel.

Sincerely yours,

Walter W. Finke
Lieutenant Commander, U.S.N.R.
Acting Director of the Dependents Welfare Division

Bureau of Naval personnel letter to Kathleen McDevitt

As soon as the fighting stopped, Seabees worked around the clock on Saipan to build five huge runways for the new, large B-29 Superfortress bomber with its ten tons of bombs and 6000 mile range. Large numbers of bombers began arriving. On the 24th of November, the first raid, consisting of eleven B-29s, took off from Saipan to bomb a major engine works near Tokyo. More and larger raids followed. By March 19, 1945, 325 B-29s took off to burn out the wooden heart of Tokyo. An estimated 83,000 Japanese died in the terrible inferno. This was massive punishment for the Japanese, but still there was no overture for surrender.

B-29 Superfortress bomber takes off from Saipan runway

One final item remains before closing this chapter on Joe McDevitt's first amphibious assault. His personnel record contains an undated copy of the following memorandum from the Office of the Commander, Amphibious Forces in the US Pacific Fleet.

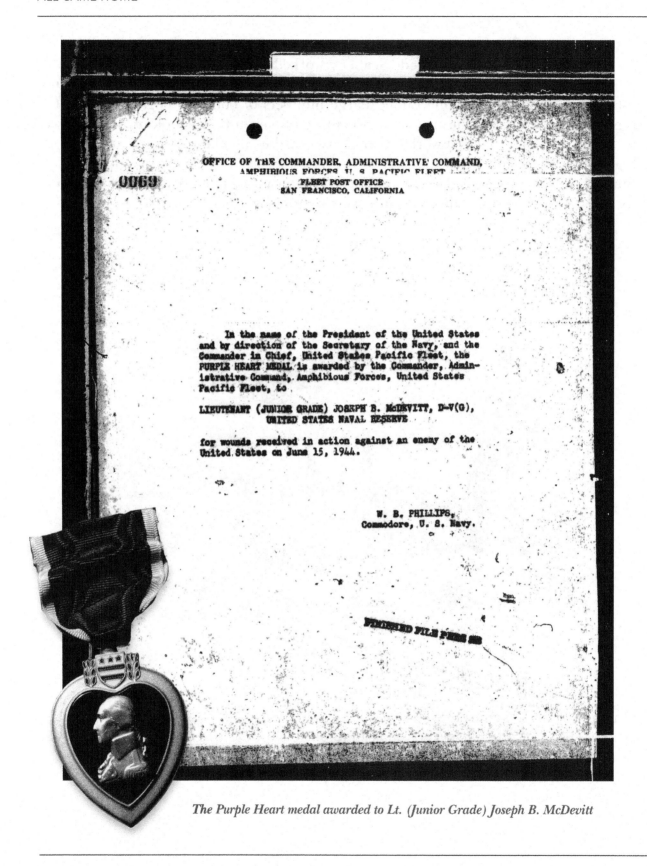

0069

OFFICE OF THE COMMANDER, ADMINISTRATIVE COMMAND,
AMPHIBIOUS FORCES, U. S. PACIFIC FLEET
FLEET POST OFFICE
SAN FRANCISCO, CALIFORNIA

In the name of the President of the United States
and by direction of the Secretary of the Navy, and the
Commander in Chief, United States Pacific Fleet, the
PURPLE HEART MEDAL is awarded by the Commander, Admin-
istrative Command, Amphibious Forces, United States
Pacific Fleet, to

LIEUTENANT (JUNIOR GRADE) JOSEPH B. McDEVITT, D-V(G),
UNITED STATES NAVAL RESERVE

for wounds received in action against an enemy of the
United States on June 15, 1944.

W. B. PHILLIPS,
Commodore, U. S. Navy.

The Purple Heart medal awarded to Lt. (Junior Grade) Joseph B. McDevitt

4

OPERATION STALEMATE: ANGAUR

A War History (cont.)

"After the Saipan operation, everybody talked about going back to the states, but it didn't work out that way. First the Leon was to be sent to support the delayed Guam operation. The crew began loading ammunition at Eniwetok. Change of plans: A day later they unloaded and went back to Pearl Harbor.

From Pearl the Leon went to Honolulu Harbor and on July 31, 1944, loaded the troops and cargo of the Army's 81ˢᵗ Division, 321ˢᵗ Regimental Combat Team. Another operation was in the works."

From August 1-3 they conducted training exercises at Lahaina Roads and Maalaea Bay, Maui. The troops of the 81ˢᵗ Division were training for their first assault. The *Leon's* crew, however, had had a taste of battle at the inferno of Saipan. The boat group had now experienced heavy artillery and mortar fire on the water off the beaches. They'd seen

Marines floating face-down in the surf and had helped retrieve their bodies. They'd transported Marines back to the ship who still had "the light of battle" in their eyes. They understood what was to come. And so they worked *hard* at the training for their next operation. Practice, practice, practice.

SOURCE: NATIONAL ARCHIVE

Marine, grimy with coral dust but the light of battle still in his eyes,
Returns to transport after two days and nights of Hell at Eniwetok

The *Leon* and accompanying transports returned to Honolulu Harbor on August 5, debarked the troops, and commenced loading the remainder of the 81st Division's cargo and supplies. The troops returned on August 8 and the *Leon* reembarked 1652 members of the 81st Division's 321st Regimental Combat Team. Four days later, *Leon* got underway with TG 32.4 to Guadalcanal where they anchored on August 24.

For the next two weeks TG 32.8 prepared for Operation Stalemate. With the Mariana Islands conquered and airstrips there already operational and pounding the Japanese, the next island-hopping target was the Palau Island Group lying some thirteen hundred miles northwest of Guadalcanal. Angaur, a small island only five thousand yards long and four thousand yards wide, and Peleliu, its larger sister island six miles away, were considered important stepping stones to the Philippines.

Operation Stalemate called for a Peleliu Task Group to land the 1st Marine Division on Dog Day, September 16, 1944. To provide the Japs with a diversion from the Peleliu assault, the Angaur-bound transports would spend September 15 and 16 cruising off the main Palau Island of Babelthaup, threatening a landing. Once released from duty at Peleliu, they would land elements of the 81st Division Combat Teams on Angaur the next day, Fox Day, September 17. The *Leon* and her 81st Division troops were designated a floating reserve force for the Peleliu attack and, if not needed, as divisional reserve for the 81st at Angaur.

In addition, the *Leon* was to provide Joe McDevitt and his LCC guide boat to lead the first Angaur assault wave on BLUE Beach.

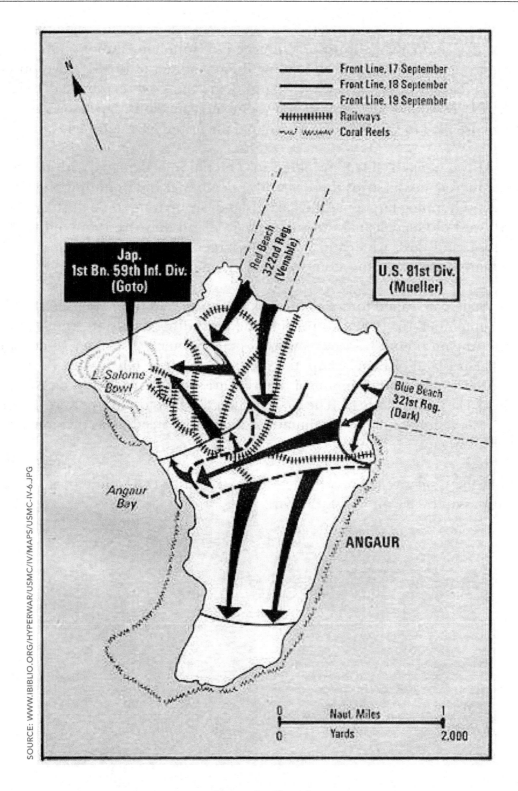

Front Line, 17 September
Front Line, 18 September
Front Line, 19 September
Railways
Coral Reefs

Jap.
1st Bn. 59th Inf. Div.
(Goto)

Red Beach
322nd Reg.
(Venable)

U.S. 81st Div.
(Mueller)

L. Salome
Bowl

Blue Beach
321st Reg.
(Dark)

Angaur
Bay

ANGAUR

0   Naut. Miles   1

0   Yards   2,000

Angaur landing plan

The *Leon* was anchored at Doms Cove, Cape Esperance area, Guadalcanal on September 1, 1944, when Joe McDevitt became a father. Rose Vaughan reported that Kathleen gave birth to her first son, Jeffrey Bryan McDevitt, at 7:00 a.m. at St. Clare Hospital in New York City. St. Clare was a Catholic hospital, founded in 1934 by the Franciscan Sisters of Allegany, to serve the working class neighborhoods of Italian and Irish immigrants.

Personal Journal of Rose Vaughan   *September 1, 1944*

> Mother went to visit Kay and Baby September 1st afternoon. I saw the baby, adorable. Kathleen was home in only 10 days owing to redecorations begun at the hospital.

On September 2nd and 3rd Angaur Task Group 32.8 went to sea and conducted final training exercises off Cape Esperance. TG 32.8 included five transports crammed with troops and cargo:

Transport Division 26

USS *Leon*	APA 48
USS *Crescent City*	APA 21
USS *Windsor*	APA 55
USS *Warren*	APA 53
USS *Callaway*	APA 35

All ships then returned to Guadalcanal to complete loading and refueling from September 4-7.

New York, NY   *September 3, 1944*

Dear Aunt Margy,

Just a short note this time - I'm not allowed to sit up for very
long yet and I still have to write Joe. My Mother was just here
to visit me and said you'd called this afternoon to ask about
the baby. We were just going to send out telegrams to you and
Poppa and Ed so that you'd know about the news. Oh, Aunt Margy
- he's the darlingest little baby in the world - you'll love him
to death when you see him for yourself. He is all Joe in looks,
and I'm so pleased. He weighed 7 lbs at birth. He's blond and
blue-eyed (and nice clear skin, not rooster red like some of
them are at first). We're going to christen him Jeffrey Bryan
and the priest who is going to do it is the one who introduced
Joe and I and then married us. Now, I have to stop as they are
bringing the babies in - I nurse him you know. Take care of
yourself.

Much love, Kathleen

We sent Joe a cable - haven't heard from him so don't know
whether or not the news has reached him yet.

Task Group 32.8 put to sea on September 8 bound for the Palau Islands. Aboard the
Leon, the pre-assault tension grew. They arrived on September 14, and, as planned,
cruised off Babelthaup Island September 15 and 16 and then proceeded to Angaur.

U. S. S. LEON (APA-48)

PLAN OF THE DAY

COMMENCE BATTLE FOR ANGAUR

Sunday 17, September 1944.

0400 – Reveille.

0415 – Breakfast for ship's company only.

0430 – Early breakfast for LCC officers and Capt. Drummond.

0445 – Set Condition 1-A.
Breakfast for troops.

0450 – Or when directed lower LCVP at rail port side #5 hatch.
Lower LCC and LCM. LCC to report to CALLAWAY, LCM to report to SUMTER.
Open #5 hatch when boats are cleared.

0500 – Up all gripes on all hatch boats and davit boats.

0510 – Hoist out all hatch boats to the rail.
Lower all davit head boats to the rail.

0530 – Or when directed secure from Condition 1-A. Set condition 3.

0545 – Wardroom breakfast.

0552 – Sunrise. Light ship.

0700 – Synchronize all watches.

0730 – Or when directed commence debarkation of Mine Platoon and RTC Reserves.
Use 4 LCVP's, these boats report to CALLAWAY.

0755 – Synchronize all watches.

0830 – Or when directed Set Condition 1-A, and commence debarkation of troops.
As soon as hatches are cleared open all hatches.
Second division be prepared to lower smoke generator in LCVP when directed
When all troops have left the ship commence unloading cargo as directed.

1746 – Make preparations for darkening ship.

1801 – Sunset. Darken ship.

NOTE: Supply department to provide all boat crew's with rations prior to
leaving the ship.

2. All hands on gun and lookout stations are reminded to have their gas
masks, steel helmets and life jackets with them at all times.

3. Food to be available at all times in crew mess and wardroom.

4. TO THE TROOPS.
Best of luck. Shoot straight and give the Yellow Bastards hell.
We have enjoyed having you aboard and hope to have you with us again.

USS Leon Plan of the day, Sunday, 17 September, 1944

At 0408, the *Leon* arrived in the outer transport area off Angaur. She anchored eight miles from BLUE Beach and set condition 1-A. They waited through the ferocious air and sea bombardment of tiny Angaur that was already underway.

Amphibious fire support was an important element of the Navy's evolving amphibious assault doctrine. Those plans called for the bombardment group to provide firepower during the pre-assault bombardment and until artillery could be deployed ashore. But there was a problem. The new heavy warships, including battleships and cruisers, carried a limited variety of bombardment shells and fired them on a lower trajectory than is normal for land artillery. Beginning with Tarawa and continuing on through Saipan, pre-assault naval bombardment had rarely fulfilled expectations. Landing troops continually met withering fire when they were most vulnerable... landing on the beaches.

After Saipan, the Navy was determined to launch all possible high explosives at the beaches in the Palau assaults.

A War History (cont.)

"The bombardment was unforgettable. Battleships, cruisers, destroyers, rocket launching ships and planes joined in some of the most concentrated firing warfare has ever seen.

Man-made thunder and lightning hit the northeastern corner of the baby island, shredding it, and finally hiding it behind a cloud of smoke and dust. Ship after ship belched flame and smoke, rolled back, waited only long enough for the salvo to land, and fired again.

Little Angaur reeled, and the warships poured in more and more and more – then stopped. H-Hour was silent. The little landing craft moved in..."

A Coast Guard photographer with a steady hand took a memorable picture as the landing craft approached the maelstrom created by the bombardment. When the photographer developed the picture and viewed the remarkable scene, he entitled it: "Into the Holocaust."

SOURCE: NATIONAL ARCHIVE

Into the holocaust: Angaur amphibious assault

What makes ordinary men forge ahead in the face of such devastation? The inferno on BLUE Beach was beyond anyone's experience or imagination. Yet the Navy's amphibious force, including LCC, wave guides, and boat crews maintained their wave discipline and their course for BLUE Beach. Full speed ahead.

A War History (cont.)

"When the smoke cleared, men were standing up on the beaches. No one opposed them. Treetops were gone. The green wooded area was gaunt. The only good observation tower on the island was battered, and Angaur was being Americanized.

The little island of one or two thousand people swelled to 15,000 without a night passing. Angaur had few casualties, while Peleliu in sight a few miles north was having hundreds, then thousands. The Leon was lucky again.

One of the war correspondents who came aboard the Leon at Angaur was a bespectacled little photographer named Joe Rosenthal. No one paid much attention to him then. Iwo Jima was still a Jap Island. And the Iwo Jima flag-raising picture hadn't been made."

September 17, 1944, FOX Day, the crew of the *Leon*—still awaiting the call as reserve force—again demonstrated the value of the Navy's new breed of citizen sailors. As Japanese resistance grew ashore, she received the order, and at 1025 she began debarking the floating reserve force. At 1220, her first wave landed on BLUE Beach. By 1303, she had completed the debarkation of her entire reserve force of 1254 combat loaded soldiers. Mission accomplished.

At 1845, the weary crew got underway to retire from the area.

From FOX plus 1 day through FOX plus 6 day, *Leon* cruised the seas surrounding the Palau Islands by night and moored in the transport areas by day to unload cargo, to provision other ships, and to receive and treat wounded.

At 1030 on FOX plus 3 day, all organized resistance ceased on Angaur Island. At 1551, the crew completed discharging the last of *Leon's* cargo. For the next two days, the *Leon's* boats and boat crews were dispatched to USS *Storm King* and USS *Jupiter* to assist unloading their supplies and cargo. Finally, on FOX plus 6 day, September 23, 1944, the *Leon's* beach party returned to the ship, the weary boat crews returned, and all boats were secured for sea. The *Leon* got underway from Angaur at 1700 as part of TU 32.19.8.

USS LEON (APA 48)

ACTION REPORT - OCCUPATION OF ANGAUR

September 24, 1944

C-O-N-F-I-D-E-N-T-I-A-L

PART V

Troops On Board

The Third Battalion of the 321st U.S. Army Regiment, which included the 306 Engineers and 316 Field Artillery, were on board for almost two months. By their high morale, splendid cooperation and good discipline they demonstrated that they were fully qualified to join the Navy. They were considered part of the ship company both in work and play. The Commanding Officer, Executive Officer, and Captain of the Ship's Guard have every right to be proud of their organization. The ship's platoon, which was newly organized and untrained, produced with a willingness and untiring enthusiasm which could not be exceeded.

Air Operations

A few night reports were received but no enemy aircraft encountered or seen. The advance striking forces were evidently so effective in cleaning the Japs out of the air, our lookouts became bored and hard to scare into attention.

Tactics

The maneuvering of these transports during the Saipan Operation under the direction of Admiral Turner continued to improve under Admiral Blandy, and it is considered that they would have no difficulty holding their own with any combatant group of ships in the Navy.

Conclusions, Recommendations

The USS Leon received all plans and orders and carried them out as scheduled. All hands were thoroughly instructed and briefed. Troops, vehicles, ammunition, cargo, and operational gear were unloaded as planned and ordered and were transported to the Line of Departure on time.

In light of the fact that all hands and all gear worked smoothly and efficiently the Commanding Officer would have difficulty again in singling out any one department, officer, or man whose performance of duty was outstanding in comparison with the others. During the operation there were no casualties on board to personnel or the ship's cargo handling gear.

Enclosure B.

From: The Boat Group Commander

To: The Commanding Officer

Subject: Battle of Angaur - Observations and Suggestions

ACCURACY OF INTELLIGENCE

Intelligence stated that the set of the current was southerly with drift of between 1 and 1.5 knots. On the day before FOX Day, Reconnaissance Teams reported the set of the current to be northerly. During the operation it was discovered that the current within 100 yards of the beach set to the north during high tide and to the south during low. Drift was as reported.

There was strong indication in intelligence reports that BLUE Beach was composed of sand. It was in fact found to consist almost entirely of coral with very little sand. However, this caused no difficulty since boats had to hit the beach hard in order to be high enough to unload.

Pillboxes were not reported on the limestone cliffs to the left of BLUE Beach. However, they were cleverly concealed and hard to recognize.

Mines not previously reported by intelligence were discovered to the near proximity to the beach. There were many such mines moored in the area between BLUE Beach and RED Beach. It is difficult to understand the reason for their location since the transports could not have been expected to close the beach to such extent. They were evidently of a type that could not be exploded by landing craft since before their discovery small craft crossed the area indiscriminately.

Beach photographs and general information on the nature of the beach were very accurate and on a higher level than for the invasion of Saipan.

ASSAULT PHASE

Since the USS Leon troops did not participate in the actual assault there are no comments upon this phase.

The troops aboard the USS Leon landed in reserve at approximately GEORGE plus 3 1/2 hours. This operation was conducted according to plan and no difficulties were experienced. Excellence of radio communications made this possible.

CARGO UNLOADING PHASE

(These observations are based upon four days' duty aboard the LCC Traffic Control Boat stationed approximately 50 to 75 yards off the center of BLUE Beach.)

The traffic control plan designed for the use of Transport Division 26 was carried out and was proven to be the correct solution to the problem of keeping the beach area clear and workable. In general the unloading and salvage of boats was at all times under easy control and the area within 50 to 75 yards seaward of the beach was seldom congested. This is a definite improvement over conditions which existed at Saipan.

The use of the 536 radio for communications between the Beach and the Traffic Control Boat was entirely satisfactory as a means for beaching boats with the right type of cargo at desired locations and for securing salvage when needed.

Credit is due to the officers and crews of the salvage boats for their hard work and splendid cooperation in keeping the beach clear of broached or sunken boats. In my opinion at least 75% of all boats which hit the beach had to be salvaged. This situation was due to three factors: (1) heavy ground swells caused the boats to broach at high tide; (2) at low tide the approach to the beach was very shallow and boats stuck on the coral shelf; (3) during unloading, the boats would partially fill with water through the open ramp and from the swells breaking over the stern, and this added weight prevented them from retracting under their own power. A Handy-Billy Pump is a necessity in every boat used for salvage in order that boats may be pumped out after retracting from the beach.

A beach salvage party should be equipped with Handy-Billy Pumps of a large size if available. On many occasions the beach would call for a salvage boat with Handy-Billy pump to come in and pump out a sunken boat. A salvage boat is far too valuable to risk beaching, especially on a beach where there is such a strong possibility of damage to screw or rudder from the coral. A pump on the beach is the only logical solution to such a situation since the boat can't be pulled from the beach when it is full of water.

It has been suggested by a salvage officer that the Beach Party should cooperate in securing the heaving line when it is tossed from the salvage boat to the boat which is broached on the beach. On many occasions the "toss" would miss by inches but would have to be recoiled and thrown again because there was no one in the water to retrieve such near misses.

It would seem that especially in the early stages of unloading, all the DUKW's; LVT's; and LCT's should be loaded at the transports with loose cargo, and that LCVP's be loaded with pallets. On a beach such as BLUE Beach, LCVP's can be handled only at certain times when the tide is favorable while DUKW's and LVT's can go inland at any time. This would prevent the "waiting" experienced by many LCVP's for periods of as much as two days or more. It is a fact that pallet-loaded had no difficulty being called in at any time and these boats were thus available shortly for new loads.

J.B. McDevitt,
Lt.(jg), USNR

In his report, Joe McDevitt noted that his observations were based upon four days aboard his LCC (**L**anding **C**raft **C**ontrol) Traffic Control Boat off BLUE Beach. Finding a picture of an LCC was a challenge, but we eventually discovered the picture below in Norman Friedman's U.S. Amphibious Ships and Craft: An Illustrated Design History. LCCs were specially designed vessels equipped to coordinate amphibious assaults and the ensuing traffic flow between the beach and the transports. Joe's LCC was a lightly armored vessel, fifty-seven feet in length with a thirteen foot beam, and a crew of fourteen. It was equipped with three twin .50 caliber machine guns, surface radar, and advanced communications systems.

Landing Craft Control Vessel used for amphibious assault

Joe's presence on the traffic control vessel off BLUE Beach suggests that his responsibilities had expanded beyond serving solely as *Leon's* Boat Group Commander. Later documentation confirms that he was also Traffic Control Officer for the BLUE beach landing area. That officer and the Beachmaster cooperated to manage all boat traffic between the transports and the beach, assuring the timely arrival of men and equipment without congesting the landing sight.

TU 32.19.8 departed Angaur and sailed the Central Pacific for three days, arriving at Seeadler Harbor, Manus Island, and Admiralty Islands on September 27, 1944. She relocated to Seeadler Harbor, Los Negros Island, on October 1st.

There was mail waiting for them.

USS Leon, c/o F.P.O., San Francisco, CA   *October 2, 1944*

Dear Aunt Margaret,

You can rest assured that your nephew Joe is the happiest man
in the Pacific Ocean these days. When we reached port this time
we had all our mail for the past month waiting for us. And Kay
had written every day beginning on September 2nd the day after
Jeffrey was born. I was certainly surprised but pleased that she
should write so soon. She must have come through wonderfully -
and in her letter it seems that my son is just perfect and coming
along fine.

Isn't it fine though. I'm so pleased to have a son though I
never stated a preference before. He was probably christened last
week - I wanted Ed to be his Godfather but doubt whether he
could make it. Kay wanted Fr. Kenealy to perform the ceremony
and since he was going into a hospital for an operation, it had
to be done before he went.

The nicest thing in Kay's letter was the group of snapshots
taken the day she left the hospital. They weren't too good but
they certainly served the purpose. Also I was tickled pink to
read that you had telephoned and chatted with Mrs. Vaughan.
That was so very nice Auntie and Kay was absolutely delighted.

Now I only hope that we will get home at least for a short leave
so I can see him before he grows up - before he starts walking.

I'm in fine health and came through without a scratch this time.
And with all the mail we're receiving I'm plenty happy.

Guess who I found here? Bob Timpany. He's been out here for 27
months without a leave. He married Joy Wilson - remember. We
have had a wonderful time together. He was my best friend at
school you know. He's coming aboard again tomorrow.

Ed writes often. He was in Little Rock again recently visiting Dad
who seems to be feeling much better these days.

Auntie I do so wish your hand would absolutely heal up because I miss your interesting letters. They were always so full of news and I preferred them over any others. But I realize how difficult it is for you to write as it is. How are things in Harrisburg and how are you? How is Uncle Bill and his family? Do you ever hear from the folks in Evansville? And Aunt Lizzie and the girls? Tell them all hello for me.

We're working hard and are all as brown as Indians. But we're certainly homesick and longing for that wonderful day when we reach the shores of the USA - and HOME.

Love,
Joe

Elsewhere in the Pacific, possibly aboard the USS *Sevier* APA 233, another Harrisburg, Illinois, sailor was also learning of the arrival of a new McDevitt. Kathleen McDevitt mailed the accompanying birth announcement and note to Lieutenant Monte Foster. Fortunately, Monte kept the announcement in a box with other important war memorabilia, and his family was kind enough to provide this important document for our story.

Birth announcement for Jeffrey Bryan McDevitt

5

THE PHILIPPINES:
LEYTE AND LUZON

<u>A War History</u> (cont.)

"The time was September 1944. In the bright tropical sunlight single-engine fighter planes from Admiral Halsey's Third Fleet carriers drone in over the green jungles of the Central Philippines, over Samar, over Leyte. Their mission: To knock down all the Jap opposition that might try to oppose the bombardment ships and transports now seizing Palau and Morotai.

While machine guns splattered and bombs dropped, cameras were busy recording the appearance of the land the Japs had held since 1942.

Results were amazing. The word of pilots plus the photographic evidence added up to only one thing: The Japs were incredibly weak in this land they had controlled over 18 months.

If there had been any truth to the "going home" rumors there wasn't now. The Leon was embarked on the most grueling months it ever saw. Lesser operations were canceled. The slates were cleared. Every available transport got ready to move into the Philippines 40 days ahead of schedule, not the Southern Philippines as first planned, but Leyte in the center.

At Manus, where she rushed from the Angaur invasion, the Leon loaded units of the first cavalry. (The word went round to expect horses in Number Three Hold and to clean up twice a day, but the cavalry came with jeeps.)

There was no time for training maneuvers. When the transports were loaded they sailed to Hollandia. Other convoys sailed from other ports, all in accord with a master timetable. At

Hollandia the Leon joined the Northern Attack Force invasion convoy sailing to Leyte, while a Southern Attack Force sailed for Dulag.

D-Day for the Leyte Force was October 20. Our target was Tacloban, the capital. Some units would land on the islands guarding the entrance to Leyte Gulf on D minus 2 day and set up navigational lights and signals. We would arrive on D plus 2 day and land our troops over beaches already opened deep in the gulf near Tacloban.

The Japs knew something was coming. Radio Tokyo, in English broadcasts, rushed out bulletin after bulletin on the annihilation of the American fleet. "If sharks could only talk," one broadcast said, "American mothers would know where their sailor sons are."

On schedule, early in the morning on October 22, we nosed through the smoke and mist of Leyte Gulf. American ships were everywhere. American planes lazed in from the sea, hurtled down in steep dives to drop their bombs, and lazed out again.

All the bombing and shelling was well inland, sign enough how the battle was going. The battered American ships reported by the Japs were not in sight. Only occasionally did a Jap anti-aircraft gun dare to send up a burst against one of our planes. When it did, methodic, wrathful planes and warships combed the area with fire.

Aboard ship, hatch crews worked vigorously. Men shouted. Winches ground. Loads of cargo moved out of the holds and over the side. Boats shuttled to the beach.

In six hours, all the troops and cargo were ashore. Boats were being hoisted back aboard. Tired, satisfied men were sweeping up the decks. There is a special pleasure in having an empty, clean ship again.

Steaming in column out of the gulf that night, the empty transports passed the old battleships, some of them resurrected from the mud at Pearl Harbor.

Two nights later those same battleships, formed in battle line across the entrance to the gulf, turned back and all but annihilated a Jap battleship force trying to enter, crossing the T on the Jap column in one of naval warfare's most classic maneuvers.

This was part of the great Philippines naval battle – the last battle in which the Jap Navy appeared as an effective fighting force. Next day, another Jap task force cut down from the north and battered one of the supporting carrier forces, then turned and fled at Halsey's approach.

The Leon that day steamed quietly to anchor in Kossol Passage, an American anchorage just south of the big Jap-held island of Babelthaup in the Palau group. We might have expected the Japs to have fired a few shots at us but they must have learned better manners. We even had deck movies.

From Kossol Passage the Leon sailed to Guam, arriving there October 31, to pick up the 77th Infantry Division whose tired troops, worn down by battle, mosquitoes, fungus, mud, and K-rations, were slated to rest and recover at New Caledonia, the cool Hawaii of the South Pacific. And the Leon crew, tired, bored, and three months without a liberty, looked forward to the trip.

We never got there. On Armistice Day when we were a thousand miles from New Caledonia a radio message sputtered in. The convoy commodore hauled up a signal, executed it.

There, in mid-sea, the transports wheeled around and headed back. At Manus, the ships pulled into Seeadler Harbor, dropped anchor, and sought more information.

The 77ᵗʰ was needed in Leyte."

In November 1944, the *Leon's* reserve officers received fitness reports. Joe McDevitt's report again assessed his performance as both boat group commander and deck watch officer. Captain Adell noted that he was now an experienced boat group commander, having served in three major operations against the enemy (Saipan, Angaur and Leyte) in an outstanding manner. He was also qualified as OOD. The captain recommended him for promotion and for retention in the regular Navy.

A War History (cont.)

"The afternoon we arrived in Manus, a new skipper arrived on board, Captain Harrison B. Southworth, USN. Time and formalities were short. After a day of inspections and meetings, Captain Southworth met Captain Adell on the promenade outside the captain's cabin.

Through a microphone, Captain Adell read his orders to report to Admiral Turner's staff. Captain Southworth read his to assume command of the Leon. With a few quick salutes and an "I relieve you, Sir" the transition was made. The Leon had a new skipper with nine months of its war travels done and (though it didn't know it) nine months to go.

A new skipper is a matter of very special interest to every officer and man aboard. The ship is his kingdom and he is its sole ruler. Good times depend on his good nature. When times are tough, the ship may float or sink on his decisions. To all the rest of the Navy he personifies the ship and is responsible for its actions and the actions of every individual under his command.

Captain Adell had been wiry, bantam-like, friendly, short on temper, long on liberty and good times. He drove the Leon like a sport coupe, never minding a few dents or scratches as we went alongside a dock or a tanker.

The new skipper was about the same size as Captain Adell but more fully fitted with gray hair. He held his cards in front of him and seemed to relish the poker game he was playing with the officers and men who (whether they would admit it or not) were trying to find out his pet peeves, his likes, his habits, and his views on a thousand things.

They soon found one story on him in a book called "And Then There Was One." As chief engineer of the carrier Enterprise in the Coral Sea days when carriers were gold dust he had rebricked a boiler in record time to give her the speed needed for a battle.

On November 23rd, a month after her first appearance, the Leon was back in Leyte Gulf. Several times on the way Jap planes had made passes at the convoy. After a raid the night before we arrived, Tokyo Radio reported three transports sunk. Actually none was hit.

Friendly clouds hid us that first day in the Gulf and the troops unloaded without incident. Not all the ships were able to unload and we stayed on a second day – a clear day.

It started uneventfully. We had orders not to fire our guns with friendly planes in the air and in such close quarters with other ships (an order that was later rescinded). About 1100 there was a sudden noise of a speeding plane. Men looked up, interested. And those with good eyes ducked more quickly than they looked – "He's a Jap!" and already the bomb was falling.

It seemed to take its time falling and it crossed over the ship in its angle and missed by 50 yards on the far side. Water splashed onto the deck. Men scrambled for guns, even though they couldn't fire.

The Jap had come low through the hills and raced out over the ship before the alarm could be passed. Now two P-38 Lightnings got on his tail, splattered him with machine gun bullets. The doomed Jap had come around and, passing over the transports again, burst into flames.

Still the pilot was not dead. He headed squarely for another transport. Then the flames won and he crashed into the water and disappeared.

To prove it could happen here – it happened again that afternoon. The air-raid warning signal – "Flash Red!" – came seconds before the plane broke through ahead. Guns tracked him but did not fire.

Down over the bow he came, only a few hundred feet high, and dropped his bomb. No fire went up to stop him. Friendly planes were knifing in again, but the bomb was falling. For some reason, just before he dropped it, he swerved and just enough. The bomb missed, landing off the starboard side aft, but not by much. Lighting circuits were knocked out in the engine room and were back in use in five minutes.

The P-38s tailed him, chasing him out to sea, and finally got him. Twice in one day it had happened and only twice, but each time the pilot had chosen the Leon for his target out of all the ships in the harbor. We felt big and conspicuous though others were as big.

"What have they got against you?" one of the skippers radioed Captain Southworth. The Lucky Leon didn't care, glad enough to have been missed, and just a little proud it was no longer a battle virgin."

Not all ships were as lucky. Two days after Leon's escape, the carrier USS *Essex* was operating in the Philippines Theater when special attack (kamikaze) pilot Lieutenant Yoshimori Yamaguchi attacked the carrier as she was fueling planes for a mission. Although damaged by defensive fire, Yamaguchi dove his Yokusuka D4Y3 bomber into the port edge of her flight deck amidst the fueling aircraft. The last image that fifteen young American sailors likely saw before they perished is reproduced below.

SOURCE: NATIONAL ARCHIVE

Kamikaze attacks the carrier Essex on November 25, 1944

Because the danger in the Philippines operations was always from above, speed was the primary emphasis for the transports. Both the transports and their valued treasure—the combat troops—were most vulnerable during debarkation. Get them over the side fast. Get them in the boats fast! Get them on the beaches, fast!! By this stage of the war, the crews of the *Leon* and the other transports were highly motivated, veteran amphibious forces, the best in the world. Their primary goal was to get boots on the beaches... safe, sound, and soon.

During the first Leyte landings, a picture taken aboard the USS *Elmore* APA 42 demonstrated a signature debarkation procedure that all boats crews had now perfected. The troop-laden LCVPs circled in the background as the empty boats waited their turn. As each boat was summoned alongside to its debarkation station, its boat team (here # 13) of thirty-six men was released to debark. With ten stations per transport, debarking was quick and efficient.

SOURCE: NATIONAL ARCHIVE

USS Elmore debarking Marines at Leyte

A War History (cont.)

"From Leyte the Leon went to Hollandia, from Hollandia to Noemfoor, there to load the 158th Regimental Combat Team for the Luzon invasion. At Hollandia, all hands from the captain down unashamedly lined the rail to look at a nurse, the first white woman most of us had seen since leaving Hawaii.

Ernie Pyle, speaking the mind of sailors as well as soldiers, said often and in many ways that war is mostly boredom and homesickness. It was early December now, Christmas and New Year were coming up.

The Leon crew had not had a liberty since August 11 in Honolulu. At Guadalcanal, at Manus, at Guam, and at Hollandia there had been brief chances for recreational parties to go ashore and play ball for a few hours on muddy, fenced-in fields and to drink the standard Pacific ration of three cans of beer.

Recreation facilities on board are limited, particularly when the ship is crowded with troops. There is a library. Movies are permitted on deck in rear area ports. There is a medicine ball and intermittently there has been a punching bag. At sea we sometimes had evening entertainments from the promenade deck.

And that's about all there is or was. Days under such conditions often have more than 24 hours. Noemfoor could not have been attractive any time but this little island outpost of the Dutch empire was far less so with Christmas and New Year at hand. Mail ships reached it only occasionally. Packages when they did come were often mashed and soaked.

Noemfoor still stands as the high water mark of monotony. Weather and the Japs caused the Luzon invasion to be postponed. We couldn't get the Leyte airfields going.

The Leon stayed at Noemfoor a month, anchored outside the coral reef just off an airfield from which raids went over to the Indies. Some days we went out and held firing practice. Other days Aussie flyers used us as a target for bombing and strafing rehearsals, nearly nipping off our upturned noses as they zoomed over the decks.

Christmas Day we got underway and went over to Mios Woendi to get fuel. New Year's Day we went down to Japen for a practice landing. Mios Wendi and Japen were both islands near Noemfoor, all in Geelvink Bay at the northwestern end of New Guinea, less than 100 miles south of the equator.

That sounds like a lot for a month, but that was all. No operation was more gratefully embarked upon than Lingayen on the Philippine island of Luzon. Nor, as it turned out, was any operation any harder on the crew. For the next 30 days gun crews were to be constantly alert. The danger came from above.

The invasion route was through Surigao Strait (over the sunken Jap fleet that had tried to enter Leyte Gulf), through the Mindanoa Sea to the far side of the Philippines, then up the west coast of the island chain to Lingayen Gulf.

For days the ships were near the same kind of hills from which the two Japs had raced at Leyte. Technical devices are of little help under such conditions. Lookouts must have their eyes open, or else. This time there were no restrictions on firing. The kamikazes were in flower. "Keep firing until you blow them apart," the orders read. As always, defensive fire was concentrated on providing an impenetrable umbrella of fire around the transports.

SOURCE: NATIONAL ARCHIVE

Umbrella of fire over the transports

Again, under the timetable, we were due on D plus 2 day. The convoys ahead of us were having trouble with the kamikazes, particularly the bombardment ships. Such word is supposed to be secret, but just enough leaked out to start tremendous rumors, with implications far worse than the truth.

The truth was simple enough. While other convoys got hit, ours steamed the whole way to Lingayen, passing en route the still-smoking beaches of Mindoro, and unloaded before we were attacked.

The attack came on the night of D plus 2, January 11, 1945. Friendly planes were grounded. A Jap was flying overhead looking for a target. Smoke generators and smoke pots burned on all the ships in the harbor to throw up a concealing cloud.

Patiently we sat at our battle stations, unable to see, unable to fire, waiting for the Jap to make up his mind. The smoke levels a greasy, oily film over everybody and everything. Men could slide like ice skaters about the decks.

Sometimes we would hear the motor of the plane or planes. One of these times a nearby transport saw him through the smoke.

A line of tracers arched skyward. The sound of the motor turned to a roar. The Jap came directly down the tracer stream, knowing he would find a ship at the bottom.

He misjudged or was hit and wasted his suicide effort flaming in the water a few feet off the transport's bow.

On the beach a heavy Jap gun opened up, sent shells whistling over the heads of the beach party and boat crews. It was an ungood night.

The first morning of our trip back to Leyte was low-ceilinged with broken clouds. Flash red had been in effect an hour when a single-engine Jap plane pushed out of the clouds.

Deliberately, he looked the convoy over while guns turned toward him. Tracers moved up to him and he made his choice, winged over, and plummeted squarely into the guide ship, two ships from us. Shells, including the Leon's, set him on fire in mid-air but this fellow's aim held. At the crash, flames shot 100 feet in the air, then died. That afternoon and the next afternoon, it held funeral services."

Fully twenty years later, as my Dad and I watched the 1964 presidential election returns together, he reminisced about his wartime experiences and described this very attack in detail and with great emotion. He recalled that the *Callaway* was the lead ship in the formation, followed by *Sumter* and *Leon*. He recalled that he was on watch duty and observed the damaged kamikaze crashing into the *Callaway*. Several days after the attack, he learned that one of his best friends aboard the *Callaway* had been killed in the attack. I have never forgotten that talk.

A War History (cont.)

"Returning to Leyte, we loaded up for a reinforcement trip to Luzon, with the First Cavalry embarked again.

One of the passengers was Captain Mark Wohlfeld, a Bataan survivor who escaped from a Mindanao prison camp and made his way up to Leyte by boat. He didn't hate Japs, he said, he just wanted to kill them. To do it, he postponed his return home until after he had marched into Manila with his unit.

Not far from Torpedo Junction at the far end of the Mindanao Sea and at far range of our land-based fighter cover, we had another air attack.

Soon after sundown, bogey reports began coming in. This one moved steadily closer. BOGEY 27 MILES CLOSING. BOGEY 23 MILES CLOSING. BOGEY 10 MILES CLOSING. BOGEY 5 MILES CLOSING.

Control passed the order to all guns: "Don't fire unless you can see the target." Barrels pointed in the direction of the bogey. Lookouts searched the stars. Men with their hands full of ammunition stood waiting.

The destroyers fired first. The transports astern of us followed. Two bombs or shells dropped near us. The night was filled with explosions, but we couldn't see the bogey. From the speed with which the fire shifted across the sky we knew he was fast. Then he was hit, a giant torch in the sky, bright orange, only a few hundred feet over the convoy, wobbling, falling. Briefly, he flamed on the surface in the middle of the convoy, then sank.

A green light blinked from the ship second astern of us. It had taken a torpedo in its engine room and had to turn back to Leyte. Later we learned that men in the engine room had time to get out and batten shut the doors before the resting warhead had exploded. No one was killed.

The moon was bright for the whole trip and we were as alert by night as by day but there were no more incidents.

Without sorrow, we sailed out of the Philippines February 2, 1945, headed for Tulagi in the Solomon Islands. And from there, no one knew what. The States perhaps—but hardly."

Night fire in the Mindanao Sea

6

OPERATION ICEBERG: OKINAWA

The next Pacific campaign would be the largest amphibious assault of the Pacific war and—though no one knew it—the last major combat operation.

War planners had first targeted Okinawa Shima in the Ryukyus Island chain in October 1944. Operation Iceberg was scheduled to commence at H-Hour 0830 on L-Day, April 1 (Easter Sunday), 1945. Four assault divisions, with three more divisions in reserve, would land on the Hagushi Beaches of western Okinawa and wrestle that island from the sixty-seven thousand men of the Japanese 32nd Army.

The Japanese were committed to fight to the death. Their motto:

One plane for one warship;
One boat for one ship;
One man for ten of the enemy or one tank.

A War History (cont.)

"A Jap meteorologist could have told the Nipponese generals and admirals an important truth: Luzon is the point where typhoons curve north and thunder over Japan, gaining velocity as they move. They form up out in the Central Pacific and move west to the Philippines, change direction there and move up the island chains to the Empire.

It was soon apparent that the man-made American typhoon was no different. The main thrust hammered to the Philippines and then drove north. Search planes, bombers, and fleets went up that way – all the way to the Empire."

New York, NY   *February 12, 1945*

Dear Margaret,

I just received a letter from Joe today and knew you'd be glad to hear that he was well and fine and had just arrived safely in port for a little while. He was pleased as punch because they were just receiving a month's batch of mail that was due them and all their Christmas cards and packages. Even though the holiday treats were arriving late (end of January when he wrote) they were just as welcome as they would have been on Christmas Eve. By the way, did you receive the package I sent you? Being that you were away over Christmas taking care of that sick woman, I was wondering if it was still at your house when you did get home. I hope it came in handy.

Well, I'm afraid the prospects of my taking the trip to Harrisburg look pretty bleak right now. To be perfectly truthful, Aunt Margy, it's just more than I can manage financially at the present moment and I hope you won't be too disappointed. I am sorry I can't come and bring Jeff because I'd like nothing better, but I think you understand that I want to come - it's just that the budget won't stand the expense. We expect Joe will be home sometime this year and maybe it will be sooner

than we think. When he does come, we are going to make
Harrisburg our first stop. We hope he'll get in this summer so
that really isn't much later than March anyway. Hope you've
been well. What do you think of the picture? Please write me
soon.

Much love, Kathleen

A War History (cont.)

"Back at Tulagi, the transports that had moved to the Philippines replenished for a new push, took on the first fresh food in months, got spares and replacements for equipment that had broken down in the long Philippine campaign, and had their first real recreation in six months.

However much they tried to minimize their effort, men were tired, grouchy, homesick, and high-strung. At Tulagi they took a deep breath, went swimming, played ball, walked through jungle trails, guzzled the usual beer ration, and spirits improved.

Compared with Manus, Guam, Hollandia, and Noemfoor, Tulagi was heaven. The climate was hot but the jungle was clean and the Americans had been there long enough to erect some nice-looking and comfortable installations, and get things into pleasant enough shape.

Tulagi was past the dusty bulldozer days and confusion that gripped the newer bases. It even had USO shows.

The ship took on new life. Underwent repairs, changed its dress, substituting an all-blue paint for the patchwork camouflage it had borne its first year.

After weeks of resting and restocking, the transports went out on February 23, 1945, to fire their guns across the warship graveyard named Iron Bottom Bay, and past Savo Island. That night they anchored at Kukombona Beach, Guadacanal, B.S.I."

While the crew prepared for another operation, the new skipper prepared fitness reports at the end of February 1945. The review period included continuous operations in the Philippine Islands, including reinforcement operations at both Leyte and at Lingayen Gulf, Luzon.

Captain Southworth's remarks suggest that the "seasoning" of Joe McDevitt continued:

> *"Lt (jg) McDevitt has carried out his assigned duties in an excellent manner. He has excellent military and personal character. He is recommended for promotion when due. An officer of initiative and good judgment who turns in a consistently superior performance."*

A separate memo written and submitted to Captain Southworth by Captain James K. Davis, commander, Transport Division 59, confirmed that Joe's responsibilities had expanded once again during the operations in the Philippines. He was now a senior member of the Transport Division Commander's staff. Captain Davis characterized Joe's contributions in the First Lingayen Gulf Reinforcement as "Outstanding."

Meanwhile, all across the Pacific Ocean, naval units were gathering and conducting assault rehearsals for Operation Iceberg. On Guadalcanal, the 6th Marine Division had been formed from numerous units, some battle-hardened, some untested. They had just finished five months of intensive training when the *Leon* dropped anchor.

The next day, *Leon* began loading elements of the division's troops and equipment. From February 24-28, she embarked forty-three officers, 1119 enlisted men, and 744 tons of cargo. Fully loaded, she put to sea and joined the other fully-loaded attack transports in Transport Division 35. The massive size of the coming operation became clear to everyone given the size of the divisions, five transports rather than three as at Saipan.

TRANSPORT DIVISION 35

USS *Leon*	APA 48
USS *Clay*	APA 39
USS *George Clymer*	APA 27
USS *Arthur Middleton*	APA 25
USS *Catron*	APA 71

From March 1 through March 7 the transport division conducted intensive training and rehearsals for the next planned operation. After the final rehearsal on March 7, the troops aboard *Leon* were returned to their camp on Guadalcanal for rehabilitation and final planning.

TOP SECRET status notwithstanding, the specifics of Operation Iceberg gradually emerged. Five transports in Transport Division 34 and five in 36 had also been conducting landing rehearsals. Altogether, the fifteen APAs in Divisions 34, 35, and 36 and their support ships formed transport group Able. They would land all elements of the 6th Marine Division on the northernmost GREEN and RED Beaches in the coming operation.

Transport group Baker consisted of fifteen APAs in Transport Divisions, 52, 53, and 54, plus all their support vessels. They would land the 1st Marine Division on the adjacent BLUE and YELLOW Beaches.

Altogether, the thirty APAs in transport groups Able and Baker, plus all of their support cargo vessels formed TF 53 NORTHERN ATTACK FORCE.

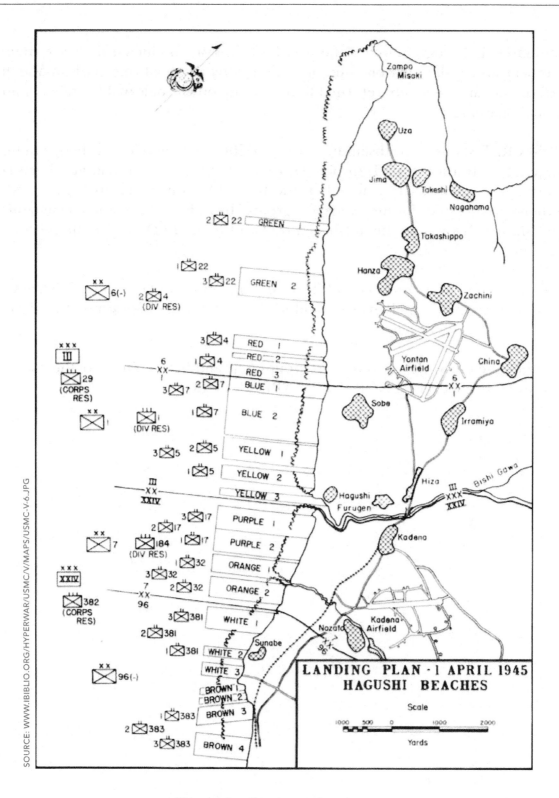

Okinawa Landing Plan: Hagushi Beaches

A parallel force, TF 55 SOUTHERN ATTACK FORCE, included a third and fourth transport groups which would assault the southern beaches. Transport group Dog and its fifteen APAs would land the 7th Army Division over PURPLE and ORANGE Beaches. Transport group Easy would land the 96th Army Division over the southernmost WHITE and BROWN Beaches.

Operation Iceberg posed the most formidable challenge yet to the Navy's amphibious forces: to plan and execute a simultaneous assault over twenty-one adjacent beaches—ten miles of western Okinawa coastline—by four full combat divisions from sixty attack transports. Such an operation was unimaginable just ten months earlier during Saipan's Operation Forager. The Navy's amphibious doctrine was by now well established, however, and its amphibious forces were largely all seasoned veterans.

Once again—and for the final time—on March 14, 1945, the *Leon* embarked fifty-three officers, 1378 enlisted men, plus thirty-six War Dogs of the 6th Marine Division. She departed Guadalcanal at 0616 on March 15 en route to Ulithi in the Caroline Islands.

USS Leon, c.o. FPO, San Francisco, CA   *March 18, 1945*

Dear Aunt Margaret,

Just a few lines this evening since I go on watch at 4 a.m. and must get a little sleep. As you know, I have not heard from you for quite some time. As a result, I worry, but at other times, I'm pretty disappointed, especially when I hear that you have written a letter and that therefore it isn't because your hand is so bad that you can't write.

Recently, I've been quite worried what with all the news of floods in the Ohio Valley. The news says that it wasn't as bad as the last one and I trust that the levee took care of the danger.

Kay told me that you had written and invited her out - also that
you had phoned her. As she has already written you, it was a
big thrill to her to receive your call and invitation, Aunt Margy.
You're a darling. She decided not to come at this time, didn't
she. But she knows she's welcome any time and will probably
accept in the spring. As for me - I'm glad she decided to wait.
It's been a hard winter at home hasn't it? And don't forget Kay
has never been into the so-called "wilderness." (Actually she's
not that narrow-minded, but plenty New Yorkers are so). I say
let her come in the spring - it's so fresh and pretty then,
and Jeff will be of an age when he isn't quite so much trouble
traveling. Perhaps I might even make it myself. I know that is
what Kay is hoping and stalling for. But I'm not counting on it!
We've been out here one year yesterday and it will probably be
several months before we get back to the West Coast. And even if
we get that far we may be there only a few days and get no leave.

Haven't heard from Ed in quite some time now. He was probably
kept busy during his 6-week period of training. But that is
finished and he's in some port of embarkation by now no doubt.
He needs all our prayers, Aunt Margaret, because the infantry is
no place to be. I sometimes think my job is one of the worst.
But in my case, it's bad for a while and then it's OK. But the
infantryman has it tough all the time up in the front lines.
I hope to have a letter from him when we reach our next port.

You've been reading of the rapid movement of the Pacific war.
So it's needless to say that I've been busy. Whenever you read
of an invasion you're safe in assuming that I was on the spot.
We seem to make one right after another, but there's still a long
way to go. The European war news is favorable, we're winning
over there, but it's costly.

There's nothing in the world I'd enjoy more than a letter from
you, Aunt Margaret. It has been many months since you last wrote
of course - letters from you could possibly be lost somewhere
along the line, but most of our old mail has caught up with us
by this time. I really haven't the slightest idea how things are
faring with you or with the home town.

Dad writes once a week and seems to be in good health. He enjoyed his visit to New York and thinks his grandson is a fine lad indeed. Everyone who has seen him says he looks like me. I'm anxious to have your opinion since you're the best judge.

I'm fine and hope you're the same. I remember you daily in my prayers.

Your loving nephew,
Joe

A War History (cont.)

"A week before the invasion we were at anchor in Ulithi lagoon, not far from the fire-swept hulk of the battered Franklin, just in from her tragedy at Tokyo. The Marine Colonel called his men together on the main deck to make the first initial announcement of our destination:

"Men, we are going to Okinawa. We will be ashore there by noon next Sunday. When the island is ours, Japan will be forever cut off from its ill-gotten empire. Our job is to land over GREEN Beach and to take Yontan airfield. I expect the airfield will be in our hands within three days. May God in his infinite mercy look over all of us."

A low "Wow!" went through the green-clad, unshaven crowd at hearing they would be ashore so soon. The rest of the speech was cheered and applauded.

Two days later, at 1400 Tuesday, March 27, the transports weighed anchor, fell into line and moved in a silent procession out of Ulithi lagoon. The Lucky Leon was sailing for her fifth amphibious assault operation of the Pacific war.

For the first time in twelve months the Leon was nosing up out of the tropics. The difference was a little more apparent each day. The days grew cooler. The flying fish were less frequent. And the water was rougher. For the first time in a year the Leon really pitched and rolled. Temperatures in the 60s sent us scurrying for sweaters and jackets and heavy socks.

We got the whole way to Okinawa without so much as a Flash Red, unexpectedly good luck that we understood better the afternoon before the invasion when we sailed by division after division of carriers in Carrier Support Group. America had moved into the Ryukyus, airfields and all."

Units of the Pacific fleet had been on the move well before L-Day. The bombardment force was already shelling the Hagushi beaches. That force included nine battleships, ten cruisers, thirty-two destroyers, and 177 gunboats. In addition, the carrier support group planned to launch thirty-one hundred airstrikes against the beach areas.

On L minus 6 day, March 26, five battalions of the 77th Infantry Division landed on four of the five islands in the Keramas chain, located fifteen miles west from Okinawa, and swept them clean of light resistance by Japanese defenders. The island chain provided a large and secure anchorage for over seventy large warships in the coming operation and would eventually become the 5th Fleet's rearming, refueling, and repair base.

Ominously, the Americans clearing Kerama Shima discovered three hundred fifty combat-ready suicide boats, *shinyos*, carefully hidden along the coastlines. Japanese documents retrieved later reported that these craft were intended to attack the troop transports should an assault on nearby Okinawa materialize.

Another 77th Division battalion landed on Keisa Shima eleven miles southwest of Okinawa and secured the island for the arrival of several Army artillery units. The artillery would support the assault forces on L-Day and throughout the bitter fighting on southern Okinawa.

Underwater demolition teams (UDTs) undertook final reconnaissance sweeps of the Hagushi beaches on March 29. On the 30th, UDTs 4, 7, 11, 16, 17, and 21 swam to the beaches and began removal of anti-boat obstacles. Meanwhile the attack transports of the NORTHERN and SOUTHERN ATTACK FORCES were gathering off the beaches to the west and making final preparations for the assault.

Finally, the 2nd Marine Division, the diversion force, arrived on the morning of March 31st off the southeastern beaches of Minatogawa—a site that the Japanese believed a possible landing spot. This feint had been reinforced by the presence and operation of minesweepers and UDTs there since March 29.

A War History (cont.)

"Convoys from the Philippines and Saipan converged on the same track with ours the night before L-Day and all four transport groups moved through the dark, past the southern end of the island, out around Kerama Retto and then north.

Dawn found our convoy heading due east, squarely into the island, aimed at our respective landing beaches, ours being the farthest north. During the night we had fired a few shots at a low-flying plane but nobody including the plane got hurt.

Air power we had never seen before came out of the sky that morning. Swarm after swarm of planes, 40 or 50 in each one, droned high overhead toward the beaches.

All the signs we could read pointed to a tough beachhead.

Reconnaissance parties reported stakes had been erected to stop boats. Preview photographs showed plenty of gun positions.

H-Hour was 0830, and the planes and bombardment ships worked up to the last minute blasting every target they could find. Then silence, familiar by now as the sign the boats were hitting the beach."

Even to war-seasoned veterans, the unfolding view of the assault was "Impressive:"

> "The approaching landing waves possessed something of
> the color and pageantry of medieval warfare, advancing

relentlessly with their banners flying. In the calm sunlight of the morning, it was indeed an impressive spectacle"[12]

A War History (cont.)

"On the ships there was nothing to do but wait for news. The Marines still aboard sang "Put on your Easter bonnet with the camouflage upon it....." and "Okinawa here we come.....," both ditties composed on route.

It was half an hour before we got the first radio report from the beach. Landings on GREEN Beach were two minutes late. The waves had separated and landed at two different spots. At 1000 the news was unbelievable. There were almost no casualties. Men were standing up, walking across the island, and Yontan airfield had already been reached. Men pinched themselves and wondered what the trick was.

But the news stayed good. The airfield was ours before noon. In two days the island was crossed. It was still unbelievable. In a few days it became apparent the Japs had withdrawn to the southern end of the island, and weeks later many of the Marines became casualties.

On the ships the unloading went slowly. A barrier reef made it impossible to land supplies except at high tide. By night we got underway and moved out to sea to avoid air attack, always returning at dawn.

No concentrated air attack had appeared. A few Jap planes scampered across the sky at sunset and dawn, fleeing the tracers and shell bursts that always rose to meet them, and only one plane came close.

Suddenly there was tremendous thunder in the sky. And next there was a splash in the water. A kamikaze had roared out of the morning and crashed in the middle of the convoy. Not a shot was fired. But his speed cost him his aim and he hurt no one."

12 Dyer, G.C. (1969) The Amphibians Came to Conquer: The Story of Admiral Richmond Turner, p. 1094. Retrieved from www. Ibiblio.org/hyperwar/USN/ACTC/actc-24.html

If you were telling the story of the Navy at Okinawa, the story would be about kamikazes and the terrible loss of life they inflicted. The early attacks at Leyte Gulf had been small and poorly coordinated, but they were nevertheless highly effective. With their backs to the wall, the Japanese High Command accepted in late 1944 that only kamikazes could halt the American fleet.

To the Americans, the kamikaze was a new and effective type of aerial warfare that was hard for the Western mind to comprehend and difficult to counteract. As kamikaze attacks continued, Admiral Bull Halsey, fearless commander of the 3rd Pacific Fleet, had declared the kamikaze, "the only weapon I feared in war."

The heaviest defensive burden at Okinawa fell upon the tiny picket ships stationed far out from the fleet to provide early detection of kamikazes.

Al Trombi was a machinist mate 2nd class serving picket duty aboard the Fletcher Class destroyer USS *Wren* DD 568 in April 1945. He never forgot the experience of kamikazes raining down on the picket ships off Okinawa:

> *"We were constantly at battle stations day and night because of the Kamikazes. I can remember this twin-engine Betty coming right at me. It was flying 20 feet off the water, waggling its wings. I could see the 20-millimeter tracers (bullets) from the Wren going right through the fuselage, but it wouldn't blow up."*

Trombi was running for his battle station in the destroyer's engine room, right where the bomber would strike. He wondered if he was about to be blown into oblivion.

L. J. Adams from Pasadena, Texas, a 40-millimeter gunner aboard the *Wren* also remembered that Betty.

> *"All of a sudden the Betty made a turn and flew right at me. I had his glass nose right in the middle of my sight as I tracked him on in.*
>
> *I could hardly wait as his glass nose kept getting bigger and bigger. My range finder, sitting right next to me, kept shouting '7,000 yards, 6,000 yards, 5,000 yards, then 4,000 yards.'*
>
> *I opened fire.*

Watching the nose of that Betty as it broke through the smoke, it was as if he was trying to get me personally. The entire war came down to this minute. I was pouring my fire into his nose and my range finder kept yelling, 'You're on him, you're on him!'

I stayed right on him as his underside filled my sight. It was like watching this dangerous spectacle in slow motion.

All of a sudden it exploded before my eyes. "[13]

The blast showered fire, debris, and body parts from the exploding bomber all over the *Wren's* deck. The destroyer escaped immolation. So did Al Trombi.

A War History (cont.)

"A storm caused more trouble than the Japs.

A ship like the Leon can't move in and out of a parking space like a Ford car. That night we virtually had to. The invasion ships were anchored close together off the beach when the blow came up.

The danger in a heavy wind is that the anchor will lose its hold on the bottom and the ship will drift aground or into another ship. Officers of the Deck check doubly-close when there is a wind.

If it's light and you can see, that's half the battle. Tonight it was dark, overcast and misty. That half of the battle was lost before we started.

Even in darkness it became apparent we were dragging, and dragging fast. In an area not so crowded we could have started the engines and moved out to sea. Impossible here, but we did.

It was like the blindfold games in which the victim tries not to step on the books. Only here there was no one taking the books away. Captain Southworth stationed two officers as lookouts on

---

13   Moore, Don. (2010) War Tales: Kamikazes Rained Down at Okinawa. Retrieved at www.donmooreswartales.com/2010/04/26/al-trombi

either wing of the bridge. On the flying bridge above, some 30 officers and men stood by as volunteer assistants.

The Captain stayed in the middle of the wheelhouse near the helmsman and the engine room telegraph, giving orders – engines ahead, engines back, engines stop, right full rudder, left full rudder, rudder amidships.

As ships popped out of the murk and the officer on that wing shouted the alarm, the Captain turned or maneuvered the ship away. If both officers shouted at once, the Captain weighed the evidence (who shouted the louder?) and made his choice.

Every ship in the area stayed off the radio circuit so we could exchange information with the ships near us. After hours the Captain got the ship clear and headed out to sea, only to be challenged by a cruiser as a possible Jap intruder.

That past, we rode out the night beyond the anchorage. Early in the melee the Captain had let go one of our anchors, chain and all, rather than risk the time to haul it in.

April 5 we left Okinawa, just as a message was received: "Stand by for mass air attack." The next day while we were safely at sea, the attack came. On our radio we heard intercepting fighters in just one area report shooting down more than 50 Japs.

The Lucky Leon was headed to Saipan and then Pearl Harbor. It was our first visit to Saipan since the invasion and we weren't allowed ashore. We had just come from a bush typhus area and were invited please to stay aboard our ship.

At the outer edge of the harbor we received mail and fuel and from there we could see the Superfort fields carved out of green hillsides and a vast military establishment where before there had been cane fields.

After a day watching the Superforts, we headed east to Pearl Harbor, all the transports on their own more or less. But the Leon was an old ship now, her bottom green with marine growth, and no match for the young fellows. Ship after ship passed us and disappeared over the horizon.

In our minds, Pearl Harbor had changed a lot in a year. When we first arrived in April 1944, it seemed an outpost, far from home. To some extent it was. The "front" was at Eniwetok, 2,470 miles west, in the next big island group.

Now, in April 1945, it was civilization. The front was at Okinawa, 4,700 miles away. None of us had walked down paved streets or into a soda fountain or looked at American girls since we left eight months before in August.

The Leon went into drydock, came out of the water for the first time in 15 months and had her bottom scraped and painted, her bent screw fixed, and repairs made throughout the ship. Supply quotas were really filled for the first time in 8 months.

Where would we go from Pearl Harbor? To the States? Men laughed. But the war in Europe ended and that's where we went – on 24 hours' notice. It didn't seem possible. No one quite believed it, but the course was east."

A War History (cont.)

"Friday morning, May 18ᵗʰ, the outer hills of San Francisco Harbor were visible. A mist glistened over them in the sunlight. The Golden Gate was a dim, shadowy outline.

Men who had dreamt about it for 14 months looked at each other. "There it is," they said.

By noon we were anchored, had mail aboard, and the first liberty party was going over to get the feel of American soil. After 427 days, the Leon was back.

Any one wondering what the crew thought of the ship got his answer in the next few days. If men don't like a ship, they will stay over leave and not come back, even though it means getting in trouble. One man did, and only one.

Transfers were to be had, transfers with 30 days' leave attached. A man turning down a bargain like that might be considered a sucker. But men did, more than one time."

Fortunately, Joe had been able to get word to Kathleen that the *Leon* was bound for San Francisco. Kathleen was able to reach the port city just prior to his arrival, which was no small task in those days of wartime travel restrictions.

During their first war leave together, Joe and Kathleen scheduled an appointment for portraits on Thursday, May 31ˢᵗ, at the Smart Studios on Geary St. in San Francisco. The results, in this son's opinion, were the most memorable and treasured pictures ever taken of them together. Kathleen was the quintessential war bride, and Joe was the veteran sailor who had not yet seen his first born child.

Joe and Kathleen McDevitt, San Francisco, CA, May 1945

New York, NY   *June 12, 1945*

My dear Margaret,

It was so nice to talk to you last night and I meant to sit right
down afterwards and write you this letter, but you can't always

arrange things like that so easily in this busy house. I got
started doing Jeff's laundry after supper and by the time I was
finished I was so tired I didn't even feel like writing to Joe,
but I did get a short letter off to him. I never did get to you,
but here I am tonight anyway.

First of all, it was just wonderful to see him. Oh, he looks so
good and healthy and in fine spirits that it's hard to realize
he's seen any action at all. I can guarantee that Joe is
completely unchanged.

We had five days together - I wasted a lot of time traveling out
there but that of course couldn't be helped. I had a Pullman
to Chicago, flew as far as Denver but couldn't get any farther
than that by air, so I took a coach on out the rest of the way.
The only train out that day was a very slow one - made stops at
all the local byposts and had long layovers of 2 to 2 1/2 hours
in several cities. It took 46 hours to make the trip - but it
was the best I could do, so I had to grab it and forget about
the discomfort. I was so glad I didn't have Jeff along, because
I would have been utterly exhausted by the time I reached San
Francisco. As it was I felt pretty bushed, but the minute I saw
Joe I forgot about feeling anything but completely happy.

It was a shame that we couldn't reach you by phone - Joe was
very disappointed but he was glad to talk to Esther anyway. He
called his father and spoke to him before he left. However, I
don't think it will be too much longer till he gets his leave
and when it does come it should be 30 days. The rumor on the
ship has it that their leave should come up in September, but do
keep in mind that there was nothing official connected with that
idea. I'm not even counting on it in the least, because I don't
want to be disappointed, but there is always hope that it might
really work out along those lines.

There is nothing I'd rather do at the moment than come out for
a visit with Jeff but there are a few obstacles in the way. First
of all, he's so hard to manage now that I get the shudders
thinking of the train trip - 12 hours or whatever it is. He's

starting to walk and is not content to sit on my lap any longer
than two minutes. Of course, if I got a bedroom it would be
easier, but from my own recent experience I know how difficult it
is to secure even a Pullman. Unless you're very lucky in getting
a last minute cancellation (and that means being at the station
all ready to leave a few minutes before the train pulls out) then
there is a standard wait of 30 days for a reservation of any sort.

Then there's something else again. I've already said I would go
away to the sea shore with my sister and her little boy (Stephen
- he's two years - they're living home here too as her husband
is in Germany) for the entire month of July. We had planned
that long before Joe ever arrived. We have already taken the
place at the shore and I can't back down on that now and leave
her to spend her vacation alone. So all in all, it's rather an
impossible situation all around and I think we'll all have to
put off the thoughts of a get together for a while longer as much
as I hate to think of that. Perhaps I can come out in the Fall
even if Joe doesn't get his leave till later on and stay with you
and wait for him to come home to Illinois.

I'm really sorry we can't work out any plan, but summing up the
situation it seems that the chances for the summer are mighty
slim. I trust that from reading this you can be certain that
I'm sincere in all my efforts but that's just the way things
stand. I hope you've been feeling well yourself and that the
hot weather won't bother you too much. By the way, I think that
any plans you want to make for renting the house should go right
ahead, because I can't see any way of being definitely sure when
Joe will be able to get home. However, you'll be hearing from
him yourself and if he has learned anything new I'm sure he'll
let you know, but for the moment the outlook is very hazy. Will
be sending you a picture of Jeff and I very shortly - had some
taken when I got home. Take care of yourself for all of us.

Best of love, Kathleen

A War History (cont.)

"In all we were in San Francisco 13 days. Some of the stevedores were on strike so we loaded our own ship. The wonder of wonders happened next.

For passengers we got 300 Waves. Men pinched themselves and asked if this was really the Navy. The Supply Officer flustered over perfumes, lipstick, and unmentionables for the ship's store.

The girls "turned to," helped type up office work that had been bypassed for months, swabbed the decks, and even scrubbed the landing boats. At night, after supper, the mess hall became "Club 48" for dancing and floor shows.

More than one sailor went looking for an engagement ring in Hawaii. As we went down the channel leading to Pearl Harbor, men from ships on both sides of us whistled and cat-called. The Leon was the proudest ship in the Pacific that day.

A week then in Pearl Harbor and we got impossible news – orders to San Francisco again. This time we carried back patients and Navy nurses. We pinched ourselves again. Was this the Leon? It was."

USS Leon, c/o FPO, San Francisco, CA   *July 2, 1945*

Dear Aunt Margaret,

I know you've been expecting to hear from me for quite some time now, especially since I tried to call you when in San Francisco. But don't forget that there is still such a thing as censorship of letters and one of the rules is that we can't write about where we've been until thirty days after we were there. And theoretically we aren't supposed to call while we are there. That last rule has been relaxed however and I didn't do anything wrong.

As you know, I couldn't reach you so I tried Aunt Esther and succeeded in contacting her. It was just before we pulled out so I couldn't take time to try to get you person-to-person in Galatia. I had tried to call you several times before so both Kay and I could talk to you but couldn't get through. Kay was hoping with all her heart that we would be together when I called, but I was on the dock just before leaving when I talked to Aunt Esther. However, I called Kay at her hotel and told her that I had finally succeeded in getting through. I also called Papa - boy was he excited, and I was also for that matter.

As Kay has probably told you she had quite a time getting to the West Coast. It took her a week to make the journey. We were very thankful she didn't decide to bring Jeff along - it would have been a terrible trip for both of them.

But the seven days we had together in San Francisco were wonderful beyond compare. It doesn't seem fair that the men of the ship should have only two weeks in the States after being gone for fifteen months - but that's the way it was so we made the best of it. I have never been quite so happy as I was with Kay. She is indeed a wonderful person and I'm longing for the day when you can meet her. She's prettier than ever since Jeff was born and just as vivacious and full of life as can be. I'm mighty proud of her.

So - I still haven't seen Jeff. But I've just received a picture of him and Kay which she had taken when she got home. I just can't believe my eyes because he looks so much like a little boy even though he was only nine months old when it was taken. I know Kay is sending you one so you'll see for yourself just what I'm talking about.

It's practically impossible to make any plans these days. The Leon has been kept as busy as any ship in the Pacific in the past and it may be about time that we get a little rest and perhaps a thirty day leave. We thought it would have already come since other ships which haven't seen as much service as we have returned to the States for theirs. But - it isn't our turn yet evidently. Several of us planned to have our families move out to San Francisco so they'd be right here every time we came in; but that's an important decision and I'm inclined to think we shouldn't do it until we know something more definite about the future.

Kathleen McDevitt and Son, Jeff
June 1945

Furthermore, with travel conditions as they are and steadily
growing worse so far as civilians are concerned, I think it best
that Kay remain right in NYC since I can travel much more easily
than she can. One of the boys has a car at home and his wife
can get gas to drive out here and wants Kay to come with her.
We're going to wait and find out what the ship does first. We
are supposed to come back for 60 days in the future sometime.
I'll have 30 days leave and will have to spend the other 30 days

in whatever port we put in to on the West Coast. That's when the car may come in handy.

Any way one looks at it - things are in a mixed up state. Planning is impossible. Kay is going to the country for a month with her folks which will do them all a lot of good. She has her hands full taking care of both Jeff and Rosemary's son Steven. Kay will just be 21 years old on July 28th so she is getting an early start in life, isn't she?

She wrote and told me that you had called her and invited her to come to Harrisburg. Gosh, she wants to get to Illinois more than anything else right now, but she first has to go with Rosemary on this vacation now. Rosemary stayed home from work and took care of Jeff while Kay came to see me, and Kay is about the only pal Rosemary has since her husband is still in Germany so it wouldn't be much of a vacation for her without Kay. And, Aunt Margaret, do you really know how difficult it would be for her to pack up with Jeff and travel by train. With this new 5-day limit on reservations it will be practically impossible to get decent space.

But, to tell you the truth, Auntie, I believe Kay really wants to wait to see Illinois when I can show it to her. It's going to be her home and she's sentimental enough to want her husband to show it to her the first time. And I can't say I wouldn't feel the same way if I were she. Also, I know that the state of her mind is very unsettled right now - she may have told you that I have been back again since San Francisco - and in fact just left yesterday. I shouldn't be saying this yet and won't say anymore until it is permissible. I called her and it was a big surprise. She couldn't have come out in time to see me and I wouldn't have asked her to make the trip anyway. But, it's just that way - she never knows when I'll be in because I can't let her know in advance. So she feels that it would be wise to stick around close to home until - as I said before - I know something more definite. One thing is certain: at my first opportunity I'm heading home to see that boy of mine!

2 Days Later

I'd been having trouble for some time with my lower left wisdom
tooth - it isn't in yet. Yesterday I got a terrific tooth ache
and x-rays showed the wisdom tooth to be impacted against the
second molar. Dr. Kent pulled the molar and it took him 25
minutes to get it out. You can imagine what I felt like when it
was all over - and still feel that way. There was an abscess and
the Doc is taking good care of me. The wisdom tooth has plenty
of room to come in now - it's been on its way for four years.
All in all, my teeth are in good condition and the rest of me is
too for that matter. Just lonesome that's all - and there's only
one cure for that.

Aunt Esther told me that Clarence was wounded at Okinawa and
was being returned home. I had just left there when we were in
San Francisco. It was pretty hot around there especially for the
Navy with all the Jap suicide planes around. I hope Clarence
isn't injured too seriously. I wrote him some time ago but never
received an answer.

You know all about Ed in Germany I suppose. He writes me
regularly now. I'm hoping he can pick up a good camera while
he's there. Those German cameras are the best.

Frankly, I'm feeling pretty low right now with this hole in my
jaw still bleeding, so I'm going to close for this time, Aunt
Margaret. I'll be able to mail this letter tomorrow I hope.
I'll not wait so long to write next time though.

You know I'm still hoping to hear from you some time. I can't
remember the last time - of course, I know you must be pretty
busy now. Say hello to all the folks and to Mrs. Edwards.

Oh - I feel terrible.

Your loving nephew,
Joe

A War History (cont.)

"After two days in San Francisco we sailed up the coast to Portland, Oregon, for eight days there. To get to Portland we sailed 90 miles up the Columbia River, through the forests of Washington and Oregon, and in sight of Mt. Hood and Mt. Adams.

Our stays were so short and so uncertain that there was no leave. But there was plenty of liberty and a great many officers and men were able to see their wives and families or at least talk to them on the telephone.

July 1 we sailed back down the Columbia River and out to sea, loaded with Army replacements, this time on the long trip back to Okinawa.

At Pearl Harbor we stopped and picked up Commodore (previously Captain) J. K. Davis, USN, and the staff of Transport Division 59 and became the flagship of that Division. Capt. Davis had also used us as his flagship during the Lingayen operation.

The route led from Pearl to Honolulu for more cargo, to Eniwetok to fuel, and then to Ulithi. At Ulithi we were held up for 16 days before we were finally ordered up to Okinawa in a large convoy."

Breakwater Bathing Beach, Mattituck, Long Island, NY   *July 23, 1945*

Dear Margaret,

My sister and I are here for a month with the children and it's really lots of fun. They are getting nice and tan and love the beach. Jeff is starting to walk now and is growing so big. Hope you liked the pictures.

Love, Kathleen

A War History (cont.)

"As we sat at Ulithi, the first atomic bomb was dropped. The day after we left, Russia entered the war. The impossible was happening. Japan's house of cards was tottering faster than any man aboard had dreamed.

By the time we got to Okinawa it was only a matter of time. Raids still went off to Japan but any one might be the last. And we still had our morning and evening quarters.

We sat out any number of false alarms. Then at 0820 on the 15th of August, 1945, the ship's public address system passed the official word: "President Truman has just announced that Japan had accepted the terms of the Potsdam Declaration."

Just as when we first saw San Francisco, there was no shouting, no whistle-blowing. It was over. And men smiled and were happy and felt chills run down their arms and legs. But everyone knew the job wasn't done.

That night we went to General Quarters as ever and a Jap plane came over and dropped a bomb in the area.

By August 27 our hopes of going to Tokyo were dashed. The occupation was already underway. And on Sunday, September 2, as the articles of surrender were signed aboard the battleship Missouri in Tokyo Bay, we waited at Okinawa with another fleet to load a force destined to occupy and accept the surrender of the Japanese in South Korea.

It was a disappointment not going to Tokyo, and Korea looked as an anti-climax to the long, long haul to Japan."

Every ship's crew in the Pacific fleet wanted to be in Tokyo Bay for the signing of the articles of surrender. Every single crew. This was not possible, of course. There was work to do. But every member of the Allied forces—soldier, sailor, and airman—was proud of the victory. Captain (later Vice Admiral) Gordon Beecher, Jr. extolled their contributions in his poem written in September 1945:

By Nimitz - - and Halsey - - and Me

Patty McCoy–an American boy–
Left his home in the old Lone Star State.
He set out to sea in a shiny DD

And he wound up in Task Force Three Eight.
He cruised for a while with a satisfied smile.
Then he took his pen in hand,
And here's what he wrote in a well-censored note
To the folks back in State-side land.

Me–and Halsey–and Nimitz
Have sure got the Japs on the run.
We're drivin' 'em wacky in old Nagasaki.
We're settin' the damn Rising Sun.
Kyushu and Kobe and Kure
Are wonderful ruins to see.
We've got 'em like gophers a-seekin' a hole.
The way that they burrow is good for the soul
And everything out here is under control
By Nimitz–and Halsey–and me.

Me–and Halsey–and Nimitz
Are havin' a wonderful time.
What we ain't uprootin'
By bombing and shootin'
Would fit on the face of a dime.
They say they're a face-savin' nation,
And that may be true as can be.
They're takin' a pushin' all over the place.
We give 'em the Arsenic minus Old Lace.
They're gettin' a kicking but not in the face
From Nimitz and Halsey–and me.

Me–and Halsey–and Nimitz
Are anchored in Tokyo Bay.
The place is just drippin' American shippin',
They stretch for a helluva way.
We hear that the fighting is finished,
And that is the way it should be.
Remember Pearl Harbor–they started it then.
We're warnin' 'em never to start it again,
For we have a country with millions of men
Like Nimitz–and Halsey–and me.

7

OCCUPATION LANDINGS: KOREA AND CHINA

By the conclusion of Operation Iceberg at Okinawa, the Leon and her crew members had earned the Asiatic-Pacific Theater Ribbon with five campaign stars. Each star signified a memorable operation: Saipan, Palau, Leyte, Luzon, and Okinawa. The Leon's five star battle history had been written in *real* time by Lt. A. A. Smyser, and that history remains today a remarkable tribute to the ship and her crew.

After Japan surrendered, Allied plans called for the immediate replacement of Japanese civilian leadership and military forces in Japan and all of the occupied territories claimed since her undeclared war against China began in 1936. The next order of business for the Navy's amphibious forces was therefore to support these "occupation" landings and to repatriate prisoners of war in those same territories. The first destination was Korea.

A War History (cont.)

"From Okinawa to Korea was a three day trip, three days of earnest searching for floating mines in the infested waters of the East China and Yellow Seas, mines laid by both sides during the war. Many were found and exploded. No ships hit them.

We carried out full wartime security measures – our ships darkened at night, guns manned, and morning and evening general quarters – but there was no interference from the now docile Japanese.

Our entrance into Korea was expected and heralded. The dawn on September 8 found our convoy at the outer islands and a Korean boat out to meet us flying the international signal for "Welcome."

The Leon pressed her unloading in the harbor. It took her until Monday night to finish. Next day, September 11, the unloaded transports steamed back down the channel toward Okinawa.

Now the war is over.

Ships could be lighted at night. Gun watches were cut to a minimum. Zigzagging was canceled. And the Navy point system was reaching out to provide for the discharge of more and more officers and men. The first seven had left the ship before the Korean occupation.

Where to next for the lady who had sailed so luckily?

China had not yet been reached. Marines waiting on Okinawa lacked only the ships to take them there.

Would the Leon go back to the States? Well, anyway – not until after the next operation."

USS Leon, c/o FPO, San Francisco, CA   *September 13, 1945*

Dear Aunt Margaret,

Well, many, many things of interest have occurred since I wrote you the last time. I have been so busy that even Kay has been neglected. But this cruise back to Okinawa is affording opportunity to sorta catch up on loose ends.

First of all, Naval Censorship has been abandoned and we are now operating on the "honor system", the only restrictions being that

we cannot reveal the aspects of any future operation or disclose
the units, Army or Navy, which will be involved. However, my
letters should prove to be much more interesting.

To begin with I shall go back a short while to July 1st. We left
Portland, Oregon on that date and came all the way to Okinawa,
via Pearl Harbor, Eniwetok, and Ulithi, prepared to participate in
the biggest invasion of all- HONSHU. But as Russia entered the
war close on the heels of the "atomic bomb" and Jap peace feelers
filled the air it became evident that the invasion would not be
necessary. So we dropped the troops we were carrying on Okinawa
where they were used as replacements for the 7th Division.

Then came a harassing three-week period of waiting while
negotiations for peace were being conducted - I say "harassing"
because despite the fact that the war was well-nigh over and
despite the fact that our planes had discontinued raiding Japan,
the "Nips" came over every night and hit something practically
every night. We saw a torpedo plane lay a "fish" (torpedo) into
the USS PENNSYLVANIA which blew off three of her four screws;
also a transport was hit not 400 yards away from us. We also saw
the specially marked Japanese plane which flew to Le Shima with
the Japanese peace delegates, en route to Manila.

However, once peace was signed the raids ceased and we started
loading the 7th Division to take them to - KOREA! We're on our
way back to Okinawa now from there. As soon as we arrive we load
for a famous port in China which you shall hear about later. So
now that the war is over we are seeing the world - at least this
part of it - although it means a lot of hard work for the Boat
Group. We're in the boats either loading or unloading most of
the time.

Korea proved to be highly interesting. We landed at JINSEN (also
called "INCHON"), a West coast port which serves the capital,
KEIJO (also called "SEOUL") 25 miles inland. Jinsen is a city
of 170,000; the capital has 1,500,000 and both cities were
surprisingly modern. We landed on the piers of the harbor and
it was with a curious feeling that I led in the first wave for the

sixth time in this Pacific war (Saipan, Pelelieu, Leyte, Lingayen, Okinawa and Korea) for right there in front of me were Japanese - out in the open for the first time: they lined all the piers, armed, standing at attention, and saluting! However, no trouble was experienced and impressive surrender ceremonies were held the second day aboard a battleship anchored in the river, as well as in the town square.

We were permitted to tour the town for the first two days, but were restricted thereafter because of riots and fights which broke out - one of which I shall narrate later.

Every fourth Jap is permitted to retain his weapons because if such were not true the Koreans would mob them. In addition, uniformed Jap Civil Policemen form a part of every American "MP" patrol. The reason for this is twofold: The Japs need Americans along for protection, otherwise Koreans would attack them and seize their weapons - we don't want the Koreans to have weapons; and on the other hand, if an American walks down the street alone the Koreans gather round him by the hundreds just to look at him and touch him and call him "Savior", making it impossible for him to accomplish his duty, whereas with a Jap Civil Policeman along the Koreans remain at a respectable distance. The people are highly excitable. Personally, I cannot distinguish between them and the Japs although they make certain that you don't mistake them: they come up to you when you're talking to a Jap (in civilian clothes) and say "Japaneessee" - the only English word they seem to know.

Another officer and I were in the center of town when we heard a big commotion around the Chinese Embassy. A group of Koreans with Japanese weapons were "cleaning house" at the Embassy. A Chinaman who spoke fair English came running up to us and shouted, "Those Korean rascals have killed my friend", and at the same time here came the Koreans dragging the dead Chinaman along after them. We flourished our .45's and they scattered like wildfire - they respect an American with a gun. We called the nearest MP squad and left the area - it was none of our business.

That night American sailors became intoxicated from drinking "saki" and found their way to the "red light district" where one of them was stabbed - not seriously. The next day the entire town was "out of limits" to sightseers.

On the day we landed the Japs killed three Koreans who insisted on staging a welcome demonstration for the American forces. I was in town when their funeral was held and it was some parade - more like our Halloween festivals. There must have been 50,000 in the mob and several people including Japs were killed.

Our occupation forces will have a merry time in that country. Those people have become accustomed to rough treatment at the hands of the Japs; I hope our attitude of benevolence and kindness doesn't lead them to resent us and take advantage of us. However, we can change our tune at the slightest provocation or hint of obstinacy, especially if harm should come to any of our occupation forces.

I was surprised to find a Catholic cathedral, school, and hospital, all in good repair and immaculate in appearance. There were two Irish Sisters, the only members of the mission whom we saw or had opportunity to speak to, who told us that they had been in Jinsen for fifteen years and that many of the Koreans were Catholic. I say "surprised" because we have been led to believe that the Japs tolerated only two religions: Shintoism and Buddism. But the Sisters talked to us with tears of happiness in their eyes and were loath to break our handclasp. We were the first people who spoke English in a free and relaxed manner whom they had talked to in many years. Their English was terse and clipped much as a Jap speaks our language. They told us that the Japs had not molested the mission to any great extent, but they had taken all the chickens, eggs, cows, etc. They had also exported the high grade rice grown in Korea to the "homeland" and substituted a much poorer grade nutritionally which caused under-nourishment among the Koreans. However, I thought the natives looked plenty fat and healthy!

As is always true, the richer class of Koreans would buy just about anything they desired: at a banquet given by one of them for Americans who had been Jap prisoners there were beef, fish, ort, egg, fowl, vegetable and other dishes as well as entertainment by "geisha" girls who are very expensive.

We are taking two Army pilots (they flew P-47's, Thunderbolts) back to Okinawa with us who were Jap prisoners for a month or so. They were in captivity for such a short time that their experiences amounted to exciting adventure rather than hardship. One was sent up to Jinsen on a routine reconnaissance flight on August 13th and was shot down by a "Jack" - a Jap fighter plane. On the 14th the other flyer went up to Jinsen, a three hour flight from their base on LE SHIMA (the small island off the coast of Okinawa where Ernie Pyle was killed) to look for the plane of the first and he also was shot down by a "Jack". Neither was hit personally and both parachuted into the water, opened his collapsible life raft and paddled to the nearest land where each surrendered to the first Jap patrol which came along. They were taken to Keijo, the capital, and placed in a prison camp. Each had to go through a mock execution: forced to kneel down, blindfolded, and then have a shot fired immediately over and from behind the head. (This is the way the Japs commit suicide or "hari kari". They do stick a knife into their stomach as we have been told, but someone else stands behind them and shoots them through the head so they won't have to suffer.) It was a harrowing experience to say the least and fully indicative of the fiendish mind of the Jap, but they're still alive to tell the story. Their capture came at a time when the Japs were scared to death; peace brought about violent rumblings from the various Korean underground movements which threatened to wipe these Japs in Korea off the face of the earth. Consequently Allied prisoners were no longer mistreated, nor even detained within the POW compounds; the pilots tell me that they walked out right past the Jap guard headquarters, and demanded and received their own personal firearms which had been confiscated previously.

It was at this stage of the game that rich Koreans, members
of one or another of the ten or twelve Korean "underground"
associations, each of which is struggling to become the official
Allied-recognized Korean government, began vying for the honor
of wining and dining the Allied Nations' prisoners of war.
Therefore, from this point until our arrival to remove them, life
was a bed of roses for our captured men - they say so themselves.

During the writing of this letter we have arrived back at Okinawa
and have "dropped the hook" (anchored) in MACHINATO Anchorage
on the west coast of the island. The mailman has gone ashore
and we're living for only one event - his return. He should
bring quite a load since none of us have seen letters in over a
month.

Under the latest modification to the Navy "point" system my total
reads: 44-3/4 points. This leaves me 4-1/2 points to go before
reaching the required total of 49, and since I gather 3/4 of a
point each month there are only five and a fraction months yet to
serve. That means March, 1946, should find me on my way home.
However, release may come even sooner if further modifications
should be made to the system which would favor me. Whew!
"Sweatin' it out"!

What I have just explained also means that Jeff will be a year
and a half old before I have a chance to see him. He should
be quite a lad by that time. Kay has been sending me pictures
of him as well as herself in almost every letter and my desk is
now lined with them. And you can be assured that the "desk" is
where I spend all my idle moments.

I know that you must be very busy, Aunt Margaret, but it would be
awfully nice to have just a few lines from you saying that you
are in good health or something like that. The trouble with you
is that you never write unless the letter amounts to a book, and
it takes too long to write that kind of a letter when one can't
sit down and complete it at a single sitting. Your finger probably
still causes plenty trouble which may be the reason you haven't
written. Do you realize that I have received only one letter from

you during the course of this war? I know nothing about what
you have been doing nor about Harrisburg in general.

Well, I must close this long-winded letter and get ready to go on
watch. We will start loading tomorrow and from that time on I
will be too busy to write. Must write Dad and Ed tonight.

Your loving nephew,
Joe

A War History (cont.)

"*After Jinsen the Leon together with many of the ships that took part in the Korean occupation were ordered back to Okinawa. One of our number, the Colbert, was diverted to Dairen, Manchuria, to lift a load of liberated Allied POWs and head directly home. The Leon and probably many of the other ships, felt she could carry out this assignment equally well – however, as things turn out later, the Colbert was not so lucky.*

The Leon was just beginning to get used to Okinawa air again when the weather stations warned all ships that "unnatural disturbances" to the southeast were fast assuming typhoon proportions – the dreaded "big wind" was heading our way. CTD 59 was ordered to round up a group of ships both Navy and Merchantmen and head for sea to ride out the storm.   As we cleared the anchorage the Colbert, with her POWs on board stood in. Seeing that something was obviously amiss she asked "What's up?" On being told "There's a big blow coming, better come along" she quickly swung about and assumed station 1000 yards off our starboard beam.

That night the Leon got her baptism of rough weather. Except when rounding Cape Hatteras two years before, she's never been in a really rough sea. As with everything else she's tackled, she took this in stride and the worst casualties were a few broken dishes and a few bruised shins.

The next morning about eight o'clock the Colbert reported by radio that there was a mine close aboard her port side and seconds later there was a tremendous explosion, a column of water shot skyward above her amidships section, and her second report, "I've struck a mine," was unnecessary verification.

Few of us will forget the sinking feeling in the pit of our stomachs and the rush of pity we felt for those poor devils aboard her who had just escaped the hell of a Jap concentration camp. Men with rosy visions of home and loved ones before their eyes were suddenly confronted with the stark peril aboard a crippled ship in a typhoon. However, the Colbert took it and came back fighting. Her skipper reported her engine room was knocked out and she was dead in the water, but that the flooding was under control and she could remain afloat. Later in the day, she was expertly taken in tow by the Butte, and we returned to Hagushi."

Joe McDevitt continued to earn strong fitness reports. In his March 1–August 31, 1945, report Capt. Southworth stated:

> "Lt. (jg) McDevitt is an outstanding young officer. He is quick to grab essentials and displays initiative, intelligence and good judgment in performing his duties. He is cool headed under pressure. He has ably trained and commanded his boat group in 5 amphibious operations. Both military and personal character are excellent. He is recommended for promotion. He is recommended for a commission in the regular Navy. He has seen this report."

A War History (cont.)

"At Okinawa, we sat for long boring days of sunshine and rain, with occasional daydreams of a revised point system that would give due credit for "overseas" duty. We finally loaded elements of the First Marine Division, destination – China. Our port was Taku, the seaport city of Tientsin, and our trip there was uneventful, except for the numbers of floating mines encountered. Luck was with us, and Officers of the Deck always managed to keep sufficient water between the mines and the ship.

On arrival in Chinese waters on 30 September, 1945 we anchored off Taku Bar – fourteen miles from the Mainland – and prepared to unload. There we faced an extremely difficult landing situation, inasmuch as the rough water and distance involved made unloading by small boats impractical and even dangerous. The larger landing craft used in unloading experienced many difficulties on their trips to the beach because of the shallow water and spent a considerable part of the time high and dry on the soft mud of the bar.

For most of us this marked our first experience with Chinese and we were all impressed with the boundless energy of their enthusiasm but seeming lack of ability for directing it along useful channels. The Chinese really put on a reception for us. They broke out their brass bands, floats, stilt walkers, waved flags and cheered lustily as our amphibious expedition steamed up the Hai-Ho. The mere fact that they were celebrating the Chinese New Year at that time didn't detract one bit from our own feeling of being the conquering heroes. We liked them and they liked us and the American dollar – especially the dollar. Taku wasn't so much, but up the river forty miles or so was Tientsin. A few fortunate souls even migrated all the way in to Peking, the "Forbidden City of China."

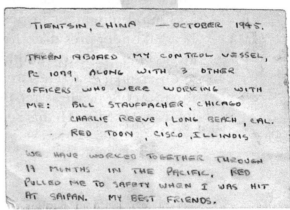

Joe McDevitt and Boat Group Officers on Joe's Control Vessel PC 1079,
Tientsin, China, October 1945

Fitness reports submitted later by Commodore Davis verify that Joe's primary duty during the China landings was Control Officer for the Commodore's Transport Division 59. Regrettably, a full picture of Joe's control vessel PC 1079 is unavailable. However, she was the same class of PC as the 472 pictured here. The vessel was a specially equipped **P**atrol **C**raft refitted to serve amphibious control duty. She was steel hulled, measured 173 feet in length and twenty-three feet at the beam, and displaced 284 tons. A normal crew included five officers and sixty enlisted men. The amphibious PCs were also equipped with the most advanced communications and radar systems available.

SOURCE: US NAVY PHOTO #NH96481

PC 472, sister ship of Joe McDevitt's PC 1079

A War History (cont.)

"The tales they bought back to the ship will be told often and probably grow considerably in the years to come. A souvenir hunter's paradise, beautiful Russian women, windows full of liquor (genuine

"Four Crown" and "Three Roses" (guaranteed best available Japanese wood alcohol)) – night clubs – oh, Tientsin was quite a city. On the ship for the majority of us, it was another long task to be completed before we could sail. The days and nights were cool, wild geese and ducks were in the sky every morning and evening, and we all were mighty homesick. At this time we were given a quarter of a point for sea duty and a few more fortunate people were eligible for the much desired rate – Civilian 1/c.

Finally, we upped anchor and sailed, not for home as many ships were doing but for Manila The third day out of Taku we slowed down and then finally turned around and headed back. Another typhoon was sweeping in from the Philippine Sea. This time we were more careful about lashing our personal gear down but with most of us that did little good. This was it – a real typhoon lasting for two days, we lived on sandwiches and coffee and moved about only when necessary.

There was a competitive spirit between the watches, each competing for the dubious honor of having the largest roll occur during their watch. Mr. Reitze scoffed at all our stories and said "Now, when I was on the Nightingale, I rolled 35 degrees one time and didn't think much about it." About 0400 the second day we were running from the storm, the Leon set her record that everyone aboard sincerely hopes will never be broken – 39 degrees. That's all the inclinometer showed but everyone aboard would have bet it was much more than that. Some claim the davit head boats hit the water and the rails on each side rolled under. It was the earliest reveille we'd had for all hands for some time. People who were not thrown out of their sacks were awakened by those who were and there was no more sleep that night for anyone.

Typhoon in the Pacific, October 1945

Joe McDevitt on the Leon's flying bridge, China Occupational landings

The storm finally passed, we made Manila on 13 October, and mighty glad we were. Here, at least, was a city that would look American, and rumor had it that liberty was pretty good.

Manila was a smashed city. Most of us saw here for the first time what war can do to a modern city and it wasn't a pretty sight. The "Pearl of the Orient" had been the victim of an extremely thorough job of destruction. Yamashita and Co. had really demolished it. The most thorough job was the Intramuros or old walled city where nothing was left intact.

Liberty was good here, at least everyone got all the liberty he wanted and a chance to spend his money and how those Filipinos rushed at the chance to relieve us of it.

Here again a few of the old familiar faces began to disappear. The much cussed and discussed Navy point system began discharging a few of the old timers (with dependents.)

For some time there had been rumors going around the ship that we were to carry Chinese troops. That rumor became fact, and we sailed from Manila to Hong Kong. Our overnight stay there was all too short and with part of a Chinese Army embarked (and plenty of rice), we put to sea and headed north. Our original destination was Darien, Manchuria but the Russians objected to that; it was changed to Hulatao, but the Communists had control there; so finally we disembarked our allies at Chinwangtao on 30 October, 1945. We left the next day and returned to Hong Kong on 7 November.

There we had a bit more liberty, but no more time, and we lost a few familiar faces. This time we took our passengers to Tsingtao and participated in what may have been the first modern amphibious landing of a Chinese Army. Here we had all the liberty anyone wanted, while the ship overhauled its power plant. We became very much at home in China and the cries of "Cumshaw, cumshaw, no Papa, no Mama, no food." became as familiar in our ears as the familiar, "Say, Buddy, can you spare a dime?" of yesteryear. We rode rickshaws, we bought souvenirs, (rare old "Ming Dynasty," very very good, very old) and we worked. The ship had to be very carefully cleaned and disinfected for we hoped our next load would be our own troops – HOMEWARD BOUND."

On November 6, 1945, Joe McDevitt received a promotion to lieutenant and another physical examination compliments of the Navy. Remember that promotion from lieutenant junior grade to full lieutenant that he expected when he went to sea from Norfolk, Virginia? More weighty matters than promotions for reservists had kept the Navy busy for twenty months. Finally, however, the Navy caught up. As for the physical, Lieutenant Lusk, (MC) USNR, of the *Leon's* medical staff concluded McDevitt

"is found physically qualified for temporary promotion
to Lieutenant (D) USNR, and to perform all duties of
his rank at sea or on foreign nations."

New York, NY   *November 15, 1945*

My dear Aunt Margaret,

I was very glad to receive your letter and to learn that you are
feeling a little better at least. Don't ever feel embarrassed that
you can't write oftener, as I fully understand how handicapped
you are with the arthritis. Mother has had the same trouble
since July, but it is not so severe as with you I am sure. It's
her legs that bother her - particularly the knees and it makes
it hard for her to get around. However, your hands must prove a
great limitation and the pain must be terrific.

I've just had mail from Joe today after several weeks of waiting.
Lately I've only been getting one delivery a month - the mail
seems slowed up everywhere since the war ended. He says that it
seems possible that he'll be home sometime in January, but of
course that is not definite by any means as yet. I wouldn't want
to spoil any plans you might be making for a vacation this Winter
by saying for sure that he'll be home in January. It might not
be till Spring but I really don't believe his homecoming is as
far away as that. I was hoping he'd make it for Christmas, but
that seems out of the question now.

Just this month Joe will have enough points to be discharged -
he needs 46 because he is an officer. The 41 points pertains to
enlisted men only. He is around China at present so he has a
long way to come to get back to the States.

Jeff is growing very fast, and gets to look more like Joe every day. He's 14 months now and has been walking since 10 months, so he's very steady by now. He does a lot of talking that you can't understand but says a few words like Da-da, bye-bye, Ma-ma, hot and ta ta, but that's about all. He's teething and having a lot of trouble with it - he has eight now but is due to get a whole lot more all at once. Will send you a new picture at Christmas-time. I know how that is, as we are always losing things around this house with the children too. Stephen, my sister's boy is nearly 3, and he hides anything he can get his hands on. It's a nuisance but there's not much you can do about it as they all go through this stage.

Well, it looks like we will be seeing one another soon so don't give up hope yet. January is not so far off and I really do believe Joe will make it by then. Hope you continue to feel good and let me hear from you again as soon as you feel like it. Will keep you informed about Joe.

Much love from Kathleen

USS Leon, c/o FPO San Francisco, CA   *November 25, 1945*

Dear Aunt Margaret,

As you can see by the card, I am in TSINGTAO China and I have just now received your letter written in September - two months after you wrote me. Our mail deliveries have been afoul for a long time now and I am presently receiving mail from Kay which is over two months old.

Now you say in your letter that you will be at 125 West Homer Street only until November 1st or 10th and it is already two

weeks after that time. I only wish this one letter had reached
me on time. I have had no idea that you were in such dire
straights. When I was in San Francisco that short time I tried
to call you but did not succeed. I hope you have not moved as
yet because financial help is on the way to you. I wrote Kay
immediately after reading your letter and told her to send money
at once.

You have written me only this one time since I came into the
Navy, so I've had no idea how tough things were going. I
have not had an easy time myself you know so far as money is
concerned. God saw fit to grace my household with a son just as
soon as possible and I've found great pleasure in him already
even though I have not seem him. He has cost a lot of money.
And the University of Illinois debt of which you write as well
as the debt to Kappa Delta Rho have been paid in full by Kay.
Perhaps we could have done without her trip to San Francisco to
see me since it was very expensive. But after all I had not seen
her for eighteen months which is a very long time. At any rate
she has done her best to build up a bank account and has done
well considering all factors. I am responsible for Dr. Klein not
having been paid before now. I completely forgot about it for
a long time and then was ashamed to tell Kay. However, I have
written him and he will receive the money in January.

You wonder where I intend to settle down. As you know, Aunt
Margaret, I will have to take the Bar Examination again and that
means going back to school for a refresher course. So as soon
as I am released from the Navy I will go to New York to get Kay
and Jeff. Then after a few days with her folks we plan on coming
down to visit you so you can meet my family, and so Kay can meet
my side of the family. Needless to say, she is looking forward
to that visit with anticipation. Then after a short time with you
we will go up to Champaign for my refresher course. This will
all cost money but is necessary. The $75 per month from the
government will not cover expenses for these so we'll have to rely
on our bank account to some extent. I cannot spend much time
working this time since that's the reason I failed my first Bar
Exam - I didn't have enough time for study. I don't know where

I will set up in practice. I would like Harrisburg but as you know I've lost all contact with businessmen and lawyers there. I know I am going to have a hard time for the next few years and I have a long way to go. But Kay will be my inspiration - she realizes just what lies ahead and will probably keep me going when things appear darkest. I'm fairly certain that I shall be in politics as well as law. How does that strike you?

Dad is getting pretty old and will not always be in good health. I have to think of him also. I have hopes that I may be able to get settled down soon enough to have both you and Dad live with us. It isn't right that he should continue to live alone either.

So you can see, Aunt Margaret, that I have not forgotten about you as you and others seem to think. I haven't sent any money and in that respect I've been wrong. But because I haven't heard a word from you until now, I've been under the false impression that you have been working steadily. The only word I've had of you is that you had fixed the house up, installed a bathroom, etc., which would indicate that you were working. We have saved every cent possible although it certainly doesn't amount to the sum I would like to have on hand for what lies ahead.

You have probably thought many times that I was foolish in getting married at a time when I was in debt and had no assets. This is no doubt the correct viewpoint except that human nature also enters into the picture. I found a girl for whom I had always been looking and she was willing to accept me knowing all the facts. I know now that I was right and am more than glad that at the age of 26 I have a beautiful, intelligent and faithful wife, and a son who is already over a year old. And I already have high hopes for at least three or four additional sons or daughters. All that plus firm intentions to perform my obligations with respect to my father and mother.

I can leave the Navy when we arrive the West Coast the last of December. But I am considering staying in for an extra six months in order to save some more money. You must realize that this would be the most distasteful decision because I want nothing more than to get out. It would delay me in getting started. I must talk to Kay first - she will probably desire the hardships of starting out as we are rather than wait those extra-long six months.

Well, Auntie, I hope you receive this before you have sold the house. If you do not want to sell it, I intend to try to keep it from becoming necessary. When Kay calls you tell her the whole story, so I can get it when I call her.

Love,
Joe

A War History (cont.)

"Finally the needed repairs were completed in the engine room and we left Tsingtao and China bound for Sasebo, Japan to load elements of the Second and Fifth Marine Divisions for transport to San Diego, Cal. For the information of any Texan who might read this, that is in the U.S.A.

There was some liberty at Sasebo but it seemed hardly worth the trouble of leaving the ship. A fortunate few were able to visit Nagasaki to see first-hand what happens when an atomic bomb hits a modern city. To borrow a phrase struck by the 8th Air Force, "One of their cities is missing." Most of the remarks by Chief Bos'n Lyons when he saw it were unprintable but the part "No wonder they gave up, y'know it?" really struck a truth.

Finally, with all the vehicles washed, troops embarked, and Imperial Japanese mud scraped off our feet, we started home. The Leon still wallows a bit and trembles a lot as befitting an old lady but she never falters. For a lot of us this is our last trip – the end of the rainbow. When the Leon reaches San Diego, she's going to lose most of her "Plank Owners." What she'll do next is anybody's guess, but whatever the assignment, we know she'll do it smoothly and efficiently because that's the kind of ship she is. For those of us who are leaving maybe the nicest thing we can say of her is:

"She made us into sailors who now know,
how and why a sailor loves his ship."

To all our shipmates – Happy Landings and it's been damn nice knowing you!"

THE END

★ <u>Transport to Tokyo: The Story of A Ship That Didn't Get There</u> ★
<u>A War History of the USS Leon (APA 48)</u>

Lt. A. A. Smyser, U.S.N.R.
1 October 1945

8

HOMEWARD BOUND

US Army Chief of Staff, General Gorge Marshall understood as early as 1943 the importance of the rapid return of American service personnel at war's end. Planning responsibility for this operation was eventually delegated to the War Services Administration. That organization developed the point system for establishing eligibility and priority among 8 million overseas personnel and began preparing for their repatriation from 55 theaters of war. The Operation was named Magic Carpet.

The first task force dedicated to Operation Magic Carpet in the Pacific departed Tokyo Bay in September 1945. TF 11 included the battleships USS *New Mexico*, USS *Idaho*, USS *Mississippi*, and USS *North Carolina* plus two carriers and a destroyer squadron. Those ships loaded up with servicemen heading home, and then they stopped at Okinawa and picked up some more. Eventually the Magic Carpet fleet would number 369 ships, including 222 attack transports.

As the *Leon* set course again for the east, carrying Marines from the 2nd and 6th Divisions, one fear remained on everyone's mind, crew and troops alike—mines. The captain's Night Order Book, which contained notes and reminders from the captain to night watch personnel, unfailingly cited the danger of floating mines. No one wanted to consider the possibility of surviving the war and then striking a mine and sinking with war weary troops from the 2nd and 5th Marine Divisions aboard.

New York, NY   *December 25, 1945*

Dear Margaret,

Many thanks for sending Joe's letter on to me and I can
understand very clearly how you came to think it was yours. The
address was certainly a queer combination of mine and yours. Joe
must have been miles away in thought when he wrote that envelope.
Nevertheless the error was his, not yours and anyway it didn't
make any difference to me that you may have read it, so enough
said on the subject.

It took me a couple of days more than was necessary to get the
telegram straightened and mainly because I've been so busy
with last minute things, but I finally did get around to it. I
haven't heard anymore from Joe as yet so there's nothing new on
him.

We had a nice Christmas here. The children enjoyed it especially.
Jeff was all eyes when he saw the tree - it's a huge one - floor
to ceiling and I guess he thought he'd never seen anything quite
as big and awesome. We were going to go to Midnight Mass but
changed our minds because we all got so sleepy. Father Kenealy
(the priest who introduced Joe and I and married us) stopped
in about 8:30 Christmas Eve and helped us trim the tree. It
was grand to have him - he perks Rosemary and I up just when
our spirits start to droop. He usually stops up to visit us on
Sunday evening - he lives near here in the neighborhood so he
comes in after he's been home. He's been a wonderful source of
encouragement to me and I certainly will feel quite lost after Joe
and I move out to Illinois.

I hope you feel much stronger now - anything like the flu is
very weakening and what you had was more severe.

I hope you enjoy the holidays - don't overdo anything till you
feel better.

Love and best wishes, Kathleen

P.S. I will send Jeff's picture later on - I still haven't had it
reprinted yet. Will get to it shortly.

December 1945 was an eventful month for Joe McDevitt. So many important events occurred that researching and ordering them chronologically was difficult. On December 20, Captain Southworth offered him the position of executive officer (XO) of the *Leon*, effective upon the departure of Lieutenant Commander Reitze who had received orders. As was customary for that position, Joe also received a spot promotion to lieutenant commander.

On January 2, 1946, Joe received another physical examination, compliments of the Navy. Two physicians aboard the *Leon* concluded that he was:

> "found physically qualified for temporary promotion to
> Lt. Cmdr. USNR., and to perform all the duties of his
> rank at sea or on foreign nations."

On January 31, 1946, Commodore J. K. Davis, commander of Transport Division 59, submitted a special letter fitness report to the Chief of Naval Personnel to clarify the record on Joe's duties and performance during the hectic period 25 October, 1945–31 December, 1945.

0036

FB7-59/ P20-2(1)
Serial 486
J.D/ces

Office of the Commander
TRANSPORT DIVISION FIFTY-NINE
Amphibious Forces, Pacific
Fleet Post Office, San Francisco, Calif.

U.S.S. LEON (APA 48)
Flagship
31 December 1945

From: Commander Transport Division FIFTY-NINE.
To: Chief of Naval Personnel.

Subject: Lieut. Joseph B. McDEVITT, (D), 226094, USNR -
          Special Letter Fitness Report - submission of.

Reference: (a) BuPers C/L No. 3-44, paragraph 16.
           (b) CominCh Conf Ltr ser 0599 of 3 March 1945.

1.   In accordance with the directives contained in reference (a)
and (b), the following special letter report on the performance of duty
of the subject officer is submitted in order that his record be complete.

2.   The period covered by this report is from 25 October 1945 to
31 December 1945, and the assignment of this officer was Division Control
Officer.

3.   An OUTSTANDING officer. During the period covered TransDiv FIFTY-
NINE has twice lifted, transported and landed divisions of the Chinese National
Army. As Division Control Officer, he was confronted with new and difficult
problems, all of which were effectively met.

4.   Lieutenant McDEVITT is considered OUTSTANDING material for a
permanent commission in the Regular Navy and is recommended for promotion.

James K. Davis
JAMES K. DAVIS

CC:
     CO, USS LEON
     Lieut. McDEVITT

Special Letter Fitness Report, Lieut. Joseph B. MCDEVITT

At the time he wrote this letter, Commodore Davis was obviously unaware that Joe McDevitt had already been promoted from lieutenant to lieutenant commander. Nevertheless, two commanding officers of the USS *Leon* and a transport division commander had now recommended Joe for a permanent commission in the regular Navy. This was especially high praise for a reservist, confirming that he's good enough to be *one of us!*

But Joe was absolutely NOT interested in further sea duty in the Navy. He wanted to rejoin his family and to resume his life's avocation which was the law. He and Kathleen had clearly mapped out their future as he explained in his next letter to Aunt Margaret.

USS Leon, c/o FPO, San Francisco, CA   *January 3, 1946*

Dear Aunt Margaret,

I have delayed writing for a few days for several reasons. In the first place I've been trying to get a call through three nights in a row and have not succeeded. And in the second place I just haven't had time to write. I happened by the Western Union Office here on the Naval Base yesterday and sent you the night letter to let you know that I had arrived on the West Coast.

I have been ashore only one night since we arrived and it took the entire time to wait for a call to Kay to get through. But I did get to talk to her. I had some disappointing news for her and it wasn't the most pleasant kind of phone call to make.

On the way back from Japan the Captain asked me to remain aboard this ship for another six months in the capacity of Executive Officer (second in command) since he did not have another officer as yet qualified for the job. I told him that if he would promote me to Lieutenant Commander I would take over - and that is exactly what he did. I made Lieutenant Commander on December 20th having been a Lieutenant for only a month and a half. It means a big increase in pay which is what I was primarily interested in.

Kay and I discussed the advisability of my remaining in the Navy for an additional period in order to give us opportunity to save a little more money before starting out in civilian life. We did not contemplate my becoming a Lt. Commander, but we did expect that I would be transferred to the East Coast for shore duty since I already have more months continuous sea duty than most officers of my class. However, in order to make the promotion I had to agree to remain on Pacific duty, and that is what I had to tell Kay on the phone. Needless to say she was quite disturbed especially since I am not receiving any leave. I had to take over immediately and it is keeping me too busy to even take in a movie.

However, the six months started on December 6th and will expire next June 6th - and you can bet your bottom dollar that I will be home just as soon thereafter as possible. It leaves only five months to go and we will be much more secure insofar as a bank account goes. I will be making almost $100 more per month.

The other day I received a letter from Kay which was written soon after I wrote her and told her to send you some money. It was written the day she sent the money and called you at Benton. You can't imagine what a relief it was to find that you had not left Harrisburg as yet, but I was sorry to hear that you had the flu. Here's hoping everything is healthy with you at this time. I will be trying to call again tomorrow night and I hope to get off long enough this time to get a hotel room, place the call, and wait for it to come through. There is something like a fifteen hour delay in getting through so one must have a place to sleep in the meantime.

If it appears that I will be able to get off long enough tomorrow night, I will send you a telegram in the morning and let you know that I will be calling in order that you will be near the phone. I want to find out just what the situation is with regard

to the home in Harrisburg and what all your problems are today.
If there is anything which I can do - it will be done.

You must understand that I am not ungrateful for everything which
you have done for me all these long years, Aunt Margaret. I
realize that I have not been sending you any financial help, but
it's not entirely due to forgetfulness. You see, as I have said
before, I thought that you were working. In addition, I have been
far away out here - letters never came from you although I wrote
you several - and when yours finally did arrive it was about four
months late. Kay and I have been striving to save every penny
possible because we were set back a long way with Jeff's arrival
and with her visit to the West Coast, and I was expecting to
be leaving the Navy very soon.   However, she understands the
situation perfectly and stated in her letter that we would take
care of everything which needed care. So you can count on us.
After I call you tomorrow I shall write Kay and tell her what I
think.

This added six months is not going to do me any good because I
am so sick and tired of this kind of life that I'm about to go
nutty. And each and every one of Kay's letters indicates that
she is almost at the end of her self-reserve. We were engaged
for six months and lived as man and wife for a paltry two
months which is no way for married persons to spend their life
- especially when there is a child in the family. But I thought
and worried about the decision for many sleepless nights before I
decided and it was solely because of the added financial security
which made me accept. Believe me - I have no inherent love for
the Navy or for the "sea". I would rather spend the rest of
my life flunking bar examinations (certainly not an enjoyable
occupation) than be forced to continue this present life.

We will be here in San Diego until 0800, January 10th, at which
time we sail for Okinawa - 5500 miles away. But we definitely
know that once we arrive there we will pick up a load of troops
and return them to some West Coast port. So I'm hoping to be
back in the USA by the last week in February and that we will
sail around to the East Coast at that time for repairs.

Tell Aunt Esther I received her very lovely Christmas card and that I really enjoyed hearing from her. No doubt the kids have grown to unbelievable proportions - I can't imagine what they must look like now. It surprised me to hear from Aunt Martha that her two girls are married. You can imagine what thoughts continually run through my mind with respect to Jeffrey. He's walking and talking and I haven't even seen him as yet! Luckily for me I'm kept too busy to mope about it extensively.

My present intentions are as follows: Leave the Navy on June 6th (assuming that we will be in the USA at that time; if not, I'll leave just as soon thereafter as we arrive in the USA), go directly to New York City (I'm changing my address in the Navy records to NYC in order that I may be separated there and therefore be sent directly there from the ship) and spend a week with Kay's folks, pack up our belongings and come to Harrisburg. While in Harrisburg I will make arrangements to return to Champaign for a short review course preparatory to taking the September 1946 Bar Examination, and we will move to Champaign for that purpose probably about the first of July in order to give me two months solid review.

Along that line, Aunt Margaret, I wish you would box up all of my Law School notebooks - the red ones - and any other papers which may be stored with them and send them to me just as soon as possible. In that way I will have three or four months opportunity to review here on the ship. When we are at sea there is plenty of spare time. I wish that I had written for them sooner although it probably would not have been advantageous since the ship has been too busy during the war. Just send them to me at the address on this envelope as soon as you can.

Papa has stated that he will come to Harrisburg when Kay and I go there. But I am wondering. He has been complaining more than usual lately and he is getting well up in years. Actually I can't remember exactly just how old he is but I know it's 70 or close to it. I just can't picture him being that old, dear Papa. A man that age can't stand up for hours on a train. Kay wrote me the same idea. So I intend to try to make arrangements to go

down there. Now that Jeff is in the family we really need a car
of our own - even if it's a Model "T". Dad wrote me a letter
early in December which was only one page long (unusual for him)
in which he merely stated that he wanted to talk to me personally
since he was intending to make a move which would be for my
future good as well as his. He didn't say what he had in mind
and the only thing I can think of is that he may intend to sell
the house and move to an Old Folks home. But that doesn't make
sense - confound it I wish that he had said just a few words.
I've been trying to call him but can't get through. I've been
doing a lot of thinking about Dad lately also. He's too old to
be living alone and he leads a very unhappy life. He wants to
be near Ed and has never been able to. I'd like to have him
sell the house and pick up his gear and come to Illinois to live,
but I'll have to talk it over with Kay first. It would be so nice
to get our whole family together for a change wouldn't it, Aunt
Margaret.

My eyes are falling shut so I'll close for this time. I think
I've said everything in my mind at present, and we'll talk
everything over on the phone tomorrow night. Dr. Klein will be
hearing from me this month. I'll write again before I shove off.
Do get well, Aunt Margaret. Say hello to Aunt Esther and Uncle
Mike for me. I'm looking forward to June with the greatest of
impatience.

Love,
Joe

USS Leon, c/o /FPO, San Francisco, CA   *January 11, 1946*

Dear Aunt Margaret,

This will be a "shortie" since I have only a few minutes to get
it off the ship and mailed before we shove off. You have probably
already received my telegram (if my friend has sent it as he
said he would) telling you that we are on our way to the Panama
Canal. We leave at 1400 this afternoon and will arrive on about
the 19th of January. We will spend three or four days there
and then proceed to the vicinity of New Orleans. We have been
ordered to report to the Commander of the Eighth Naval District
which is at New Orleans, but may be assigned to any port on the
Gulf of Mexico. This ship was built at Pascagoula, Mississippi,
and it may be that we are being sent there to be repaired and
overhauled. We may also be sent there to be decommissioned
that is, taken out of the Navy and turned over to the Maritime
Commission.

In either event it means at least a month and probably more than
that. As far as we know, transportation north from New Orleans
(or vicinity) is not half as difficult as to or from the West
Coast. And it's comparatively a short trip home from down there.
So I'll be doing my best for a leave while we're there. It also
means that I'll be able to see Dad - I'm worried about him.

I've wired and written Kay and I know that she will be mighty
pleased with this news. She was heartbroken with the thought of
my returning to Okinawa. I have ideas that she will be down
in the sunny south with me as soon as I find out just what the
situation is down there.

So I'll close now and get this off. Just wanted to enlarge on
that telegram. You can understand that much is still left to
the imagination. We know for certain that Panama is next and
that being assigned to the Eighth Naval District means somewhere
on the Gulf of Mexico. At least it means the USA - and a little
nearer home than we are out here. Let's hope for the best. If
you haven't shipped my books as yet don't do so although it's

OK if you have. My present address will continue to reach me
although it will change once we go through the Canal. I'll
keep you informed and you can expect to receive a wire or call
long about the last of this month. The trip will require at
least sixteen days including stopovers.

Love to all,
Joe

The *Leon* departed San Diego on January 11 bound for the Canal Zone. She steamed in formation with her sister ship, USS *Sheridan* APA 51, with whom she had served in amphibious assaults at Saipan, Leyte, Luzon, and Okinawa.

The *Sheridan's* deck log records that *Leon* and *Sheridan* executed their final joint maneuver together beginning at 0947 on January 15, 1946, en route to Balboa, Canal Zone.

Read this entry carefully or you'll miss it. The war was over. Showtime!

Deck Log Remarks Sheet   USS Sheridan (APA 51)   15 Jan. 1946

04 - 08

Steaming independently in accordance with Com. 11. NAVAL DIST. Routing
Instruction en route BALBOA, CANAL ZONE on base course 117 True, 117
pgc. At 14.5 knots (full speed), 80 rpm's.

08 - 12

Steaming as before. 0800 Crew mustered on station. No absentees. 0800
Received daily magazine temp report. Conditions normal. 0947 Changed
speed to ahead two-thirds. 0954 Engines stopped. 1000 Lying to. Boat
lowered to exchange movies with USS LEON (APA 48). 1014 Rolling
engines ahead 5 rpm's. 1031 Hoisted boat aboard. 1032 Changed speed
to ahead full, 14.5 knots, 80 rpm's. Changed course to 166 True, 116
pgc.

DW Riley
Ensign USNR

On February 1, 1946, the *Leon* entered the welcome waters of Mobile Bay, Alabama.

New York, NY   *February 18, 1946*

My Dear Aunt Margaret,

My sister was just up to the hospital this evening and told me
you called - so sweet of you. I am feeling so much better now
than a few days ago - every day helps that much more. Was so
heartbroken when I had to cancel my plans to go down with the
baby to see Joe in Mobile. The luck of the Irish seemed to run
out on this occasion. I guess I'll get out of here the end of
next week, but won't be able to travel for about two weeks after
that. Don't know how I'll have the patience to wait all that
time - seems so long, after we've waited so long already!

Oh, I miss Jeffrey so terribly. My sister brought him outside the hospital today and I looked out at him running around - so cute now. He looks like he's grown even in these few days.

Joe will stay down there now until he gets out of the Navy in June. I was so glad to know he wouldn't be going to sea again. It's a good location as it's near Little Rock, and you in Benton, and as soon as I get down there we'll see if Joe can't get a leave so that we can visit you. How I dread this delay - such a waste of time to be lying here. I do hope you'll be feeling better, honey. Take it easy all you can. I'll let you know when I get out of the hospital and what my plans are after that. Best regards to Esther, Mike and all the kids and very fondest love to you.

Kathleen

At an unknown date in February or early March 1946, Captain H. B. Southworth, USN, was detached from duty as commanding officer of USS *Leon* and ordered to the EIGHTH Naval District in New Orleans. Lieutenant Commander McDevitt became the commanding officer of the *Leon*. His first command! We don't know whether Captain Southworth's departure preceded or followed the *Leon's* final cruise from Mobile to Chickasaw, Alabama, but wouldn't it be nice to imagine that Joe enjoyed even a short cruise as the *Leon's* commanding officer?

One of Captain Southworth's final duties prior to his departure was fitness reports, September 1, 1945 through March 7, 1946. He noted:

"Lt. Cmdr. McDevitt is outstanding among Reserve Officers. He has the ability to grasp essentials, organize, delegate, and lead. He is loyal, courteous, and possesses high moral courage. His military character is well developed. He was given a spot promotion to his

present rank to perform the duties of Executive Officer.
He is recommended for a regular commission in the
Navy. He has seen this report."

Joe's last official act aboard the *Leon* was to decommission the ship on March 7, 1946. The picture below shows Joe—resplendent in dress whites—receiving the decommissioning party aboard ship.

Lt. Commander Joseph B. McDevitt
receives Decommissioning Party, March 7, 1946

For a contented crew, a ship decommissioning is a sad event. For the few remaining "Plank Owners" still aboard, the *Leon* had been their home for nearly two years. She was the Lucky Lady who had delivered them safely from the Japanese Imperial Navy, from coral reefs, and from Pacific typhoons.

Many years later, CM2c William Janega, who was present the day she was decommissioned, recalled clearly the feelings of those original crew members as they walked down the *Leon's* ramp for the last time. "The Plank Owners, the men who had been aboard since her commissioning, those men were crying like babies as they left the ship that day."

The *Leon* was transferred to the war shipping administration on April 2, 1946. Like so many other ships that survived war duty, she was eventually put up for sale. The Isthmian Steamship Company purchased her in 1947 and renamed her *Steel Chemist*. After plying the high seas for fully twenty-four more years, the vessel was scrapped without military honors or recognition in 1971.

The Lucky Leon

But the *Leon's* crew never forgot their ship or their service together. They shared war stories and tears at reunions many years later. Joe McDevitt proudly displayed a framed picture of the *Leon* for the rest of his career. And in their hearts and minds, her few surviving sailors still have hallowed memories of their ship:

"What helmeted, life-jacketed ghosts roamed your silent rusting decks and passageways in those last inglorious days afloat? In Naval history yours was a small role and your deeds went mostly unsung. Those who trod your decks often cursed and reviled you. But now, at last, the few of us still left will remember you and honor you as long as we live, and be proud we trod those decks. Perhaps after all, in the deep shadows of your humble history, a tiny flame of heroism flickers. Perhaps a small gleam of glory shines through your rust."[14]

14 Adapted from George S. Gibb. A Battle History. Retrieved from www.oocities.org/uss_sumter/georgegibb.html

9

AT LAST – THE LAW

We don't know how he managed this, but Joe McDevitt was reassigned to the district legal office in the Navy's EIGHTH Naval District, New Orleans, LA. He reported for duty on March 9, 1946. The district legal officer immediately appointed him to the general courts martial review section with responsibility for reviewing general court martial records.

New Orleans, LA   *March 13, 1946*

Dear Aunt Margaret,

The past three weeks have been the most hectic in my life. Kay told me that you called her and she told me to write. But I have not had time to write - even to write her, and for over two weeks I just didn't feel like writing anyone. I was confined to my room with a throat infection. She doesn't know about it - I didn't tell her because as you know she's been in the hospital herself.

I came to New Orleans last Friday completely worn out and slept for two days. On Monday I went to work again. I am now in the Legal Office of the 8th Naval District here in New Orleans.

Since my promotion was to be effective only so long as I served on the USS Leon, I will be a Lieutenant again tomorrow. It means a reduction of $120 per month in my pay which leaves me feeling pretty low. I could resign from the Navy today as a result of losing the promotion but I feel that I can't afford it with hospital bills and the cost of living such as it is now. And I couldn't go back to school at this time of year.

By Friday I will send you a money order. This pay day will be the first time I've received more than $30 myself. The money has always gone to Kay, but I canceled the allotment this month since I expect her down here before the month is over. We are really maintaining two homes now since my rent and food are now coming completely out of my own pocket.

I will be so glad when she arrives since we can then sit down together and formulate some plans as well as balance the budget. Frankly I am very worried about the future especially since I'll have to go back to school which will be very expensive. Though I dislike the Navy very much I'm sorely tempted to remain a while longer until we can get solidly on our feet and have such items as Dr. Klein taken care of. I wrote him and told him I'd be home in January and would pay him then. That was before I signed over for six months. Please tell him that I will send the money by the end of this month. I must get these things cleared up. Now that Kay will be joining me finally we can take care of them - even if we end up like the proverbial church mouse.

I can't go on tonight. I'm rambling all over the paper. I'll finish tomorrow. I really should have taken some leave and rested up. But every day of leave I take now means a loss of $10 per day later. I'm thinking too much in terms of pennies to use up

any of my leave now regardless of the situation. Good night, dear
Aunt Margaret.

March 14 - 8:30 p.m.

Well, as usual, I'm pretty tired after a long day. But I enjoy
the work since it deals with law and legal matters. There was
some talk of sending me to Washington to learn Admiralty Law - a
branch of Naval Law. I can't understand why that should happen
since I'm due out of the Navy in June.

Aunt Margaret, from Mobile I sent two boxes to you by Railway
Express. One contained two cases of pineapple juice which have
traveled all over the world with me - I've never had a chance to
mail them. The long box contains a souvenir Japanese rifle which
I may give to one of my friends someday. I had very little time
for packing or else I would have sent more things home which I
will not need here. There are three big boxes coming to New
Orleans which contain many items which will be of no use. But
when I left Mobile I didn't know where I would end up so I could
take no chances. Probably sometime soon I shall ship another box
or two home. Railway Express is very expensive. It would be much
better if I had an automobile to load all my junk into, but that
is out of the question with cars as expensive as they are today.

I haven't heard from Kay now for over a week due to my change
of address. I hope she is okay and that no infection has set in.
An operation for a pilonidal cyst (?) must be a very painful one,
is that true? Kay never complains.

I'm enclosing $20 since I want to mail this letter before Friday
which is payday. I've been so long in writing as it is that I
can't delay any longer.

Now Aunt Margaret I know that you want to talk to me and that
you desire me to take some leave and come home. But you can
understand why I don't do so since I told you how much money
I would lose in doing so. So won't you please write me just a
one page letter and tell me exactly what the situation is with

you at home. I write very seldom but you know that I am a very tardy correspondent. And I am working hard which wears me out at night - the only time I have to write. I want you to know that I am ready to do anything in the world for you - everything I have is yours. And Kay feels the same way. I can show you her letters to prove it. Write just a page - no need for your usual long letter since I know it's almost impossible for you to write. For the first time during the war I'm beginning to be in a position to help you out and I intend to do so. Whether it was wise or not, I did marry Kay and we did have a child and I'm now the happiest man in this world because I did so. I have a perfect wife and a handsome son (I think so from his pictures anyway - and Kay says so. He has a big head just like me!) and she is now and will be in the future a person who keeps me on the right path. I will say that I am a much better man as a result of her influence. And she loves you, Aunt Margaret, even though you and she have never seen each other. You will adore her and I know of course that she will fall for you hook, line and sinker.

So, again, write me a line. You are as much a part of my future plans as is my family - so I must plan the budget accordingly. Telephoning is too expensive and we can't get everything said.

Though I don't write often, I'm always thinking of and praying for you.

Love,
Joe

Personal Diary of Rose Vaughan   _March 1946_

Joe returns again (war ends) and Kay joins him at New Orleans with Jeff. Joe sees his lovely boy for the first time. Oh yes – he thinks Jeff's OK!

New Orleans, LA   _April 13, 1946_

Dear Aunt Margaret,

Just a few lines this Saturday morning. I am at the office which is not the usual thing on Saturday mornings, but there was some unfinished business to clear up and besides it gives me an opportunity to write you (which is rather difficult at home with Jeff nosing around) and furthermore to use a typewriter and send you something that you can read for a change.

I received all the letters which you have written me - some of them were delayed quite a bit due to my moving around. And I didn't mind the one which you warned me about the least bit. You had a right to be a little peeved at me.

Well, Jeff is just about the nicest little youngster I've ever come across. He had been quite ill prior to coming down to New Orleans, in fact Kay took him out of the hospital only an hour before their plane took off. Consequently, and as a result of the trip, he was in bad humor for a couple of days. I had begun to wonder whether he would ever "make up" with me - and it did seem that he must be a spoiled young'un. But I should have realized that such a sudden change from winter to summer, plus his illness would serve to make him cranky. About the third day he began to snap out of it and now he is really his Daddy's little boy. He's going to be a mighty fine one and Kay has certainly done a good job raising him thus far.

Kay is in fine spirits also. She is well satisfied with the little apartment which we have. It is completely furnished even down to bed linens and towels, and all utilities paid. It cost only $1 a day, or $30 per month. As you might guess, there is only one place in this country where one can live at that price - it is managed by the Navy and is for Navy families. We will be able to remain there for the sixty days that we will be in New Orleans. Jeff had more space than he ever dreamed existed to romp and play around in and this hot sun is making him look like an Indian already.

I received a wire from Ed yesterday stating that he is now in Little Rock. We will call him up tonight. I was hoping that you would be able to make the trip down with him, but on second thought there really wasn't much point in it since I won't be in Little Rock. Perhaps Ed and Dad will be able to drive down here for a couple of days - they would enjoy the trip and this city immensely.

About Mr. Combs. I have written a letter to him but haven't mailed it as yet since his address is at home. Will mail it tonight. I do wish I knew more about the situation before I write. I think I shall wait until I talk to Ed on the phone before mailing the letter. He may have heard something about it in Benton. I remember Aunt Esther saying that there was a position open and that Uncle Mike was trying to hold it open for me. It probably is the same one.

When I get out in June, things will be moving fast since I will have to head for Champaign immediately to prepare for the September Bar Examination. While I'd like to take a little time off it just can't be done by a man who has my responsibility.

By the way, I have been offered the opportunity of remaining in the Legal Branch of the Navy at a salary of approximately $700 per month. That, dear Auntie, is rather hard to turn down, and Kay is of the same opinion. It will be a long time before I am making that much every month practicing law. Of course, it would be Navy the rest of my life, at least until I retired in 16 years. I'm considering it, but as you can see from the fact that I'm also writing Mr. Combs, I'm also considering leaving the Navy in June. Before we make any decision along that line I shall talk it over with you. Security is an awfully important item and that's what the Navy would offer more than anything else.

Well, I must close now. Will write shortly after the first of the month. Will also have Dr. Klein paid in full by that time. Write when you find time.

By the way, Aunt Margaret, don't say anything to anyone about the things which I send home. Some of them came from the Navy and people might talk. These tools, for example. While I acquired them in a perfectly honest manner, many men in the Navy are picking them up illegally and the Government is hot on their trail. Mine were given me by the Supply Officer, but everyone doesn't know that so let's just say nothing.

Love,
Joe, Kay and Jeff

New Orleans, LA   *April 21, 1946*

Dear Aunt Margaret,

Happy Easter Sunday, Aunt Margaret! The McDevitt family has certainly had a full day, but now that we've finished the supper dishes and Jeff is tucked away soundly asleep I'll spend this time before retiring to send you the latest news from New Orleans.

We've been having the most wonderful time - living for the first time as a real family. Kay is just as happy as can be and is completely pleased with our apartment. Jeff needed a few days to become accustomed to the change in scenery and he didn't come to me for quite a few days. Of course he wasn't feeling up to par and that had something to do with it. But he's right up there with his dad now and I'm sure mighty proud of him. You'll really fall in love with him, Aunt Margaret.

Yesterday afternoon we took him to the Easter Egg hunt over on the Naval base. He was too young to understand just what was going on but he found nine Easter eggs all of which he smashed up very completely. He stuffed himself with ice cream, cookies and candy - I guess it doesn't do any harm once in a while.

I called Ed when he was in Little Rock. No doubt he has been over to see you by this time and has told you what I talked to him about. I mentioned to him the aspects of the future which exist at present and I told him that nothing has been decided as yet.

I have a chance to stay in the Navy as a Legal Specialist which means that I'd have purely legal work and none of the type of duty which I've had in the past. There are many things to be said in favor and others against. As you know, I have to go back to school and review for the bar examination before I can practice. I'm writing Chas. Combs as you suggested and what I decide will hinge in part on what he says. The Navy does offer security and I'd start out at approximately $500 per month which is hard to turn down. And, furthermore, in 15 years I could retire at about $300 per month at least and I'd still be a young man ready to practice law or go into business. I have liked the Navy the whole time - you know that - and I'd like being in the Navy and Kay feels the same way as I do. We both realize that there are disadvantages that for example we couldn't build a home for the next fifteen years and that we would move around quite a bit. But even so we're both young and would enjoy the adventure.

Now today we sat down and read your letters over again. I can see where this news I'm sending you can be disappointing at first but don't worry, Aunt Margaret, we won't be making a decision until after we come up in June. I intend to go ahead and review and pass the Bar Exam regardless of what happens in order that I will be eligible to go into practice whenever I decide to do so. Now if I should stay in we have said that you are to join us wherever we are - you'd have just as much fun as we would. And I'd send you money each month - which I probably couldn't do in practice for quite a while.

I'm not going further into it by letter. I probably won't do anything about it anyway - and certainly won't until I see you and talk to you.

Kay wanted to add a few lines tonight but she has fallen asleep - she was dead tired. Jeff really keeps her busy.

Cousin Ray said he could get me a new Ford. But we have decided not to buy a car - I know you'll be pleased to hear that. Frankly, the hospital bills have made it impossible anyway. But - we didn't decide this without disappointment because believe you me, it's sure difficult getting around with Jeff on public conveyances. He's now at an age when he gets into everything in sight.

Well, I'm falling asleep myself, Auntie. Must close and get some sleep. I'll be writing soon. Hope the enclosed M.O. fits in somewhere. I'm trying to build up a little reserve for when we have to start traveling around in June. We'll take your suggestions as to how to kill all birds with a few stones. (Kay will write).

Love,
Joe and Kay

Documents obtained from Joe McDevitt's personnel file confirm that he applied on May 24, 1946, for a transfer to the regular Navy as a commissioned officer, legal specialist. This application actually consisted of two separate requests: a transfer to the regular Navy and an appointment as a legal specialist. His application enumerated an impressive set of accomplishments since joining the USNR on December 7, 1942.

1. **Postings Assigned and Duties Performed:**

   - Midshipman's School, Columbia University
   - Training for amphibious warfare, Little Creek, VA
   - Assistant boat group commander, advanced amphibious warfare training, Ft. Pierce, FL
   - Boat group commander in charge of training amphibious boat groups, Little Creek, VA
   - Boat group commander in charge of advanced training of amphibious boat group, Ft. Pierce, FL
   - USS *Leon* APA 48 with duties as boat group commander, senior watch officer, legal assistance officer, and executive officer
   - District legal office, EIGHTH Naval District, New Orleans, LA

2. **Ranks Held:**

   - Lieutenant, USNR
   - Lieutenant Commander USNR (Spot Appointment)

3. **Campaign Ribbons Entitled to Wear:**

   - Purple Heart
   - American Theater
   - Asiatic-Pacific with Five Stars
   - World War II Victory
   - Philippine Liberation with Two Stars

4. **Academic Degrees Earned:**

- Bachelor of Arts, 1938-1940, University of Illinois
- Bachelor of Laws, 1940-1942, University of Illinois

5. **Report of Physical Examination:**

- A physical examination administered at the EIGHTH Naval District, district headquarters from three Navy physicians attesting, "We hereby certify that this candidate is physically qualified for transfer to the US Navy."
- A chest x-ray to confirm the absence of pulmonary or cardiac disease and to confirm the absence of parenchymal or pleural reaction to two shadows of metallic density observed over the chest shadow

New Orleans, LA   *May 25, 1946*

Dear Aunt Margaret,

I would have written sooner except for the fact that there was little to say prior to today. But today I have some news for you indeed and I certainly hope that you won't be disappointed.

As you know, Aunt Margaret, I have mentioned several times before that I had not definitely made up my mind as to just what my future plans should be; and I have also mentioned that I was somewhat skeptical about having to proceed immediately up to the University, without rest, proceed with my law review, take the bar, and then start out in practice. Such a future didn't seem at all bright. And I had good reasons to be uncertain and skeptical in view of the fact that I would be leaving a good-paying, interesting, and comparatively easy position in order to pursue that plan. Well, I have made up my mind, and Kay is in full agreement, that I am going to keep what I have at present and join the Navy as a Legal Specialist. And I'm sure that after I have pointed out the advantages of such a course in comparison with becoming a civilian lawyer, as well as the comparative disadvantages, you will agree with me.

First of all let me tell you that I made my application yesterday and it is entirely possible that I will be turned down by the Selection Board although my Commanding Officer assured me that he would give me the very highest recommendation possible and also stated that he was highly pleased with my decision since I was the type of individual the Navy, especially the Legal Corps, needs. They may decide that I am not qualified physically or that I have not had sufficient legal experience - that remains to be seen.

Also let me tell you that Kay, Jeff and I will be coming up on thirty days leave June sixth - providing the railroads are running again. It would be ideal if we had an automobile, or if you could drive down to pick us up, since we have so many things to transport that the Railway Express charges would more than cover the expenses. But it's too far to think of that and besides we can get on the Illinois Central right here and get off at Carbondale where you can meet us easily. Also in view of the fact that we will be coming back down here I think that I shall just place most of our belongings in storage instead of carting them back and forth.

I called Uncle Mike night before last because I wanted to talk to an Illinois lawyer and get his opinion on just how things are in the legal profession. As you know, I have no real contacts or assurances that I would go into practice even after the Bar Examination was passed. And furthermore I couldn't hope to equal the money I'm making now even in the next five or ten years. Let me tell you just what it amounts to.

In my present rank I make $430 per month which after the pay increase goes through will amount to $460 per month. In addition to that the medical and dental expenses for the family are free - I recently had my eyes diagnosed and obtained two

pairs of glasses, one for work and one for dress at a total cost
of $10 whereas the market value of the prescription and glasses
would be at least $50. We purchase all our food at the Navy
Commissary where there are no shortages and where prices are
very low. We buy all such things as toilet articles, cigarettes,
sheets, towels, pillow cases, blankets, hosiery, negligee's, jewelry,
pocketbooks - in other words practically everything we need, from
the Ship's Service Store at greatly reduced prices. We receive
an automatic $1500 exemption in figuring income tax. And in
addition to the above financial advantages, remember that I am a
Legal Specialist which is entirely different from what I served as
during the war. The Legal Corps is set up to run in six year
cycles: five years in the USA and one year at sea. And "at sea"
means aboard ship or on foreign station. There are very few legal
officers "at sea" - most of the legal billets are at foreign naval
bases or on the staffs of Naval Governors. And when I am sent
overseas, say to Hawaii, China, the Philippines, England, South
Africa, South America, etc., my family goes with me. Of course I
may be assigned to the staff of some Admiral afloat, in which
case Kay and Jeff couldn't go along. But even so, in peace time,
we would have a home port and would actually be at sea but a
short part of the year. Kay realizes that.

Anyway when I told Uncle Mike that I was making $430 per month
with an increase in sight, he told me that I would have to make
at least $700 per month at law in order to pay office and other
expenses and end up with what I am making. It would be a long
time before I could expect to make that much. But perhaps the
most important factor is that I like the Navy, and I like the
work I am doing. And Kay is well-pleased with the type of life
that we are leading now. It carries a lot of prestige, as a Naval
officer and his family are held in high regard. Also I have only
sixteen years until retirement if I choose to take it then. At
that time I can retire at one-half of my pay and allowances.
Assuming that I will be at least a Commander - it would amount
to over $300 per month, and if I should make Captain it would be
considerably higher. If I so choose at that time I can continue
on duty for another ten years and retire at three-fourths of my
pay - I would then be fifty-three years of age drawing between

four and five hundred dollars per month, retired. I'm convinced
that it's something to work for.

If I were on my feet financially at the present, perhaps I
wouldn't hesitate to accept my discharge from the Navy and go
into the practice of law. But I do not feel secure enough at
present to do so. The Navy offers security in the best possible
manner. Maybe after ten years at law in Illinois I might be
making $20,000 per year or more - which I won't be making in
the Navy. But I will be making all that's necessary to enable
me to give my wife, children, and you everything needed to live
a comfortable and pleasing life - and furthermore, it starts now
and not five years from now.

At any rate I've thought out every angle completely and have
decided that it's the thing to do. It's done now and I have
no regrets. But I wanted to tell you in detail just what the
decision was based upon. I've thought of the angle of Jeff's
schooling - that he will necessarily obtain his learning in an
assortment of schools. But I see nothing wrong with that: I
attended eight schools in eighteen years myself. And travel is
still one of the best teachers. I've never met children of a
Naval, Army, or Marine Corps Officer yet who weren't bright and
interesting and self-assured. I've already taken out a College
Education policy for him and as soon as he reaches five years
of age he will be guaranteed $50 per month for four years at
college, whether I continue to live or not.

Now all of my plans have included you. We will discuss
everything fully when in Harrisburg shortly. But at this
time I see no reason why you can't plan to come back to New
Orleans with us and make your home with us from now on. The
benefits would be mutual since I need an automobile. You see
I'm planning on attending Loyola University Law School at night
by way of review and then passing the bar just as soon as I'm
prepared. In that way I will be licensed to practice in case I
should decide to leave the Navy - or in case I should get a good
offer.

I have no money with me. Kay put me on a budget and it ran short. But I'll send some the first of the month. And I'll write soon and let you know the details of our arrival. If the railroad strike should continue, I'll probably be calling you long distance to see if you can make the trip down. I should stop by Little Rock on the way up because I told Dad I'd see him in June - and he's living for the day. Traveling by train will make it rather difficult. But don't plan anything unless I do call you.

Write soon. I'll be anxiously awaiting your opinion.

Love,
Kay, Jeff and Joe

Mrs. Rose Vaughan, New York, NY   *May 27, 1946*

My Dear Aunt Margaret,

For a long time I have been meaning to write you, and now that you are going to have my family with you, it's as good a time as any to start. I do hope you are feeling better as Kathleen told me you had not been so well. You may be looking forward to a lively time when the family arrives, as Jeffrey will make himself heard. He is very sweet - a 2nd Joe - and I know you will love him.

I truly miss him even tho Stephen is still here with me, and Stephen misses him too. They were really like brothers and when Kathleen sends snaps of him, Stephen immediately says I want Jeffrey to come home. I am sending Kathleen mail in care of you, as she has mentioned they expected to leave New Orleans soon. Please remember me to Mr. McDevitt and Ed. Best wishes from all the family with love.

Very sincerely,
Rose Vaughan

More work followed with courts martial review, and soon Joe was being trained for further duty as an admiralty lawyer. He had transitioned quickly from serving as executive officer of the *Leon* to the world of legal research and analysis. Both his work ethic and his legal research and analysis were favorably received at the district legal office. Early fitness reports confirmed that his casework was thoroughly researched, his legal reasoning was sound, and his conclusions were logical and proven to be correct. The district legal officer strongly supported Joe's application to the Navy as a legal specialist, observing that he would be a "credit to the naval service."

On June 3, 1946, the Commandant of the EIGHTH Naval District submitted to the Chief of Naval Personnel via the Local Review Board the following endorsement of Joe McDevitt's application to the regular Navy.

In reply address not the signer of this letter, Lt Commandant, Eighth Naval District, Federal Building, New Orleans, La.

HEADQUARTERS EIGHTH NAVAL DISTRICT

FEDERAL BUILDING

Refer to No.

NEW ORLEANS, LA.   JUN 3 1946

ND8/226094/(65)
JWV/lt
Serial No. PO-7- 24584

End-1   (Lt.Cdr. J. B. McDevitt's application for transfer to Regular
          Navy, dtd 24 May 1946)
To: The Chief of Naval Personnel.
Via: Local Reviewing Board, EIGHTH Naval District.

Subj: Lieutenant Commander Joseph Bryan McDEVITT, 226094, D, USNR –
          Application for transfer to Regular Navy as Commissioned
          Officer, Legal Specialist Officer.

1.   Forwarded.

2.   It is strongly recommended that the request of the subject officer
for transfer to the Regular Navy as a Legal Specialist Officer be approved.
Lieutenant Commander McDEVITT has been assigned to duties in the District
Legal Office, Eighth Naval District, since 8 March 1946 primarily involving
the review of general courts martial records. He has energetically and
studiously applied himself to these duties with the result that the number
of cases reviewed in the month of April 1946 totaled 85 as compared to 30
in March 1946. The backlog of cases for review has been reduced and records are now reviewed in from 7 to 10 days after receipt. He is methodical
in his work and his legal conclusions are logical and sound.

3.   Lieutenant Commander McDEVITT entered the naval service on 7 December
1942 and has had considerable active duty at sea including duty in the
Asiatic-Pacific Theater as a deck officer. He has high officer like
qualities and military character.

4.   On 20 December 1945, Lieutenant Commander McDEVITT was promoted to
Lieutenant Commander while serving at sea as Executive Officer of the USS
LEON (APA 48) under a spot appointment. It is strongly requested that he
be continued in that rank and inducted into the Regular Navy with the rank
of Lieutenant Commander.

5.   It is considered that Lieutenant Commander McDEVITT is an outstanding
officer and that he will be a credit to the naval service. He cannot be
recommended too highly.

By direction of the Commandant.

E. T. EVES
Captain, U. S. N.
Director of Distribution

CC: District Legal Office.

Endorsement – Lt. Cdr. J. B. McDevitt's application for transfer to Regular Navy, dtd. 24 May 1946

On June 10, the EIGHTH Naval District Review Board interviewed Joe McDevitt and forwarded its own unanimous endorsement of his application to the Chief of Naval Personnel.

As the Navy personnel process moved forward, Joe, Kathleen, and Jeff made their long awaited first visit to Harrisburg, Illinois, in mid-June 1946. All across the nation there were family reunions celebrating the return of veterans. In Harrisburg, we know that many Zimmers visited—from near and far—to greet Joe and his new family. Kathleen was not feeling especially well during their visit or afterwards upon their return to New Orleans. She must have suspected that she was pregnant with her second child—Paul Killian McDevitt.

Joe, Kathleen, and Jeff visit Harrisburg, June 1946

New Orleans, LA   *July 16, 1946*

Dear Margaret,

Many thanks for forwarding Mother's letters on to me, and a
sincere apology for not having been able to drop you a line
sooner than this as I had intended. To tell you the truth I
haven't been feeling very well and the weather here has been
extremely hot since we returned here, so I just had to wait a bit.

We've been here in the Quonset Hut for 2 weeks now and there
is nothing new on the house we had hoped to get. The present
tenant is willing to turn it over to us eventually, but his orders
still have not come thru, so there is nothing to do but sit by
and wait till they do. In the meantime I suppose we'll have to
find something else, as you know this is only temporary housing
that we are in now. Never a dull moment!

Joe is back to work again and I believe enjoying it after his
vacation. It really did him so much good to get away from the
same old routine for a whole month, and we ALL benefited from it
greatly and enjoyed ourselves immensely. It was a big help for me
not to have to do much puttering around the food preparing angle
- I believe my worst days are finally over and I'm settling down
to only a rare "bad day" now. I hope you have been taking it a
little easier since we've been gone, and that the thumb is doing
better these days. I know it involves a lot of extra work to have
guests - I shouldn't say guests really but just extra people
around the house, and I wanted you to know that we appreciated
all that you did to make our stay enjoyable. Did you get to St.
Louis the weekend following our departure?

Jeff has not been too well the last two days and ran 103 temp
on and off yesterday and last night. I finally got it down today
to normal but he has quite a few spots on his face tonight, and
I'm wondering if it could be measles. By tomorrow, I'll know as
he'll be in full bloom if he has them, and I'm rather uneasy
about him. I'll take him to the Dr. in any event but I'm
keeping my fingers crossed. I wish you were here as you could

probably tell right off what it was. I hope my fears are 100% wrong.

Will keep you posted on our activities Margaret. In the meantime take care of yourself and let us hear from you whenever writing is possible. I understand how it is though.

Much love, Kathleen

New Orleans, LA   *July 27, 1946*

Dear Aunt Margaret,

Well, I've finally found a little time to write. When we got back, I went to the office and found my desk piled high with back work and it's had me tied up ever since. We felt that we should write all those whom we had visited on leave and so we decided to divide up. Kay wanted to write you and did so I'm sure. I used one Saturday to write Ed and the Kleins. We still must write to the Evansville folks - we've been waiting until the pictures have been printed.

Well, as you know, we moved back into a Quonset hut when we returned, and I immediately began searching for a house or apartment. It was very discouraging because there were but few places which would allow children and they all rented as high as $105, $125, or $150 per month plus utilities. Any other places weren't fit to live in and didn't have good locations. But, last Wednesday I found just what we wanted in an apartment, five rooms, practically brand new and completely modern with tile bath, hardwood floors and all. The present tenant is leaving August 5th or before and we are buying his furniture for $275, a living room suite, two bedroom suites, and kitchen table with chairs all maple and practically new. It's easily worth $500 and would cost $700 if purchased today, so we're mighty happy about the whole deal. The apartment rents for $41 per month with water furnished. We pay for lights, gas and telephone. And the nicest thing is that it is located only two blocks from the Navy Commissary Store where we do all our shopping. Butter still sells for 51 cents per pound and milk for 14 cents per quart there, and those are just samples of how other items are priced.

We have a big front yard and back yard and we're just two blocks from the bus line which I take to go to work. We'll send you pictures of it.

I had intended sending you the rest of the money, but will have to wait for a while in view of the furniture.

Have you decided as yet what you're going to do with the house? If you should decide to sell it, Aunt Margaret, and go to a city to work where you won't need your car, be sure and let me know. I'll be willing to pay you as much as you could get from anyone else.

I may be inviting trouble, but I haven't contacted Railway Express as yet to tell them where to deliver the boxes you sent down. I've been waiting in order not to have to move them twice, but will call them today and give instructions. Our crates are here from New York too and the Navy is storing them for me until we move in next week.

Well, Aunt Margaret, don't be too long in writing us and let us know how you are and what is happening. Dad is fairly well and can see a little better but he no longer writes his letters. I'm going to write him now.

Love,
Joe, Kay and Jeffrey

Joe had warned Aunt Margaret of the possibility that his application might not be accepted by the Navy. That said, naval personnel office staff would study Joe's complete record since his commissioning as an ensign in the USNR. That record included strong and unanimous endorsements by all his previous and present commanding officers and by all Review Board members:

- Captain B. B. Adell, commanding officer, USS *Leon*
- Captain H. B. Southworth, commanding officer, USS *Leon*
- Commodore J. K. Davis, Commander, Transport Division Fifty-Nine, Amphibious Forces Pacific
- Captain Harry S. Butler, District Legal Officer, EIGHTH Naval District, New Orleans, LA
- Local Review Board, EIGHTH Naval District:
  - Captain Everett K. Patton, USN
  - Captain Andrew C. Shiver, USN
  - Captain John W. Marts, USN
  - Captain Martin A. Heffernan, USNR
  - Captain Jack H. Gilbert, USNR
- Rear Admiral A. S. Merrill, Commandant, EIGHTH Naval District

Could the Navy *possibly* not listen to its own?

Of course, the Navy could do whatever it chose, but ultimately they accepted the collective wisdom of these endorsements. In August 1946, the Chief of Naval Personnel informed Joe that he had been accepted into the Navy, though not at the rank of lieutenant commander which had been a spot appointment. On May 6, 1947, Joe accepted an appointment as lieutenant in the US Navy, stationed at the EIGHTH Naval District in New Orleans.

The appointment as a legal specialist took a bit more time. But on August 7, 1947, Joe accepted a new position as special duty only, LAW. This was his dream at last!

In short order, the Navy learned that it had hired a pretty darned good lawyer who would indeed be a credit to the Navy. Joe earned promotion to lieutenant commander in 1950 and to commander in 1951. He became a recognized Navy expert in international law and was promoted to captain and head of the International Law Division in 1958. He was an intellectual force behind the legal rationale for the quarantine of Cuba, and during the Vietnam War he served as the Navy's top attorney for the United States Pacific Command. Joe was proud to be instrumental in the creation of the Navy's

Judge Advocate General Corps and served four years as rear admiral and head of that corps. He was a successful lawyer who loved the Navy until the day he died, February 26, 2006.

Joe McDevitt also enjoyed a rich and productive personal life in addition to his professional success. He and Kathleen had ten children together, including eight boys and two girls, before Kathleen died unexpectedly in 1961. Fortunately for all the McDevitts, Kathleen's sister, Rosemary, stepped forward at a time of great need, moved into a crowded household with her daughter, and provided love and support for a large family of young McDevitts.

Four years later Joe met and married Catherine (Cathy) Beatty of Wilmington, Delaware, with whom he had one son. After retiring from the Navy Joe accepted a position as Executive Vice President, General Counsel, and Secretary of the Board of Trustees at Clemson University in Clemson, South Carolina. Cathy McDevitt died in Clemson in 1981.

Joe was fortunate in love again to meet a wonderful southern lady, Mitzi Moody, from Charleston, South Carolina. They were married in 1982 and lived together for 24 years in Charleston, where they held memorable reunions at the Stiles Point Plantation house for the McDevitt and Moody families. Joe and Mitzi also attended five reunions of the crew of the USS *Leon*, including one that they hosted in 1985.

Mitzi McDevitt, loved and treasured by all the McDevitts, resides in Charleston, South Carolina.

Rear Admiral Joseph B. McDevitt,
Judge Advocate General of the Navy, 1968–1972

AUTHOR'S NOTE

Many people helped with the research for this book. Some of you are librarians, including genealogy specialists and reference librarians, at libraries across the country. Others include archival specialists at the National Archives or at the three archival units at the University of Illinois. Staff at the University of Illinois School of Law and the National Personnel Records Center at St. Louis, MO, have also assisted. All of you are indispensable for those of us who research. Thank you.

I am especially indebted to three individuals who are particularly knowledgeable about the naval amphibious forces in World War II and who helped me throughout this project. All three of them have built and maintained web sites devoted to sustaining the memories and accomplishments of those forces. They are: John Clingman, web master for the USS *Sheridan* APA 51 site (www.ussheridanapa51.com); Randy Trahan, web master for the USS *Ormsby* APA 49 site (www.ussormsby.com); and Russ Padden, web master for the Amphibious Ships (Gators) site (www.rpadden.com/gator.htm). Russ's site is a clearing house of sorts for links to many APA sites. These three fellows helped answer numerous questions, provided leads, and contributed some of the documents and pictures in this book. John, Randy, Russ, thank you for sharing generously with a newcomer.

Thank you, Marilyn Seidel. Many years ago you and Sam hosted the first of several reunions of former USS *Leon* shipmates. Later, after Sam passed on to a higher post, you kindly shared all your reunion materials with me and helped move this project along. I discovered the very important document cited below in your basement!

Lieutenant Adam A. Smyser, USS *Leon* 1St Division and watch officer, wrote and edited arguably the most important document ever produced about the *Leon*: <u>A War History of the USS *LEON* (APA 48)</u>. This war history provides a detailed, first-hand chronology of the *Leon* from her commissioning in February 1944 to October 1945, when Lieutenant Smyser apparently accumulated enough points to ship home. His story is a singular contribution to naval history.

Thank you, Bill Janega. Thank you for everything… especially for your service those many years ago and for your warm support and encouragement for the last four years. You're the best, my friend.

Rich Carnahan, my Creative Coordinator at Publish Pros, has been a welcome partner in this project for the past year. His enthusiasm helped me struggle through the rough patches that occasionally arise when researching and writing non-fiction. More importantly, his superb creative design contributions are evident to all. Thanks, Rich. You're a great partner!

The letters that my Dad wrote during those six years of his life provided the inspiration for this book and the continuity for his story. We have reproduced his letters exactly as hand-written, except for minor punctuation changes.

You were a faithful correspondent who moved me to action, Dad. I hope you're happy with your story. It's the best I could do.

Finally, I want to thank my family and friends, especially my son, my daughter, and my wife—Bryan, Kimberly Ehlert, and Barb—and Rear Admiral Dusty Miller. They all encouraged me to *stick to the story and finish it*. Barb also scoured the Internet, typed, proofread, and never complained when I disappeared down the basement stairs for hours at a time, day or night, year in and year out. And Mitzi McDevitt and Betty McDevitt provided *first hand* confirmation for many of the events in this story.

Barb, I'm back. And the basement floor is clean!

LT(JG) J. B. McDEVITT
USS LEON, c/o F.P.O.
SAN FRANCISCO, CALIF.

MISS MARGARET K. ZIMMER
125 WEST HOMER STREET
HARRISBURG, ILLINOIS

PASSED BY
NAVAL CENSOR

CPSIA information can be obtained at www.ICGtesting.com
Printed in the USA
LVOW03s1550240915

455583LV00002B/50/P